Sh!t
D@mn
Hëll

Insist...persist...consist

Six Stages to Recovery and Freedom

KARL-HEINZ AUGAT

Copyright © 2025 Karl-Heinz Augat

All Rights Reserved

Thank you for supporting the creativity and benefit of all beings.

Author Karl-Heinz Augat
Cover Design by C:Rhodes

No part of this book may be reproduced, distributed, or transmitted in any way, shape, or form by any means electronically nor mechanically, including photocopying, recording, or by any information storage and retrieval system. All images and text may not be reproduced by any publisher, printer, or company for the purpose of sale.

ISBN 978-1-963012-44-6

Published by GroovyRoads Publishing

.first printed edition 2025.

I dedicate this book to all versions of myself; past, present, and future.

I'm proud of the work done thus far and this dedication serves as a reminder to be consistent and persistent in my personal evolution.

With so much acceptance and love,
Karl-Heinz Augat

CONTENTS

CONTENTS	2
FOREWARD	8
Profound Apology	10
CHAPTER 1	**12**
CODEPENDENCY	12
Denial, the "I Know" Disease	14
Society Chronology of codependency	14
Pre-1935	15
The Plastic Age	15
The Mother of all Addiction	18
THE FORMATIVE YEARS (development)	19
THE ADOLESCENT YEARS (crisis, conflict, and rebellion)	20
DEVELOPING INDIVIDUALITY (ages 19 to 24)	21
THE STAGE OF COMMITMENT (25+ years)	22
Erikson's Stages of Psychosocial Development	23
ABUSE	24
CODEPENDENTS	24
THE ISOLATOR	26
FANTASIZERS	28
THE CARETAKER	29
IN A "NUTSHELL"	31
SUFFERING	32
CHAPTER 2	**36**
WHAT IS NORMAL?	36
The Seeds of Codependency in Relationships	38
UNDOING THE ROOTS: CHANGE	42
GEOGRAPHICAL CHANGES	43
PERMISSION	44
THE DISEASE of "Splaining!"	44
REAL CHANGE: SPIRITUAL DEVELOPMENT	46
YOUR GUIDE TO CHANGE: HEALTHY VS. UNHEALTHY	48
CHAPTER 3	**50**
HOW TO PLAY!	50

THE VALUE OF HEALTHY PLAY	50
HEALTHY PLAY: CHALLENGE Your "DEFAULT SETTING"	51
GETTING IN TOUCH WITH FEELINGS	51
CARPOOL KARAOKE	54
POSITIVE ATTITUDE, RIGIDITY, FEAR OF DYSFUNCTIONALITY	55
SOME EXERCISES	56
ACCESS THE INNER CHILD	58
THE BULL AND THE CHILD	60
BALANCE	62

CHAPTER 4 — 64

CODEPENDENCY ON RELATIONSHIPS	**64**
THE FACE OF CODEPENDENCY	64
CODEPENDENCY EQUALS CONTROL	64
Let's call it a: CASE STUDY	66
1 + 1 = 3	71

CHAPTER 5 — 74

ROLES THAT CODEPENDENTS PLAY	**74**
THE POWER OF ROLES	74
CODEPENDENT ROLES IN RELATIONSHIPS: OPPOSITES ATTRACT	75
BACK TO THE REFRAIN: CHANGE!	81

CHAPTER 6 — 84

SIX STAGES TO RECOVERY AND FREEDOM	**84**
Preparing for Recovery	84
Approaching the Six Stages	85
THE SIX STAGES	86
Total Child/Total Adult	88
Stage 1: SELF Knowledge/SELF Awareness	**89**
Working the First Stage	89
Stage 2: Developing a Support System	**91**
The Pitfalls	92
Fake it Until You Make It	93
My Celebrity Recovery Family	95
Stage 3: Self Parenting	**98**
Meeting your own Needs	98
Failure to take Responsibility: The consequences	98

Stage Three, Step One	99
Surrogates	101
Ask for what you want, then Do What You Want	102
Stage 4: Develop PMA	**104**
Three Basic Principles	106
Affirmation Techniques - SELF Statements	107
In Summary: Be Creative!	109
OG Family Exercises	110
The Seven Essene Mirrors of Self	111
Stage 5: The OG Family	**114**
Approaching the Process	114
Your Perceptions, Your Issues	116
Inventory and Journaling Techniques	118
Share your inventory with Safe People	119
Composing Lists for Journaling	120
Cemetery and Fire Therapy	123
Stage 6: The Inner Child	**126**
Final Stage of Recovery Process	126
Simple Definition of Inner Child	128
Getting in touch	128
The Gene Schematic	130
CHAPTER 7	*132*
SHAME, SHAME, & more SHAME!	**132**
ORIGINAL SHAME	133
TRAUMATIC SHAME	133
EXPECTATIONS	134
COMPOUND SHAME	136
THE SHAME WARS	137
TOXIC SHAME	140
TOXIC PEOPLE, PLACES, & THINGS	141
Means of Change	144
Bringing our Past into our Future	145
CHAPTER 8	*148*
SHAME REDUCTION	**148**
USING ALL THE TOOLS	148
Boundaries	149
Acceptance	150

- Love 151
  - The Grieving Process 152
  - Twelve Steps Tools of Recovery 154
- **Clichés, WTF?** **155**
  - Let's Talk About Batteries 161
  - Serenity 163

CHAPTER 9 .... *166*

THE SERENITY PRAYER **166**
- My Serenity Prayer! 166
- The most powerful Shame Reduction tool 168
- God Grant Me 171
- The Serenity to accept the things I cannot Change 171
- Courage to change the things I can 173
- Courage in Recovery 174
- And Wisdom to know the difference 176
- Practicing the Prayer 176

CHAPTER 10 .... *178*

GOD, AS I UNDERSTAND GOD **178**
- The Taboos 178
- Taboos Keep you from your higher Power 179
- One Ultimate Authority 181
- Three Principles 182
- GUT Theology - I can feel it in my gut! 184
- The experience of Simplicity 188

CHAPTER 11 .... *192*

WILLINGNES TO CHANGE AND GROW **192**
- The simplest Principle 192
- The Recovery Triangle 195
- H.O.W. (Honesty, Openness, Willingness) 196
- Ownership 198
- The Greatest Movie you'll ever See 200

CHAPTER 12 .... *202*

Tools: What's in your toolbox? **202**
- You want to borrow one of my tools? 202
- 12-Steps (as per The Big Book) 203
- 12-Steps (as per Russel Brand) 204

Be Like Water! Bruce Lee	205
Radical Honesty, How free do you want to be?	208

Shame vs. Guilt — 210
- Guilt — 212
- Blame — 214
- Self-awareness — 216

Suffering — 218
- Kabbalah on Suffering — 220
- I-Ching on Suffering — 222
- Buddhism on Suffering — 224

Kabbalah — 226

The I-Ching, Book of Changes — 228

A Fathers Journey — 230

FORWARD

First, as we get deep into my thoughts, my Ideas, my experiences, I am going to be referring to my recovery, my growth and my evolution, particularly to some techniques and processes taken from the Twelve Step Program, The Seven Essene Mirrors of Self, Chinese Book of Changes (I-Ching), Kabbalah, Human Design, Gene Code, Astrology, The Dao, etc. These are my processes; these are my tools, etc. I hope to really demonstrate lasting change by means of these tools throughout this book.

Second, and I'll repeat this later because it's important to my recovery and hopefully your recovery as well, that my past is not about blame and shame. I did not want to be stuck in the mud, blaming my parents, teachers, friends, wife, sisters, brothers, uncles, aunts, cousins, the girl at the 7-11, whomever. Blame is a stage I went and still go through, I needed to identify and think about it, feel it, and experience it. I feel that its important and I did not want to skim over it.

Third, I'm going to use my personal journey as my core story. Not to blame people in my own past. But to share my perceptions, right or wrong, they are my perceptions, and those perceptions influenced my discovery, development, and ultimately my newfound forgiven identity.

Finally, I write this book as an honest means to my personal sobriety. It is a sobering thought to write and share your life mishaps and lacks of judgment to people you don't know. Opening myself up for judgment and ridicule. I think this is why I always perceived celebrities as some of my heroes. To have your life story, the good, the bad, and the ugly, under constant scrutiny by paparazzi and fans, to watch them overcome their addictions so publicly takes tremendous courage, more than I feel I could ever muster.

I wanted to write this book using me as a case study of what not to do and what to do. I started this book while in rehab. And all I wanted to do was to find solutions and ways to communicate, of ways to peel back the emotional layers and to heal and to learn how to embrace relationships. I learned early in business that stating problems without possible solutions is a waste of time. I did not want this to be a confessional of all my life's transgressions. My goal was to create my process, a simple process to ultimately achieve that which I have always wanted and desired, Self- Acceptance, Self-Love, and Freedom. I can say in pure radical honesty that my journey was NOT an elegant one. My human design states I have to touch the hot burner in order to know if it's hot. Yep, you guessed it, I touched that damn burners, over and over and over, until I learned it was hot and why not to touch it again.

I will tell you it gets so confusing on what SHAME and your NORMALS drive you to do. On the Surface, I was obsessed, like complete OCD on how to take care of my wife a certain way, to take care of my kids another way, to help my Mom and Dad over here, and then to dedicate myself to work over there, so that I can provide. I kept OCD'ing on taking care of everyone and for a while, as noble as all my actions were, deep, deep down I was overcompensating. I was screaming at my family systems to look at me, look at what I am doing for all of you, but again deep down I had no fucking clue how to take care of me. So here is the Big Question; How the fuck can I take care of anyone outside of me if I do not know how to take care of myself? That is when I hear all the Zen teachings about, once you know how to take care of you, you can take care of others. You have to give up control to get control. These existential sayings started to make sense. So, then the journey of Discovery begins. And, I didn't want to stop until I finally felt the one thing that could make me stop all this insanity. A love and respect for myself.

Profound Apology

In dedication and persistence of my process, I have apologized so many times for all the family, friends, and strangers that I affected and took down with me, down this dark hole of codependency and addiction. So many of you offered so many kind words and actions and none of those deeds went unnoticed to me and it most definitely led and assisted in my path to sobriety, recovery, and ultimately freedom. Addiction of any kind is very real and it requires a very personal and radical honest approach. I have hurt people all over the world. I have been on 5 continents, 35 countries, and 48 states always searching outside myself for the magic bullet of connection, relationships, and ultimately love. Unconditional Love. And it wasn't until I committed to the greatest adventure of all. The most ambitious and courageous journey of traveling inside my mind, body, and soul that I began to find what I was searching for. ME! As humans I discovered that I am capable of anything, overcoming fear, pain, loss, depression, chaos, insanity, etc. It has been the absolute adventure of my lifetime, and now I feel. Like I truly feel. And it's time to live in harmony and peace within myself and to those I meet and have relationships with. Again, this is my profound and public apology to all of those I have hurt. You know who you are, and I am grateful to all of you, and I truly love you all. For being in my life at different times that I needed. I apologize for not being what you needed me to be or wanted me to be. I fully accept and take full responsibility of those regrettable actions. Sincerely, my profound apologies!!! Please have a full and joyful and fulfilling life. To all, please look inside and take care of yourselves.

With unconditional love,
Karl-Heinz Augat

CHAPTER 1

CODEPENDENCY

> *"Codependency is the disease of lost selfhood.
> It is a disease of the self, that causes great pain
> to the self, and all who care about the self."*
> — ***Anne Wilson Schaef***

In dealing with my addiction and personal deep dive (self-discovery), which I call the *"recovery"* process, I had a problem with the term "Codependency." For me, it was a difficult term to understand, to get my *"feels"* for. Yet it was so important that I understand the term. I could read it, spell it, say it, but I could not define it. This term is so important to me, because it will be used to describe many of my challenges I experienced. I made it a label (tool in my toolbox). In our world, when we put a label on it, *"like you're a crack head"*, *"you're and alcoholic"*, or *"you're a codependent!"* it helped me better understand and relate to 40 plus years of addictive behaviors and my life problems. It helped me understand why the cocaine and opiate use was a ***fait accompli!***, *"WTF! What does this mean? I'm an addict, please use small words and big pictures!"* I love the French language, it makes my addiction sound so elegant.

Definition of fait accompli
    fait accompli
    ˌfed əkämˈplē, ˌfād əkämˈplē/
    noun
    a thing that has already happened or been decided before those affected hear about it, leaving them with no option but to accept.

In addict-English, *"Hell, I was going to eventually abuse crack, smack, and cognac for not dealing with my codependent shit (challenges, issues, character defects), and I was going to take everyone down with me."*

So, in the words of Beyoncé *"all you single ladies (guys to), put a label on it!"* And now my recovery process begins:

If you are reading this, please don't over think this; I already did that for you. If you are having a tough time understanding the term or label, don't feel alone, don't worry about it. Work on your growth (your personal process) and understanding will come. Codependency is not the only psychological term that others and myself have problems with. I took hold of a person in my therapy group who was constantly obsessing, yet when I grabbed his face and said "Just fucking STOP!, your obsessing!" he had no idea what "obsessing" meant, and it took time for him to get it. The same with a person who lacks intimacy in his or her relationship, most understand intimacy as some form of sexual intercourse (that means "SEX"), and he or she already has that, many times hopefully and healthily with their partner, but they don't, they are feeling pleasure but not "intimacy?" So, how in the hell, can they understand "intimacy?"

So, for my, purposes, I'm going to offer up, a simple, personalized definition of the label, codependency:

If any person, place, or thing
that I am dependent on
creates insanity or unmanageability in my life,
I am CODEPENDENT!

Also, for my purposes, I consider everyone codependents, so I will use *"we,"* since all people are. And I would also like to get one other thing straight: **codependency is an addiction**. To me it is the **Mother of all addictions**; I believe it appears at the root of all addictions. As an addiction, it is not something we suddenly cure and then forget about. The recovery process is an ongoing thing. To plagiarize from the Twelve Steps Program of recovery, we look for **progress, not perfection (cliché)**. The good news is that progress can mean hope, happiness and peace in our lives. Drinking, drugs, over-eating, not-eating, anxiety, shopping, depression, sex, work, social media, control...and all the rest of the insanity and unmanageability caused by codependency...can be put behind us...as can the inevitable failure of so many relationships we try so hard to build.

So now me in my addiction mentality, initially, I do not want take responsibility and accountability for my actions and decisions. I automatically want to blame someone or something for why I am an addict, so I went back before I was born:
(Such and addict, RIGHT?)

Denial, the "I Know" Disease

Denial. *"I Know, I know!"* We all *know*. I put this Denial paragraph at the beginning for those reading that just said *"I know; there is nothing wrong with me, this is life, deal with it: I know, I know, I know"* this disease will prevent you from working on your personal growth, or *"my shit"* according to addicts. We are all wicked smart and have intellectual knowledge. But we use it against ourselves. I did, all the time. Probably because it's easier than really working on our issues, working on our character defects are problems. It's so much easier to help others, but that is because *"I know"* my problems are different, because I see them differently. As an example, *"I know"* that certain people are such negative influences in my life. But I still hang around them. I literally get irritated and annoyed hanging out with them. But I don't let go. I hang on. It's a ridiculous relationship. Horrible. It fucking sucks! I know that logically. But I can't let go. Because I'm afraid. I don't know any other kind of relationship. This is my normal. This is unconsciously comfortable to me. That's the only kind I learned about when I was a kid. The beat-up spouse, not only physical, but verbally and energetically, I feel this is worse than the physical.

Sometimes the **"I Know"** disease *"has"* us. I have met so many great human beings that have experienced unbelievable challenges and face huge, disturbing trauma in their lives, but pretend to just accept them. No bad feelings here. Not working through them. Like, *Nothing's wrong here!* They try, in vain, to intellectualize (not emotionalize) their emotional pain away. And when that doesn't work, they get depressed. Then they rationalize that they're so depressed because life, in itself, is depressing. It's as though they'd accept *anything* rather than get out of their intellects (head) and deal with their feelings (soul communication).

The "I Know" disease will kill you

Society Chronology of codependency

For some weird reason, it helped me to understand why we as a society today (1900s to 2020s) are the way we are. How civilization's past dealt with the same addictive behaviors 2000 to 3500 years ago as we do today. I learned that the concept of codependency and how to treat it evolved over time. It is not our fault. It actually might be in our DNA. I am a product of my environment and generational upbringing. Not only individually but society as a whole has defined and created codependency. So really, I was destined to use, no matter what, but ultimately, feel better about my life, such an addiction thing to do, blame society. But I did! So please be patient with the following history lesson, I promise it will make sense in later chapters.

Pre-1935
In my research, prior to the founding of Alcoholics Anonymous (AA) in 1935, society approached problem behavior with what I call, *"hide that shit"*, or *"bury that shit"* syndrome, a secretive mentality (CIA tactics): Out- of-Sight, Out-of-Mind. For example, if you were a disgrace to your family, you were dealt with in a very simple way. You were *"shelved."* If you were depressed and dysfunctional, you were placed in Psych ward in a mental institution. Pregnant and out of wedlock, shipped off far away to a distant relative, where you'd save the immediate family any embarrassment. A Thief? Prison.

Even in the mental institutions of the time, where you might expect some insight into treatment, *"a patient"* mostly received medication, and if you were lucky and the institution was, loosely defined as progressive, *"the patient"* received drugs plus electrical shock treatment (have you seen a beautiful mind starring Russel Crowe, Holy Shit!).

It was only after AA, in the mid-1930's and 40's, that we finally made a shift to a new mentality. With alcoholism, at least, we acknowledged the concept of addiction. But society still saw it as an evil, a lack of will power, a moral defect. Why? Because it challenged the only solution society could think of: **CONTROL**.

Maybe it's understandable that society had that attitude. If it had really accepted the idea that an addiction was a disease and not merely a character flaw or from the devil, it would have felt obligated to offer an effective treatment rather than judge and label the addict. There simply didn't exist, that I could find, an effective treatment.

The Plastic Age
The concept of addiction as a disease saw minimal progress after World War II, during the period from 1945 to 1960, often referred to as the **"Plastic Age"** by psychologists. It seemed that society, having witnessed

immense turmoil during the war, sought to avoid further chaos. This mindset can be described as *"bury that shit"* mentality, driven by the desire to keep troubling issues out of sight. Society operated under new slogans, such as *"A Place for Everything and Everything in Its Place."*

To illustrate how this mindset manifested, let's consider two real examples. African Americans were segregated under the notion of being *"separate but equal,"* confined to their own neighborhoods, schools, and limited job options—an empty and unjust claim. Homosexuals were forced into the closet, similar to the contemporary "Don't Ask, Don't Tell" policy— a form of virtual denial.

During the Plastic Age, a culture of **"Sacred Ideals"** or **"Sacreds"** also emerged. Everything was expected to be ideal and perfect. For instance, the prevailing slogan of the time declared that *"Policemen are Your Friends,"* suggesting that police brutality didn't exist in this ideal world (which was far from the truth!). Another ideal was the perception of priests as saintly figures who would never engage in any form of abuse, particularly towards children, male and/or female (a belief that has since been shattered).

However, the plastic facade began to crack, or more accurately, shattered during the 1960s. Suddenly, the youth embraced a new anthem captured in the lyrics of a popular song: *"The Revolution's Here!"* The internal pressures that society had repressed for so long, along with the denial and control, exploded within the younger generation. They became paradigm breakers, out-of-the-box thinkers, and iconoclasts challenging cherished beliefs and institutions. They dismantled the old idols, **"the Sacred Ideals"** with conviction. The police were viewed negatively as *"cops."* Homosexuals demanded recognition and came out of the closet with Gay Pride. The Black community fought for their rights, sometimes resorting to violence and armed resistance, just to protect themselves.

However, the pendulum of the revolution swung so far. For instance, where sex and drugs had been taboo, it was now flaunted under the banner of *"Free Love,"* leading to excessive promiscuity, and the introduction of AIDS. Drug abuse became rampant, with figures like Timothy Leary, a discredited psychologist from Berkeley University and Harvard, leading the LSD movement with the slogan *"Turn On, Tune In, Drop Out."* This period has been described as a civil war, with the younger generation clashing against the older. The songs of the youth, particularly the *"hippies,"* vividly expressed their disdain for the older generation and its way of life.

Yet, some positive outcomes emerged. By the 1970s, the pendulum began to swing back, and the older generation started recognizing the validity of the younger generation's concerns. The uproar of the 1960s subsided, giving way to meaningful conversations. It became evident that the Plastic Age had failed. In 1983, this notion received a significant boost with the release of the book *"Adult Children of Alcoholics"* by *Janet Geringer Woititz*. The book courageously portrayed what it was like to grow up in an alcoholic household and became a bestseller, resonating with many individuals who suddenly realized they were not alone and not crazy.

The book also sparked another phenomenon. Many people who did not have alcoholism in their families found themselves relating to the traits of alcoholic children, prompting them to question why these characteristics applied to them. This suggested that a broad range of problems shared a common root. In fact, the author provided a list of these problems:

Adult children of alcoholics;
struggle to define normal behavior; have difficulty completing projects they start; often lie instead of telling the truth; are excessively self-critical; have difficulty experiencing joy and having fun; take themselves too seriously; struggle with intimacy in relationships; overreact to uncontrollable changes; constantly seek approval and affirmation; feel different from others; exhibit extremes of responsibility or irresponsibility; demonstrate unwavering loyalty, even when undeserved; act impulsively, often without considering the consequences, leading to confusion, self-loathing, and a loss of control over their environment. Cleaning up the aftermath of their impulsive actions consuming excessive energy.

From here, it was a short progression to what I consider a movement in the 1980s known as ACDP (Adult Children of Dysfunctional Parents) as mentioned earlier. This, in turn, led to the concept of Codependency as defined in influential books like "Facing Codependency" by *P.M. Melody* and "Codependent No More" by *Melody Beattie*. These groundbreaking books revolutionized the understanding and treatment of dysfunctional behavior, establishing several key principles:

1. Addiction can manifest without the use of substances like alcohol or drugs. One's "drug" can be anything from your phone, social media, food, sex, power, and gambling to abusive relationships or any other unhealthy dependency that creates chaos in their life but is impossible to live without.
2. Codependency lies at the core of these addictions, serving as a common thread.
3. A significant number of people experience codependency.
4. If left untreated, codependents tend to move from one addiction to another in an ongoing and destructive cycle.

Considering the third point raises an important question: If codependency underlies all addictions, is there a shared root cause for codependency? *Identifying such a root cause could provide valuable insights for effective treatment.* And indeed, there is a common origin of codependency. However, before examining that, let's revisit the fourth point. Sadly, although many individuals are codependent, they often face an additional barrier to seeking treatment—the **"I Know"** disease mentioned earlier.

The Mother of all Addiction

Codependency doesn't simply emerge overnight; it evolves gradually over an extended period. It revolves around the absence of a distinct individual identity. To comprehend this, let's explore a widely accepted theory regarding the development of a healthy individual. We consider *"healthy"* as encompassing physical well-being, mental and emotional equilibrium, and spiritual fulfillment, where spirituality pertains not only to intelligence or cognitive processes but also to the realm of emotions. These three aspects form the foundation of our individuality.

First, the body-our physical existence. As physical beings, we have certain needs and requirements. **Second**, our emotions play a vital role in shaping our identity. We are beings capable of experiencing a range of feelings. **Third**, we possess a soul, and spirituality entails embracing our unique essence, awakening our spirit, and recognizing the qualities that set us apart as individuals. It is what makes each of us special and distinct from others.

Now, let's dive into my theory of a healthy individual. However, it's crucial to remember that this is merely a theory. We should not become confined by the notion that it defines our specific path. Eventually, we will reconcile this theory with reality. The fundamental concept is that each individual progresses through various stages of personal development. Upon reaching adulthood, one should possess a clear understanding of their identity and desires. This clarity empowers individuals to make healthy choices in relationships, fostering their well-being. Moreover, it grants them the strength to terminate toxic relationships and move forward. The theory identifies several stages in this development process:

THE FORMATIVE YEARS (development)
I researched so much about Human Development. I was so disturbed by who I was and the conflict within and the decisions I was making I kept asking, why am I like this? Did I come like this? Was I raised this way? Was I taught this, or not taught this? So, words cannot describe the emotional release I had once I understood the development of a human being from birth to late adulthood. However, it also impressed upon me how important, I mean how critically import it is to new parents on how you parent your child, ages newborn to five. Like you have no fucking clue the impression you make on your newborn baby to the age of three actually. I believe all of a person's trait and behaviors are defined and programmed from how a child was raised from birth to age 3. So, the following is my research summarized.

We were all born totally **DEPENDENT**. Babies are dependent. They have needs and expectations of their family, whatever their family is, biological or otherwise. Babies are not logical. Their expectations are to have their needs met and met *Now!* I'm hungry at 1 AM. Feed me at 1 AM. If you decide not to feed me till 8 am, guess what? It's gonna be a long night. And those same expectations persist through childhood.

Between Ages 0-11 I expect and *demand* that my family system meets my needs. Some of these needs have physical aspects, they nurture the body, but basically, they are all **SPIRITUAL**, and five of them are fundamental. **First, I need SAFETY.** If you don't feel safe you can't grow. Not really. Your body might grow, but you are not really growing as an individual. **Second, I need LOVE**—*unconditional* love. No matter who I am. No matter what's happening. No matter if I'm sick. I need my family to love me. *Unconditionally.* **Third, I need SECURITY**--food, clothing, and a roof over my head. These are the basics I need to be able to grow and learn, to expand as a human being. **Fourth, I need** to learn basic **LIFE SKILLS.** And of life skills, it's broken down to the three most basic: to **socialize**; to **play**; to have **intimacy**. To socialize is to interact, connect, share, and be part of other people, a sense of belonging. To play may seem trivial, but in playing as a child you become spontaneous, you let your free spirit out.

Intimacy. This is a tough one. Kids know what it is instinctively. But by the time we're adults we think it means sexual intercourse of every kind, when all it really means is being able to share your deepest thoughts and feelings, honestly and without fear, without judgment.

Safety, Love, Security, & Life Skills are FOUR of the five basic spiritual needs, with the fourth, the life skills, broken down into socialization, play, and intimacy, and finally Identity, being the FIFTH spiritual need.

Fifth, the last life skill: **I need an IDENTITY**, who am I? What am I all about? Where do I come from? What is my history? What is my connection to life, to humanity? A little child has to be taught his or her history. It is so important for their growth. And owning your history, all of your history, including everything you have done, good or bad, right, wrong, or indifferent…is essential to continued growth as an adult. Identity is so critical. If you do not have a clear sense of who you are, you lack **Serenity**. Without *serenity you have sadness!* When that persists, you develop depression, anxiety, addictions, and all other aspects of codependency. So, you basically enter relationships as *"needy"*, looking for someone or something to give you a sense of wholeness, of fulfillment, even in a relationship you desperately love and want. This process begins in childhood and continues through subsequent stages of your life.

THE ADOLESCENT YEARS (crisis, conflict, and rebellion):
Holy Shit, these years looking back, were the scariest, because it depended on how traumatic or safe my childhood was. I'm hitting puberty, my hormones are raging, and now I have all these undeveloped emotions feeding my body changes. The journey through adolescence is no joke, and we all have to navigate our way through it. Now what **Identity** I have, is shattered. To me, these are years **12 to 18**. I am no longer a kid. I am in between. I am not an adult. Should I play video games, or chase the opposite sex? Are my feet too big? Do I look awkward? OMG, what about Halloween? What do you mean, no more candy? And what about the really deep stuff like: drugs, sex, and just plain growing up in this scary world of war, pandemics, social influencing,

and economic uncertainty. *"OMG Toto, I am not in Kansas, anymore."* I am no longer a little kid. Now looking back seems not so bad. However, I really need someone to guide me along, someone to talk to, and someone safe.

Here is where that *Intimacy* enters in. And the theory is, remember, not reality, says that a male child should have this with his mother, while the female has it with her father. Why? Because the first love relationship the boy (Mommas 'boy) has is with Mom, and the first for the girl (Daddy's girl) is Dad. Or, in today's world, whoever stands for Mom and Dad in todays **Family System**. So theoretically, through these relationships, kids will go through this Adolescent Journey stage with parents (Moms and/or Dads) as their guides. Fortunately/unfortunately, this is where one parent has to step up and become the saintly dominant parent figure. Statistically, this sucks, because one of our parent figures will start to demonstrate codependency trauma, and do the best they can. I only say this from what I hear and see. One of the other Parentals (my daughter coined this term) falls short. These teenage years are brutal; it's literally a war zone, because this stage is where the little kid is no longer a little kid. I can now process thoughts; emotions, ideas and now I come into conflict with the family system. This is my War of Independence. At this point theoretically, I should be healthy enough, strong enough, confident enough, to challenge my family system beliefs and values and take from them whatever the hell I feel is right for me. Since, *in theory*, I experienced **unconditional love** and **intimacy** and I am no longer afraid of expressing my deepest thoughts and feelings. This is the family system structure. I should be able to get not only the guidance on all these changes, but also lock down the real concept and rules of intimacy itself. It is at this point that *"shock and Aw"* happens, possible feelings of abandonment, *"maybe my Parentals did or didn't have my back."* They did a great job or a poor job of guiding me, or not guiding me at all, etc.

DEVELOPING INDIVIDUALITY (ages 19 to 24)
Again, according to my research, and I don't know where Psychiatrists and Psychologists define these precise age groups. However, it's the rebellion stage that leads to the development of the individual. It's the stage that purely tests the family system. In this stage the child becomes a young adult, with a chosen value system, the confidence to act on it, and a clear sense of who he or she is. And this is the threshold for the final stage of life.

THE STAGE OF COMMITMENT (25+ years)

Notice there's no number after the 25. This stage is supposed to persist through the remainder of life. **WRONG**! People who have passed through all of the other stages can now make real commitments. **WRONG**! They know themselves well enough to choose relationships that suit them best. **WRONG**! To marry or not to marry, to have or not to have children, what job to accept or reject, their individual lifestyles, *real* commitments, because these people are *independent?* They know what they want. They go for it. Not for what somebody else wants. They are not approaching relationships on the basis of what they *need,* but of what they can *offer* and what they want to *share. I say* **WRONG***, because most of the time we haven't done enough work to be so lucky and healthy. Our family system of spiritual development is remedial at best. That's why this is the end of Theory. In theory, this will work if you were able to receive the positive nurturing and healthy family system that never failed you. You received your spiritual education at home as is designed. You developed* how people are supposed to develop. You can even forget the ages. But remember the process, because there is validity to it. Here's the key. I don't care if you're 21, 31, 51, or 61: *You cannot grow or move on in your life until you DEVELOP your basic spiritual needs.* FYI, I attached some additional research on Human Development or what Erikson calls psychosocial development. I have so many of these but I resonated with how he breaks each column and row down.

Erikson's stages of psychosocial development, as articulated in the second half of the 20th century by Erik and Joan Erikson. A comprehensive psychoanalytic theory that identifies a series of eight stages, that a healthy developing individual should pass through from infancy to late adulthood.

Approximate Age	Virtues	Psychosocial Crisis	Significant Relationship	Existential Question	Examples
Infancy Under 2 years	Hope	Trust vs. Mistrust	Mother	Can I trust the world?	Feeding, abandonment
Toddlerhood 2–4 years	Will	Autonomy vs. Shame/Doubt	Parents	Is it okay to be me?	Toilet training, clothing themselves
Early childhood 5–8 years	Purpose	Initiative vs. Guilt	Family	Is it okay for me to do, move, and act?	Exploring, using tools or making art
Middle Childhood 9–12 years	Competence	Industry vs. Inferiority	Neighbors, School	Can I make it in the world of people and things?	School, sports
Adolescence 13–19 years	Fidelity	Identity vs. Role Confusion	Peers, Role Model	Who am I? Who can I be?	Social relationships
Early adulthood 20–39 years	Love	Intimacy vs. Isolation	Friends, Partners	Can I love?	Romantic relationships
Middle Adulthood 40–59 years	Care	Generativity vs. Stagnation	Household, Workmates	Can I make my life count?	Work, parenthood
Late Adulthood 60 and above	Wisdom	Ego Integrity vs. Despair	Mankind	Is it okay to have been me?	Reflection on life

OK, I know this history and psychology lesson is a bit dry and is a bit boring but please stay with me throughout the next few chapters, it's so important to understand early human development. I promise it will make sense. I will tie together if I can figure out how to write it. Just Kidding. It will!

Karl-Heinz Augat   Sh!t...D@mn...Hëll   23

ABUSE

Before I move on to Codependency, I believe that most of us *do not have our basic spiritual needs met by our family systems.* Most of us *grew up abused. No matter how **small** or **large** the abuse.* Now, I am going to apologize for the massive definition of the word ABUSE, such and addict thing to do, to apologize. But I believe it's important to understand what the word abuse encompasses and all its variants and similarities.

Definition of abuse:
> a·buse
> verb
> verb: **abuse**; 3rd person present: **abuses**; past tense: **abused**; past participle: **abused**; gerund or present participle: **abusing**
> /əˈbyooz/

1. **use** (something) **to bad effect or for a bad purpose; misuse.**
"*the judge abused his power by imposing the fines*"
Similar: misuse, misapply, misemploy, mishandle, exploit, pervert, take advantage of
   o make excessive and habitual use of (alcohol or drugs, especially illegal ones).
2. **treat** (a person or an animal) **with cruelty or violence, especially regularly or repeatedly.**
"*riders who abuse their horses should be prosecuted*"
Similar: mistreat, maltreat, misuse, handle/treat roughly, knock about/around, manhandle, mishandle, maul, molest, interfere with, indecently assault, sexually abuse, sexually assault, grope. Assault, hit, strike, beat, injure, hurt, harm, damage, wrong, bully, persecute, oppress, torture, beat up, rough up
   o assault (someone, especially a woman or child) sexually. "*he was a depraved man who had abused his two young daughters*"
   o use or treat in such a way as to cause damage or harm.
"*he had been abusing his body for years*"
3. **speak in an insulting and offensive way to or about (someone).**
"*the referee was abused by players from both teams*"
Similar: insult, be rude to, swear at, curse, call someone names, taunt, shout at, scold, rebuke, upbraid, reprove, castigate, inveigh against, impugn, slur, revile, smear, vilify, vituperate against, slander, libel, cast aspersions on, offend, slight, disparage, denigrate, defame, slag off, trash-talk, miscall

CODEPENDENTS

Abused, Physically. Emotionally. Mentally. Spiritually. As you can see by the above definition and its similar examples, it doesn't have to be a major episode or episodes. It doesn't have to be blatant sexual abuse: rape, or major assault. It doesn't even have to be the chaos of an alcoholic or drug- addicted parent. Sometimes you were abused by your parents' best intentions. An example. You're a child. Your father or mother has to work two jobs to make ends meet. But you're a child and you miss, Dad and/or Mom. You cry. You are ignored. Or, worse, you're spanked into silence instead of being hugged and comforted and given an explanation of why Mom/Dad has to be away so much. You were just taught that your feelings don't count, and you will be punished if you express them when other people don't want to hear them.

Another example. Sexual abuse. You're a girl hitting puberty and the only way the male members of your family can handle it is to make fun of your body. This is a time when you need intimacy, not ridicule, especially public ridicule. And it's worse if your father is one of the perpetrators. Instead of learning to take pride in your development, instead of learning intimacy, the chance to talk about what you're feeling, you experience **SHAME**. Shame means, basically, that you start thinking, feeling, that there is something wrong with you, that you are a bad person, not that you did or are about to do bad things, but that you are (a state of being) the things you are told as a child.

As a result of our abuse, of not having our spiritual needs met, we go into life searching to have our needs met. We don't have a steady foundation. We're not sure who we are as individuals. We can't handle conflict, because it echoes the terrible internal conflict we grew up with. And we can't handle crises, *personal* crises.

That last one is interesting. As codependents we can function for a period of time in society, do our jobs. It's just ourselves we can't handle. Inside we are hurting, sometimes falling apart, and sometimes even killing ourselves physically. I have been a father and a businessman for over 35 years. I could negotiate multi-million-dollar deals, project manage massive multi- million-dollar relocations. But I couldn't negotiate my own life. I was killing myself with an addiction, a drug and codependency addiction. But I couldn't even face that, let alone manage it. For me as for so many others, I feel, it was way more convenient to run around taking care of everybody else rather than taking care of myself. Eventually, even taking care of others falls apart. I can put this another way: I was so out of touch with myself, my own identity, that I did not have an intimate relationship with *myself*. And if you don't have a relationship with yourself, how can you expect to have one with anyone else? My lack of identity was pointed out in different ways, people would notice my shift in walking or talking and it was because I would take on the strong identity traits of those I would hang out with, work with. It drove people fucking crazy.

Codependents can manage billion-dollar companies. They can manage schools and hospitals. They can even manage whole countries. But they can't manage themselves or real relationships with others. They can't face what's going on inside: the unfinished business of childhood and the new business being piled on each day that reflects the old hurt of childhood. Codependents have frozen feelings. They numb themselves with substances, their *"drugs of choice."* And they have many drugs of choice, not just alcohol or pharmaceuticals, but social media, phones, any type of media.

Codependents develop survivor techniques. Behavior patterns. There are three that I have been myself. I personally dominate in one of the three patterns that own me: I am the consummate **Caretaker**, but add a splash of **Fantasizer** and a dash of **Isolator**, and now you know me. Can you be all three? Sure. Typically, one will dominate, but we adopt the others, like a chameleon, to get through the different crises of our lives. It's really not that hard for us codependents. We don't know who we are anyway.

THE ISOLATOR
Isolators can be called the Children of Loneliness and Fear. Growing up, they experienced fear of abandonment. They got messages from their family systems like, I wish you were never born, you are a burden on the family, you cause all the problems in this family. They typically experienced this emotional abuse, as well as physical abuse. They grow up empty, afraid, and lonely. *As* adults they will search for the LOVE they never got in their family system. In regard to relationships, isolators are like little terrorists looking for a hostage. The first person that comes along and shows the slightest inclination toward love has to be captured and held by the isolator. They develop their own peculiar forms of codependency, of addictions.

For example, they easily become addicted to institutions. See, if we never had a real family, institutions become good substitutes. Isolators migrate to the mental health industry, as patients. They will Rent-a-Parent. Find a therapist. Adopt him or her as a surrogate parent. And never let the sucker out of their sight. Take your cell phone when you go on vacation because I'm going to call. And if I get to the point where I can't function without you, you'll sign me into the hospital. That will be even more like the family I never had. Three meals a day, constant attention, and they'll even take you out to a movie once in a while.

Another institution Isolators love is the military. It's a known fact that abused children make great soldiers. The military gives them a few things they never got at home, like an identity and a Drill Instructor (DI) to be my surrogate parent, Structure and **SECURITY**. All of a sudden, the Isolator goes from being a nobody to a well-defined somebody: a soldier. And no matter how rough the DI is, the DI is nothing compared to how bad my real parent made me feel.

Isolators can find a family in the prison system. Why not? It's a crazy place, and isolators are used to crazy family systems.

Isolators can also migrate to religious cults. Isolators can become workaholics; the company gives them their identity. That's what happened to me. My job had become my identity; it gave me a sense of purpose, my *only* sense of purpose. To me, once my contract was complete, I had no other Job to go to. This was my Identity. I sold my Dads Company for millions; I had a 3-year contract making great money. Once I got to the end of my contract, working my ass off, they did not want to renew. It absolutely destroyed me. I had no Idea at the time that this was my entire Identity. I felt abandoned, I felt down, almost depressed, and I was frustrated. Why did they not want to keep me? I did amazing work, hell; I even saved a 100 million dollar division from being shutdown. Are you fucking kidding me? Jesus Christ, Seriously.

Isolators migrate to another relationship addiction: **Love Addiction**. We'll cover it in much more detail later, but it's worth touching on now. I have read about so many different examples. Here is an example, which is very prevalent, of a girl raised in a large family, say ten children. There was never enough of anything to go around, especially attention from her parents. So, she grew up feeling abandoned. And she tried to hold onto every man who came her way afterward. They became her Possessions. Her issue became Control or Ownership.

Isolators will also trend toward a particular food addiction. Food is used just like drug, to give temporary comfort by altering body chemistry. But isolators are afraid that people will see their drug addictions, or the effect of the addictions, like obesity. So, after they gorge, they purge:

bulimia. Their addiction is kept secret. To preserve their outer image, they hide it and try to avoid it.

Finally, isolators will migrate toward alcohol and prescription drugs. Why? Because these are *"acceptable"* drugs. Especially the way isolators use them. Isolators are secretive addicts and functional addicts. Professional addicts. They use drinking and prescription drugs as sedatives, a way to numb the pain of a lonely life. Oh my God, I was the bestest professional addict ever. The Best. You got to be fucking kidding me. My wife and kids could see it a mile away. I mean, looking back, who does shit like this, seriously? I did! I did! I did!

FANTASIZERS
Fantasizers are the Children of Shame. They experience shame in their families in childhood from all sorts of turmoil and insecurity. They begin to deny the reality of the craziness in their family. At the same time, they don't bring anyone home because of the shame they feel about the craziness, and they look for other families to belong to, as though trying to change reality. If anyone asks about his or her families, they provide a cover-up; they lie about a fictitious family. And soon they begin believing the lies. They are off in their fantasies. It wasn't always like this for me but I was and I am still a big fantasizer, I wanted to be a bodybuilder, I wanted to be a martial artist, I wanted to be a concert pianist, but I really wanted to become an actor. I loved acting, pretending to be someone else, fantasizing of being someone other than me.

I think when Fantasizers become adults, then, they are susceptible to certain influences. For example, turmoil and craziness are all they know, so they look to duplicate that environment. They get a rush from it. It's a paradox that as much as they are repelled by the shame they felt in their family, they are also attracted to shame because it's the only thing they know. It's almost as if by seeking shame they are caught in a futile game of trying to prove that the shame in their family system wasn't so bad after all. The key word is *futile*.

Fantasizers are targets for the Disease of the Lie: Alcoholism and Drug Abuse. But, unlike isolators, fantasizers are unmanageable addicts. They are also drawn to what are called Power Addictions, and Image Addictions (for example, I knew a man that literally lived and slept in a room with mirrors on every wall and ceiling in his room), behavior that gives a sense of power but ultimately results in shame. Shoplifting. Gambling. Compulsive Spending. Sex Addiction. You can get away with them for a while, but eventually they catch up with you. Then you're hit with the shame of unmanageable debts and lies and the exposure of your cover-up behaviors.

A more painful example was a friend of my son. He was maybe 14 or 15, just the brightest, smartest, handsome boy. Every time he spoke with me; he was just unbelievably kind and polite. He would come to the house and skateboard with my son. And, Oh My God, he was so good. Like professional good. But man, you could see the pain. He never wanted my son to go to his house. I remember this one moment, my son and I, went over to pick him up, I had the opportunity to meet his father. Anger and rage, does not begin to describe the man. My son's friend never had a chance. He took all that rage and all that shame and put it into his skateboarding, he didn't care if he got hurt, and if he did, it would probably, temporarily, mask the real pain. I know he fantasized in becoming a great boarder but his anxiety and rage were so far off the spectrum, he felt he only one option left. He killed himself. It still destroys me to this day, that he felt that he had no other option; he didn't have that Intimacy with a parent he needed to overcome what he was enduring. I mean, just writing about him, still makes me cry.

Anyway, for fantasizers, that's their **"normal."** We'll talk more about **"normals"** in a later chapter. Adults tend to seek what was normal for them as children. For the fantasizer that was craziness, turmoil, unmanageability; the lies and fantasies devised to hide all of that; the rush, the high of getting away with the fantasies; and, finally, the shame of discovery. All of these can be wrapped into one word: Anxiety. For the fantasizer, their normal is ANXIETY.

THE CARETAKER
Caretakers are the Slaves of the World. They're the kid! Who never really had a childhood, who went from 3 to 33 overnight. Somewhere in their family system they became parents when they were still kids. You see this in families where one parent died and the other had to go out to work, leaving one of the children in charge. You also see it in families where the parents are immobilized by illness, mental or physical or by drugs and alcohol.

Caretakers are the kids who came through for the family. The goody-two-shoes. Kids that everybody's proud of, that always do things right. They are the ones who took care of everybody else, who rescued the family, who fixed people. Caretakers grow up to be Control Freaks. Inside they are full of rage for the childhood they never had, for all the responsibility laid on them as kids. But they don't show it outside. And they don't want anyone to look inside and see it either: *Don't get too close!* We say that for caretakers everything's fine. *"I am fine!"* My personal favorite phrase, I would say this all the time and it was a lie, it literally drove my wife nuts, my daughter had a boyfriend that would say he was fine, better yet he would always say; *"I'm Golden!"* I loved this kid, but it was such bullshit and we all knew it, but he would never admit it. That was the day I witnessed one of my mirrors. Specifically, the Seven Essene Mirrors of Self that I reference in a later chapter.

Ok, I read this definition of FINE below and it stuck with me:

FINE = Frustrated. Insecure. Neurotic. Emotional.

Many caretakers don't know how to play; they never had the opportunity to learn. They can't relax. They over think. They bum out. They're caught in a dilemma. They hate fixing things, fixing people, but they're addicted to it. They're conditioned to it. It's their normal. Anything else is too uncomfortable. And yet the constant fixing, the incessant responsibility, causes such internal rage. Myself, on the other hand, I loved to play, but I usually got irresponsible with it. I didn't play for the right reasons.

If isolators are drawn to the mental health industry as patients, caretakers are drawn as workers. They also make good nurses, teachers, mothers, secretaries...They never ask for their worth. Some bitch and moan and complain all day long. They get old before their time and get crusty and grouchy as they get old. And if isolators are one type of love addict, caretakers are another: Professional Victims. They fall in love with the sick, the damaged. The more damaged, the better. Like, *bring me you're sick, your damaged, and your deprived and I will take care of them. The* issue is: **Control**.

Caretakers, left untreated even start to decide who is damaged and how they are going to be fixed, they stay in relationships long after they are over. They sacrifice for their damaged and emotionally unavailable partners. They become martyrs. They play the victim role. Many battered women are caretakers: You can beat me into the ground but I'm going to stick with you until I fix you! Sometimes they're the ones who beat their partners into the ground trying to **"fix"** them.

Caretakers are the toughest people to work with in recovery. They never think they need recovery. How could they when they're so good at taking care of everybody? Even when they see the description of the caretaker, like the one laid out here, they say something like, *Yeah, I know people like that, My uncle, My aunt, My friend*...But never them. Not until they get desperate, really desperate as in major depression.

Even as addicts, caretakers are "goody-two-shoes." They tend to alcohol, but you never see them drunk in bars. They tend to abuse food in their own way: the over-weight, jolly person taking care of everyone else while he/she destroying himself/herself physically with food.

And they use caffeine, Adderall (prescription meth in my book), and cocaine, big time, to just keep up, to perform. As a businessman, I was just like that; I drank coffee constantly, morning, noon, and night. The only time I *"rested"* was to get the energy to go on another tear. I justified and rationalized cocaine and Adderall in my professional life because the pressure to take care of my work and my family was so great. I just did not have the energy. SO, I used substance to accomplish my caretaking priorities. I would go, go, go and then crash and then I required more substance. All with the help of my drugs, food, caffeine, cocaine, alcohol, work. The work was as much a drug as the substances. They all had the same effect: numb me, anesthetize me, block out my true feelings and what was causing those feelings.

IN A "NUTSHELL"
I'll sum this part of it up by saying that there are all sorts of diseases common to codependents. Some are physical, like those already accepted as stress-related diseases: hypertension, ulcers, colitis, and irritable bowel problems. And those coming to be accepted as stress-related: arthritis, obesity, cancer, and many, many more. Basically, if you hold your feelings in, they will eat away at you. If you are beaten emotionally, your body will soon show it. Your body never lies. Your body will always tell you the truth. According to Buddha your body is literally screaming at you to listen. You are suffering and your body is letting you know.

We're going to go into some other disease common to codependents. These are non-physical. Like procrastination, why we can't finish things we start. And lying, when we don't need to. And a fun little disease I call "**Splaining.**" Ok, I am going to really date myself but, I love TV, and I love

Cinema, if you have ever watched **"I love Lucy"** with Lucile Ball and Desi Arnez. And there is much debate if he even said this. I don't give a shit. This is my normal and this is how I remember it. When Lucy did something wonky or not according to the norm, Ricky Ricardo would find out and he would look at Lucy and say, in a Cuban accent: **"Lucy, you have some splaining to do!"** Even if it didn't happen, I love it as a reference to explain another disease among codependents. Anyway, ever since I was a child, I never forget this phrase, I thought it was so funny, and it stuck with me my entire life so far. Why, because I was big **"Splainer."**

Codependents are compulsive explainers **"Splainers"**, even when nobody's asking them too. And again, as with the physical, there are many, many more. What they basically do is undermine us as individuals. They are the manifestations of our *"neediness."*

SUFFERING

But before I move onto further ideas and topics, there is this constant theme of suffering. No one wants to suffer, least of all me. In all my readings, and watchings, and listenings, suffering seems to be the constant catalyst to change. I noticed this first when I first researched **Buddhism**, then again in the **I-Ching Book of changes**, and then off to some really light reading (yes, this is Sarcasm) the **Kabbalah**. Holy Shit my eyes opened. For some reason I believed that the ancients of 2000 to 3500 years ago, these vast and widely diverse mystical geolocated cultures had the secrets to how to become sober, find self-love and freedom and discover why I am the way I am. Suffering, being core to each one of these beautiful and enlightening mystical teachings. But they are not mystical any more. They are translated and interpreted and I can read them in English now. Fucking Awesome.

So, when I learned that suffering is critical to my journey of personal growth and ultimately to me loving myself. Yep, I said the words: Shit, Damn, Hell and Fuck, I am tired of suffering, but it finally helped that I accepted the fact I had to suffer to change. This was a huge step and turn for me. So, **First** step, **Awareness**, **Second** step, **Acceptance**. And it begins, the stages write themselves.

Suffering, as described in the I-Ching, Kabbalah, and Buddhism, shares some common themes while also offering unique perspectives on its individual nature and purpose.

1. **Suffering in the I-Ching (Book of Changes):**
The I-Ching acknowledges suffering as an inevitable part of the ever-changing and cyclical nature of life. It recognizes that both joy and suffering are interconnected aspects of existence, represented by the principles of Yin and Yang. Suffering is seen as the Yin aspect, contrasting with the Yang aspect of joy. The I-Ching teaches that experiencing suffering can lead to growth and transformation. By maintaining a balanced and composed mindset, individuals can navigate through difficult times, *just as water flows around obstacles with adaptability and resilience*. "Be Like water my friend" Bruce Lee reference. I wonder where Bruce Lee learned it? Mmmmmm, I-Ching is ancient Chinese learning, Bruce Lee is Chinese. See what I mean. He Knew!

2. **Suffering in Kabbalah:**
In Kabbalah, suffering is understood in the context of Tikkun, the concept of rectification. The material world and the human soul are considered fragmented and imperfect due to a primordial event. Suffering is seen as a consequence of this brokenness, and the human soul's purpose is to participate in the process of Tikkun by elevating and reuniting divine sparks through acts of kindness and ethical living. Suffering is also viewed as an opportunity for purification and spiritual growth. Challenges and difficulties in life are seen as opportunities to refine the soul, learn valuable lessons, and develop virtues.

3. **Suffering in Buddhism:**
Buddhism identifies suffering as the core problem of existence, referred to as Dukkha. It encompasses physical suffering, emotional dissatisfaction, and existential unease. Buddha's Four Noble Truths explain suffering as arising from craving and attachment, leading to the cycle of birth and rebirth (Samsara). The path to liberation (Nirvana) involves recognizing the nature of suffering, understanding its cause, and cultivating the Noble Eightfold Path, which includes ethical conduct, mental development, and wisdom. In Buddhism, suffering is a central concept that guides practitioners to seek enlightenment and transcend the cycle of suffering and rebirth.

In summary, all three traditions recognize suffering as an intrinsic part of human life. While the I-Ching emphasizes the balance between suffering and joy in the context of change, Kabbalah links suffering to the process of Tikkun and the elevation of divine sparks. In contrast, Buddhism identifies suffering as the core problem and focuses on its understanding and cessation through the Four Noble Truths and the Noble Eightfold Path. Despite the different approaches, these traditions share a common thread of seeking wisdom, transformation, and spiritual growth as individuals navigate the challenges of suffering.

(**Chapter 12; Suffering**; you will find even more supporting data that you can add as a tool for recovery and freedom)

CHAPTER 2

WHAT IS NORMAL?

"Normality is a paved road:
It's perversely comfortable to walk, but no flowers grow."
— **Vincent van Gogh**

"Normality is a fine ideal for those who have no imagination."
— **Carl Jung**

I want to go back to another concept: What Is Your Normal? You see, whatever your "**normal**" is, no matter how insane, you will seek it in every aspect of your life, especially your relationships.

Normal, what is Normal? I just want to be Normal. I always love hearing people say, I just want to be Normal. If they don't say it, then they actually try acting normal, or pretend to be normal (acting), like in the movies, we are all actors in our own movie. We control our narrative. In order for us to understand Normal as the world defines it, we need to first understand what Normal is personally. We have as many normals as we are honestly willing to look inward and be radically honest with ourselves. Are we willing to peel back the layers of an emotional onion. First layer of normal hurts, your eyes are burning and you cry for the vapors to disappear. It's painful and overwhelming and ever changing, however, hard work, truth, and time will transform those bitter painful layers to an absolute sweet and loving center.

My favorite question to ask, at the many coffee shops of where I conduct my research is; <u>What does Normal mean to you?</u> At first, looks of confusion, so I refine the question; <u>what is YOUR normal?</u> <u>Normal, as it pertains to your childhood formative (ages 0 to 11) years?</u> Then the light bulb switches on as they begin to describe what it was like growing up. Of which, Society, media, and our family systems shaped what normal means to us, and in most cases, a normal world of dysfunction. As, I bring up normal, normal is all about your past and your past environment, your family system. How were you raised, so it's very important that we don't place **Blame** on our past. **Blame** is part of process for recovery, it's very easy to get stuck in the gutter of blame. At the beginning I wrote about the past, I wanted to blame the past. So, as we confront our own *"honest normal"* It's important to not blame our parents, teachers, peers, the internet, whomever. Blame is a stage to go through, to think out, feel, and experience. It's important. It's not to be skimmed over. But it can also be a trap. Throughout the book I will continue to share some of my personal experiences and coffee talks as examples. Not to blame people in my own past. But to share my perceptions, right or wrong, they are my perceptions, and those perceptions influenced my development.

Finally, about the question itself: *What Is Normal?* I've had many coffee talks with men and women, mostly at a coffee shop (caffeine, still the addict), and I pose that question. Sometimes it's hard for people to understand what I'm asking. And when they get it, and answer it for themselves, you can get some extreme reactions. Some laugh. Some cry. Many do both.

For example, I explained to one person about how important the formative years are for human development, ages 0-12. And how looking back at a time where he had no control of his family system. What did a Normal day look like for him?

The amazing thing is, that these adults, we're just starting to realize that their childhood "normal" affected them as adults. In the one case, it created anxiety, which became clinical anxiety and depression. In the other, it created shame, the feeling that you are the **"Black Sheep"** meant that something was fundamentally wrong with the *person fundamentally,* meaning something that the person had no chance of changing. This had the same ultimate effect on him as suffered by the person in the first case: clinical anxiety and depression, and both of them, to escape the pain of the anxiety and depression, *"self-medicated"* with their own forms of addiction.

So, the NORMALS of your PAST, shape your PRESENT

Our normals come from our family system, and we are basically part of **Five Family Systems**: *Family-of-Origin (OG Family), Society, Religion, Peer group, and Media (All types).*

Our OG Family consists of the people who raised us. It can be parents, stepparents, or other surrogate parents: foster parents, institutions, even friends of the biological family. Society is our immediate environment: neighborhoods, regions, nationality, and cultures.

The religious family system is fairly obvious. Different religions impart and insist on different norms, and as children we have no choice but to accept them. Next, the peer groups, one of the most powerful systems to influence us. We all want to be accepted. So, we try to fit in. Fitting in means doing what everyone else does. Consequently, because of our peer groups, we wind up doing things that we really don't want to. Finally, Media: Social Media, Internet, TV, Movies, Phone, Radio, but mostly now Internet...The media has a powerful effect on what we accept as normal. Social Influencers on Facebook, Instagram, twitter. So Powerful.

The Seeds of Codependency in Relationships
The seeds of our codependency were sown by our family systems. They were planted deep inside of us, in our very spirit; when, as children, we tried to find out what normal was so we could fit in, find our own **Identity**. There were a lot of problems with that because, remember, we had five families, each with its own demands, often giving us conflicting and confusing messages. And each sending its messages with the same dire warning: **Don't change the rules!**

So, we ran into things like Mom and Dad not going to church but insisting that we go, or smoking or drinking but insisting that we don't smoke and/or drink or a religion that says not to kill but blesses troops as they march off to war. And often the same church was blessing troops on both sides.

Then we had the differences in generations. People grow older. Birthdays stay the same. A common source of confusion when labeling generations is their age. Generational cohorts are defined (loosely) by birth year, not current age. The reason is simple, generations get older in groups. If you think of Millennials as college kids (18 to 22), then not only are you out of date — you're thinking of a stage in life, not a generation. Millennials are now well out of college, and that life stage is dominated by Generation Zs.

Another example, a member of Generation X who turned 18 in 1998 would now be over 40. In that time, he or she cares about vastly different issues and is receptive to a new set of marketing messages. Regardless of your age, you will always belong to the generation you were born into.

The breakdown by generation stated on kasasa.com:

- **Baby Boomers**: born between 1946 and 1964; ages currently between 57-75 years old (71.6 million in the U.S.)
- **Gen X**: born between 1965 and 1979/80; ages currently between 41-56 years old (65.2 million people in the U.S.)
- **Gen Y**: or Millennials, born between 1981 and 1994/6; ages currently between 25 and 40 years old (72.1 million in the U.S.)
  - **Gen Y.1** = ages 25-29 years old (around 31 million people in the U.S.)
  - **Gen Y.2** = ages 29-39 years old
  - (around 42 million people in the U.S.)
- **Gen Z**: is the newest generation, born between 1997 and 2012. ages between 9 and 24 years old (nearly 68 million in the U.S.)
- **Gen A**: Generation Alpha starts with children born in 2012 and will continue at least through 2025, maybe later (approximately 48 million people in the U.S.)

The term *"Millennial"* has become the popular way to reference both segments of Gen Y. Sometimes labeled with the moniker *"Zillennials"*, those wedged at the tail end of Millennials and the start of Generation Z are sometimes labeled with this moniker, a group made up of people born between 1994 and the year 2000.

Originally, the name Generation Z was a placeholder for the youngest people on the planet, although Generation A has now taken over that distinction. However, in the same way that Generation Y morphed into Millennials, there is certainly a possibility that both Generation Z and Generation A may adopt new names as they leave adolescence and mature into their adult identities. While the label Generation A makes discussion easier, it may not be the last word on this group of humans.

My point is that I have lived and been a part of all "Sacred Ideals" from "Baby Boomers" to "Generation A" and every defined group in between each group has a different set of "**Sacreds.**" The world and what has changed is so drastic. What was so important as "**Sacred Ideals**" to a Generation X born in 1965 is drastically different than a Generation Z born in 2012. Each group has a different set of rules than the group before it. And to complicate things further there were differences within each of those groups as well. In the 40's you were taught to be patriotic. In the 60's Vietnam changed much of that. In the 40's if the cops caught a kid with a Beer it was a major scandal. In the 60's they were almost relieved when it was only Beer, not Marijuana or LSD or something. In the 70s it was Heroin, and in the 80s it has been cocaine and meth, now we are in the 2020s and Marijuana and Magic Mushrooms are becoming legal in the US and already legal in various countries, and heroin, meth, and cocaine are overwhelmingly global and way to accessible. Again, what used to be unacceptable as a Boomer or Generation X is now becoming acceptable as a Generation Z and Generation A. So are belief system, are intellect, our souls as we come into this world is being influenced across many different generations, and Parents today will have conflicting teachings then maybe the Peer Groups or Media is teaching them as they are born into a different set of "**Sacreds**" than their parents, and/or grandparents.

In my own case, I was a child-twin in a Mormon-German-American family. I had some interesting rules laid down: *Can't be out late on Saturday night, due to church on Sunday. Because our guide, the Holy Ghost goes to bed at midnight. Can't smoke, can't drink, can't curse, no type of sexual intercourse whatsoever, and don't get me started on masturbation shaming as a Mormon teenager. Shit, Damn, Hell, seriously!* Basically, do what you're told, be the perfect Mormon child. I joke about it now, but it's no joke. I grew up trying to live up to that fundamental message. From trying to be the perfect child, I went to trying to be the perfect student, perfect Mormon, perfect person. I beat the hell out of myself trying to get everything right. In school, a Mormon in Salt Lake City, Utah, we had seminary, religious studies, as a required course. So, Mormons everywhere, and there is plenty of Mormon peer pressure to be a good Mormon 24/7. Actually, we had a lot of rules; the word of wisdom, law of chastity, Priesthood responsibility, etc. This was engrained into us even at school, which influenced how I lived and learned. Hell, you couldn't be a kid; you couldn't be a teenager, because if you said a bad word in school, or kissed a girl in school, someone was going to tell your Bishop. Not even your parents, literally someone would rat you out to your bishop?

I had an interesting relationship with God at the time. Looking back, I was taught that He was an angry God, a vengeful God, and a punishing God. And maybe this was the only thing I could hear. He was a tool to keep me disciplined, to keep me in line with the rules laid down by a person or institution defining Him for you. And, yes, God, of course, was a *"He,"* a male figure. Once, I actually thought it would be nice to have a "She" God, loving, caring, compassionate, understanding. Just for fun I started referencing God as a She in my **"Splaining"** to others as I began to learn and change. So hilarious, people would stop and say your God is a she? Hell yeah, and she is beautiful and loving and compassionate. They had nothing to say to me after that. Who wouldn't want that? Just that simple gesture started to change my programming and change my normal.

The point is this: If you think back to your *"normals"* you will see where a lot of your problems come from. Try to put face on your *"normals"* so you can more easily see the confusion they can create. I am trying to give some examples to prime the pump, to get you thinking and reflecting on your own normals. Let's just go through a few more general examples. They're common enough. Let's just list some of the things, society accepted as normal over the past two, three, or four decades. You'll see for yourself how they've changed.

- *Women can't perform high level jobs; (Bullshit)*
- *Mixed marriages, mixed by gay, race, religion, or ethnic group can't work; (Again bullshit)*
- *Men shouldn't show emotion; (So much bullshit)*
- *Kids don't know better until their adults; (The ultimate in bullshit)*

It's absolutely fucking mind blowing that these belief systems still exist and I have an exercise for you. Go to the Internet and dig up songs, movies, magazines, newspapers, social influencers, news sites, blogs, etc. It has all changed drastically; people change their opinions and thoughts like a feather in a windstorm. You can find an argument both positive and negative for any argument. It can drive you crazy. Everyone has something to say. Ultimately, every person wants to be heard and validated. They want to feel they matter. They want to be loved by all their family systems. They want to be secure and have an identity.

It's upsetting to see conflicted souls declaring suicide notes on YouTube. The Internet is this amazing knowledge base, but can also be our biggest crutch, even our addiction. Oh my god, you have to be so careful, online marketers and advertisers have finally figured out in order to make real money and to hook as many as people as possible, you market to their addictions, Its genius, but horrible. This is why we need to start having a real sense of self and personal awareness.

UNDOING THE ROOTS: CHANGE

Why? Because we CHANGE! People change. Consequently, our relationships *should* change if we are to remain healthy. Yet as codependents, that's one of things we have the hardest time with: **Change**. Remember how it happened. As children we experienced shame, fear, guilt, and a host of other negative feelings that weren't balanced with the positive: open displays of love, intimacy, clear messages of encouragement. For example, the mother that couldn't be there for us because she had to work two jobs, she could have sat down and explained her motives until they sunk in. But that wasn't done then. Then *children were seen but not heard,* and *they wouldn't understand anyway.* Yet even if children don't understand certain words, they understand actions, they understand "the feeling" at that moment in time. An attempt to explain things would have gone a long way to making the child feel secure.

But again, as codependents, we didn't get the *feeling* of security or other positives. We didn't get them from our primary family or our other family systems. What we did get were "**the Rules.**" Follow the rules and you'll be accepted.

And the Mother of All Rules: Don't Change the Rules!

Now you wonder why you don't like change? Codependents don't like *any* change, Major or minor. Have you ever seen a codependent get a divorce? It takes about eighteen years (longer than it should). We know it's over but we won't let go. Why? Because of a lot of things, one of which is a normal we learned a long time ago: *You don't get a divorce! Divorce equals failure!*

But I can do you one better from my own experience. Married over 30 years, it took a therapist to show me what I was doing, what codependents typically do. She told me I was living with one foot on both sides of the proverbial picket fence. That's a pretty painful journey, right? But that's what we codependents do. We keep one foot in the past and one in the future, and we hurt like hell in the middle. Of course it hurts, my legs are literally split across a sharp picket fence. And the sharp picket fence is digging into my precious twig and berries, and I would suck it up and not say anything to anyone, but I would act out in different ways. I was like a water balloon filled with too much water. The pressure was too much and I did not know why. I did not want the water balloon to break or I'd suffer some kind of catastrophic synaptic shutdown. Instead, the water (emotions) would force its way out in unhealthy ways, Anger, Frustration, Conflict, Work, Sex, and eventually Drugs and Alcohol. Here is something I hear a lot now. I hear people, staggering, groaning, complaining, and bitching about it. But that's what we codependents do. The weight we drag is from our past, from our normals. We won't give them up. We won't change.

And it's not only the major changes we fear. It's not just about divorce and career changes. It's about the smaller things, too. It's as though in learning to doubt ourselves on the larger issues we also learned to include the small ones. And here we are stuck, with these very common codependent diseases, the **"I Know"** disease and the **"Splaining"** disease. Why change? We already *"know it"* and keep *"splaining"* it to everyone and even more seriously, to ourselves.

GEOGRAPHICAL CHANGES
So often codependents substitute geographical change for a real, complete change. I say it and think it all the time, if I'm being honest. I did it like 16 times and guess what, it worked for a little bit, but let's say I did move or change jobs, I am still carrying a dump truck of my underlying causes of those addictions chained to my ankles. So, what did I really change? My address? And what good did it do me? Eventually I had to face the fact that I wasn't happy, or **healthy** *and* that's a key point I want to get to, and that I wouldn't have much of a life until I made a real change. Making that real change meant giving up the **"I Know" disease**. It wasn't enough to say, for example, I know my OG Family had their quirks and they affected me, but I should just get over it and get on with it without taking the time to really explore those *"quirks"* and how they affected me, how they made me *feel*. And how my feelings made me act. And I had to give up the myth of a geographical change being enough to set my life straight, make it healthy.

I see people who blame the Job for their codependency. I know I Did. *If only I had a different job, getaway from these assholes.* But guess what? I quit and my problems didn't go away. I still had them. Or take the person who says, *I just need a change of location. If I lived in a Fiji making t-shirts, the seashore or country, my problems would go away.* You think so? The Unabomber lived like a hermit. Did his psychological problems go away?

If you really want to shed your codependency, get used to the facts. You are going to have to identify and inventory your issues. You are going to have to feel feelings that you buried long ago and that can be and probably will be very painful. You are going to have to **own your past, hold it, look at it, so you can finally let it go**. That is the change that will work, that will enable your relationships to work.

PERMISSION
Permission. I have to inject that phenomenon here. It might sound silly, but psychiatrists, psychologists, counselors, and therapists at all levels have noticed something about many of their clients: they feel that they don't have *permission* to change. Remember. The Mother of All Rules: *Don't Change the Rules!* That message was given long ago. And now there's nobody there to take it back, to give permission to change. So, we get stuck. Stuck with our old normals.

THE DISEASE of "Splaining!"
We codependents won't even give ourselves permission to make the small changes in life. And here's where the **"Splaining"** comes in. Codependents have to explain every little thing to other people. Somebody asks us to come to a party Saturday night. We really don't want to go, but we say *"uh, um, uh"*, got to go check and see if I can make it, then maybe even say we'll make it, then Saturday comes and we call and say *"I can't make it because the carburetor in my car is shit!"* or *"my cat and dog require special feeding times, I can't just leave them!"* The truth is the car's fine, the cat is fine, the dog is fine, but we Splain and then we lie. Oh my god, as a child, I was the most horrible liar, it would absolutely destroy me every time I felt I had to lie.

Or ask a codependent to go to a movie when they really don't want to. Instead of just saying they don't want to go, they go into another *"uh, um, uh"*, I really would like to go but I have to go here and I have to go there and hey, by the time you finish your explanation, you'll miss the movie! We explain when we don't have to. We explain when no one asks for an explanation. We explain to other people because we're afraid that they won't like us if we say no, if we make an honest choice. And guess what? We explain to ourselves even when we don't need it. Oh my God, I was the epitome of **"Splaining."** Hell, I am still doing it writing this fucking book. But the difference now is my radical honesty and acceptance of my normals and past and who I am today to make the required and desired changes.

An example. Have you ever decided to call in sick to work when you're not sick? Say you've been working hard, you just need a day, you have plenty of time saved, and nothing really critical is going on in work that day anyway.

I'm telling you, if you live with a codependent that's going to call in sick. They can make TV sitcoms out of this. The codependent will have like thirty-three anxieties the night before they have to call because they already feel guilty about it. And between attacks they start getting their story ready. It starts out like a one-line message and ends up like a book: explaining again. Rehearsing the explanations they're going to give when they call in, while explaining to themselves that they're entitled to the day off, the story will work, no one will guess that they're really not sick, and on and on. Now, remember. This is all in preparation for a day *off*.

After a sleepless night they make the call. But the guy on the other end maybe just worked the night shift and only wants to get home, so you start your explaining and he cuts you short. He notes that you'll be out sick and cuts the rest short and hangs up. Now you got a major problem. Nobody listened to your story and you're wondering why. So, you spend all day polishing the story, getting ready for the next day at work. And this is your day *off. The* next day you finally get to work, exhausted from all the explaining and worrying, and guess what? Nobody knows you were gone. Nobody cares. You sign in and go to your workstation. But you can't work. You have this great story even though it's not true and you have to tell it to somebody. You have to explain why you were out sick just so you can feel better!

And we wonder why our relationships don't work?

It's insanity. Insanity isn't just rotting in an asylum somewhere. It's the craziness we create in our own lives. The **"Splaining"** is one form of it. If you suffer from it, try something. Try answering somebody without giving an explanation. Just say what you feel and let it go. But I warn you.

It's going to be scary. That's what the child in you will feel. Because **giving up Insanity** creates a very uncomfortable situation, very uncomfortable. **Which is SANITY!** Because the little child inside of you, your past and all its *"normals"* is not used to sanity: That's why people report that the Second Step of the Twelve Steps Program, where it says, *"...will be restored to sanity..."* becomes so frightening to them. They just aren't used to it. I know I wasn't.

The other thing to remember about your recovery, the process by which you move from insanity to sanity, is that it is an *ongoing* process. Addicts have a saying about it: *Progress, not perfection (cliché)*. Because your insanity, your codependent patterns, will keep pulling you back (relapse). For example, when I was a kid, I was poor, not hungry, my Dad was starting a new business, I had a twin brother and 2 younger sisters, my Mom went to Goodwill to get us clothing and shoes, my parents were doing what they had to in order to provide for their family. But in getting this hand me down clothing, I was out dated, and I was constantly teased about it. I would leave home out the back door to go to school and then go to front porch and I would destroy my shoes so that my Mom would get me a newer more socially accepted shoes. Consequently, I developed a fear about anyone seeing me with hand me down clothes. Now today I dress respectively nice, some brand names of course. But I still, now and then, crawl back into that little kid worried how people see me in my clothes. That's an idiosyncrasy from my past. Those things linger. What should we do about them in recovery? Very simple: **Accept them.**

REAL CHANGE: SPIRITUAL DEVELOPMENT

As I noted before, this book will often refer to the Twelve Steps Program of recovery, to Buddhism, to Kabbalah, to Chinese I-Ching, and other shit I figured out. But no matter what program you follow, maybe one, maybe many like myself, you are going to find some common denominators in all the forms of your personalized treatment. One of the most important is that you are going to have to take a **personal-inventory.** In the Steps Program and Kabbalah, they encourage this critical stage of self-awareness and that you should write an honest inventory and share it with at least one other person you trust. In traditional therapy, the inventory might be verbal, with a therapist, a psychologist, a psychiatrist, or performance coach. The point is that you must look at your past, and *own* it, see how it made you who you are today. With that knowledge of your personal history, you will begin to get a sense of that thing that is so elusive to us codependents: **Identity.**

But the knowledge alone won't be enough. You have to *do something* with it. That's one of the most frustrating parts of traditional therapy and why I like these programs, Twelve Steps does a great job with this. Clients often complain to therapists that though they've gained a great deal of self- knowledge they don't know what to do with it. It's as though we expect the knowledge alone to release us from our depression and anxiety and other codependent patterns. But it doesn't and we get frustrated. Remember when we talked about the other codependent disease, the **"I Know" "disease"**? So many people walk around depressed and angry but are in total denial about the effect the past had on them. It's as though they're afraid to challenge the **"normals"** they were brought up with, afraid to admit that maybe their parents weren't perfect parents. Hell, I am a grandparent, and here I am writing a book about my addictions and my many failures. I am far from perfect. So, whose parents are perfect? The answer is: No Parents are perfect, just **Human**. So, when you tell them that their past affects them, they say *I know, I know,* but they're afraid to take it any further. So, they start believing that life is as all of us have said many times in our life: *"Life's a bitch and then you die!"* Carry that philosophy into your relationships and see what happens when the initial glow of those relationships wears off no matter who or what those relationships are with. It is no less than insane to live so negatively.

In a good recovery program, you will learn how to use your self-knowledge to change. You will learn that you have rights, the right to choose *and change* your own normal, the right to your idiosyncrasies and nuances and to that private part of yourself, which is protected by boundaries that you set. And you have the right to serenity and to end things in your life even if somebody else wants to hang on and not end them. You can choose healthy relationships and let the unhealthy go. Basically, you learn the:

New Mother of All Rules: You can Change the Rules!

---

*This reminded me of a movie I watched with Denzel Washington and Chloë Moretz called **The Equalizer**. He is in a café early morning reading a book when Chloë Moretz character (Teri) breaks protocol to talk to Robert McCall (Denzel Washington). She has accepted that being an escort is who she is and that's all she will ever be, but she really wants to* be a singer. Watch the movie, it really is a beautiful scene. Here is the dialogue:

> **Teri :** You and I know what I really am.
> **Robert McCall :** I think you can be anything you wanna be.
> **Teri :** Maybe in your world, Robert. Doesn't really happen that way in mine.
> **Robert McCall : Change your World!**

You'll learn something else, too. When you do change, 25% of the people will not like what you do, 25% will like it, and 50% won't care one way or the other! Not exactly sure of the percentages, but you get the point. So, you don't have to be afraid of change. That fear is another of your old *"normals"* that you have to get rid of. It is something you were taught.

YOUR GUIDE TO CHANGE: HEALTHY VS. UNHEALTHY

How do you know if you're making the right changes? Remember earlier in this chapter when I emphasized the word "**healthy**"? That one word is a good, basic guide to choosing what changes you make. Forget talking about things in terms of good and bad or whether something is a *"SIN"* or not. This leads to Guilt and Shame. Talk in terms of Healthy vs. Unhealthy. That alone will be enough to make a start toward real spiritual development, real growth. And if you make a mistake with your changes, we all do, just make another change. ***You'll get the hang of it.***

CHAPTER 3

HOW TO PLAY!

> *"You can discover more about a person in an hour of play than in a year of conversation."*
> — *Plato*

> *"Play is the highest form of research."*
> — *Albert Einstein*

THE VALUE OF HEALTHY PLAY

I *feel that healthy* play is one of the most important things you can do. I completely forgot to play how a child plays. So powerful, once you have children, and grandchildren, playing becomes a trigger or a second chance to be a kid. Main points I observed:

- ➔ Playing helps you get in touch with your feelings, especially your *positive* feelings.
- ➔ Playing helps develop a positive attitude.
- ➔ Playing helps shatter rigidity.
- ➔ And playing helps shed your fear of dysfunctionality.

One thing I do now is wear a Fedora, It's my Hat, It's simple, but it reminds me to be like a child, to wear a hat every day that most would think is silly or not fashion chic. That's my point! Children don't care that they are miss- matched. They will wear that Spiderman T-shirt or ballerina dress all day everywhere because they love it, it makes them happy, and I as a parent/grandparent do not judge them for it. I encourage it and love it. So why in the fuck did we forget to do this, as we become adults? Try being a kid again and who gives a shit of the judgment, just be a kid and own it, it is truly liberating. I remember attending rehab in Florida and it started to rain. I loved the rain, so I literally went out in the rain half naked just getting wet and standing in puddles, I went full Gene Kelly in the movie, "Singing in the Rain," and every recovering addict is like *"Karl, what the fuck are you doing?"* I said, *"I'm playing and dancing in the rain."* They could see how much I enjoyed it; I asked them all to come join me, there were at least 50 in my rehab all staring and watching, only a few ended up joining me. I remember how sad I was that they could not even be a kid again for just 15 minutes and soak in literally the beautiful rain. Afterwards, when we were all in therapy, and I explained it to them, and the next time it rained, we were all kids again, playing in the rain. I'll never forget it.

HEALTHY PLAY: CHALLENGE Your "DEFAULT SETTING"
I want to go back to that word I used above and mentioned in the last chapter: **Healthy**. Why do I put the emphasis on it? Because codependents generally forgot what they learned in childhood: how to play in a healthy way. While in my recovery, our recovery, and, don't get turned off by the word recovery. I'm not just talking about recovery from alcohol or drugs. I'm talking about recovery from codependency in general, from anxiety and depression and all sorts of destructive behaviors. Anyway, recovery, codependency, addictions is all consuming. We need to take a break and play, stop the insanity, the madness. Take a day or night off and make a little effort to remember the healthy things like: boating, a movie, camping, lunch, a ball game, bowling, something healthy and positive.

This isn't a rare phenomenon. One of the problems in treating addictions is that we have developed an automatic mode, what can be called a "**Default Settings.**" Like a computer, these are things we do when we don't give ourselves a clear command to do something else. And our defaults kick in especially when we're under stress. For example, a codependent stressed by a situation at work or home will automatically and strongly turn to his or her particular addictions: alcohol, drugs, overeating, compulsive spending, work, gambling, porn, sex. As codependents, we need to learn, or, more accurately, relearn how to lower our stress through healthy play.

GETTING IN TOUCH WITH FEELINGS
I'm going to stress another point here: getting in touch with **positive** feelings. Remember, recovery is about getting in touch with your feelings, especially those feelings you buried long ago, from ages 0 to 12, because they were too painful to face. You've probably heard the term "**Inner Child.**" I remember when I started hearing about my inner child. So foreign to me, deep down, I knew I did not want to go there, that it was painful, and this is why I abused substances way longer than I should

have. I did not want to be self-aware; I did not want to face or find my inner child. However, that's whom we are all trying to get in touch with, our own Inner Child as we were years ago. To do that, as we said, you are going to have to recall your history. This is where your personal-inventory comes in. And you have to own that history. Remember it, Acknowledge it. Accept it. Feel it. Really *Feel it*. *In fact, you might have to sit in that discomfort, as per my therapist in rehab (God, I hated her at the moment she said that, I Love and adore Her now, but Jesus not that moment).*

Buddhism states, in order to find yourself, and be at peace, you have to:
Go back to the beginning!

Don't go past this last point lightly. Yes, you are going to *feel* things that you buried and denied long ago. For example, if you were sexually abused and blocked it out or made excuses for the perpetrator, you are going to go back, look at it, and accept it as something that happened *to you*. And you're going to be angry and depressed and guilty and shamed.

In my case, I had repressed memories that I had been sexually abused by a 12-year-old girl, when I was maybe 9 or 10, that lived on my street. She was probably sexually abused as well. I faintly remember her telling me about her father or grandfather, I remember how upset I was when she told me as we were at the playground on the swings. Those memories were very real and I can remember many of those moments now in vivid detail. Talk about being upset. Shit, Damn, Hell! Yep, like you got to be fucking kidding me!

So, you are going to recall things that aren't nearly as traumatic as something like sexual abuse, maybe a forgotten birthday that someone forgot or even a game that you didn't get for your birthday, and that's going to hurt, too. In fact, there's a growing school of thought that even without exceptional trauma in our lives, the small hurts and disappointments alone are enough to erode us psychologically, enough to depress us and make us anxious and give in to our defaults. If we let them.

How do you not let them? By **taking your inventory.** By going through the things that affected you and putting them into perspective. We call that *"processing"* the past. When you do that, you will come to the point in the Grieving Process, which we will cover in some depth later, that we call **Acceptance**. That's when the depression and anxiety and other insanity evaporates.

So, the beginning of the recovery process is getting in touch with feelings. Healthy play will help with that. **Healthy play has to become a tool in your toolbox.** Because it is spontaneous. You might see a movie and cry, or laugh. Or see a ball game and cheer. Or go camping and be awe struck by nature. Or go to an amusement park and just yell your head off on the roller coaster. None of that can be planned. And feeling what you feel in those instances is like priming the pump to get your feelings flowing again, or, to use another analogy, banging away at the rust that has built up on your engine: **your feelings**.

Better yet, you will be experiencing *positive* feelings. And you're going to have to learn how to do that to soothe some of the pain you're going to experience in doing the inventory of your past, and the pain of today's stresses as well. In plain words, you will need a healthy outlet for stress. Otherwise, you'll keep reverting to your defaults to numb your pain.

There is another reason why writing your Inventory is so important, I call it, **The Tangled Mind**, Buddha calls it, **The Monkey Mind**. Your mind and your thoughts are so powerful, you literally have every emotion and every thought, and everything you have ever felt, heard, or learned, swirling around in your head, since the day you were born. You have to extract it. If you leave it in your head and you don't say it, write it, process it, accept it, and let it go, it becomes intertwined with other thoughts. It can become its own emotional animal. I call it **The Tangled Mind**.

It's like getting ready for Christmas, you start pulling out the boxes and you find the ornaments and the tree and then you pull out this tangled mess of Christmas lights. First thought and words are SHIT, DAMN, HELL! I have to untangle these lights, and then I think, I probably have broken bulbs too. This is what inventory is. You have to patiently untangle and unweave these lights into a single line on the floor, and then one-by-one, you start fixing the light bulbs, each time you fix one, that particular light comes on, then you move to the next one, until you have a complete line of Christmas lights and then after constant patience and hard work, all the lights are bright and shining, beautiful. And then you decide to decorate and put them on the tree. And once, on the tree, you get to look at them and reflect on how beautiful the lights are, how beautiful the whole tree is. Yep, you did that. You did the work to untangle each inventory item, and as you work through each emotional inventory item, a light turns on. Clarity, understanding, compassion, and love to yourself for creating something beautiful again. Thank God for Christmas and Christmas lights. In the words of a beautiful singer and recovering addict, SIA; *"Shine bright like a diamond!"*

CARPOOL KARAOKE
Ok, I have an exercise for you, this is one of my favorites, imagine that all your *"Normals"*, your *"Inner Child"* and your dysfunctional adult is a big giant water balloon. Inside the balloon are all these emotions, and pains, and frustrations, and sadness, and anger and depression. Like seriously, it's too much. And as each day passes that balloon keeps filling up, If we do not instigate healthy play to release the pressure. And, also as some of those releases happen like pain and sadness, you need to couple that with positive healthy tools. So here is the exercise, and I am fucking serious, you need to do this. It really works. This needs to be a tool in your toolbox.

If you feel like you are going to explode or you are going to isolate yourself, drag your ass up, get dressed the best you know how, because I know you don't want to. Get in your car, just you. And put on a song, or singer you really like. Not something that looks acceptable to your peers or what social media says, or what parents says is acceptable. I am in my 50s, I will get in my truck, and then I will literally put on Cardi B and *Hip-Hop Out!* I will roll down all the windows, rain, snow or shine, I don't give a shit and then I will sing **'I Like it'** by **Cardi B, Bad Bunny, and JBalvin** at the top of my lungs. Or I will do this to Michael Bublé, Andrea Bocelli, Miley Cyrus, then I will start in on my Latin Hip Hop artists (I am a huge Bad Bunny fan), then I progress to my French Hip-Hop artist (47ter). I literally sound like shite, but, Oh My God, music has a way of getting into your happy Inner Child. It taps into when you first heard music, when as kids we loved to dance and sing. Music is a soul language, and emotional language. You have to carpool karaoke without judgment. I am not talking external judgment, others people's judgment, I am talking about the judgment you impose on yourself. This has always helped me overcome heavy pain moments, instead of wanting to drug and drink, I used Carpool Karaoke to help make those feelings pass. Add this to your own toolbox, I promise it will work. Seriously, I am in my 50s, can you see some dude, in his 50s, in his truck rapping to Cardi B. Absolutely!

POSITIVE ATTITUDE, RIGIDITY, FEAR OF DYSFUNCTIONALITY

These three points can be covered quickly. They're related closely to what we already discussed. But pay attention to the last one: **fear of dysfunctionality**.

First though, **Positive Attitude**. We'll get into this later in the book. For now, in my research, as codependents, not always but codependents generally live with a negative attitude. Codependents are oriented to three things: **chaos, catastrophe, and faultfinding**. We find fault with ourselves as well as others. And even when things are going right, we look over our shoulders waiting for something bad to happen. It's like the line in the movies where the characters are strolling through a forest with no danger in sight, when suddenly one stops and says in fear: *"I don't like it. It's too quiet."* Why are we like this? Because of the dysfunctionality in our OG Families. Those families were chaotic and faultfinding. They taught us to expect the bad, if not the worst. Learning how to play again in a healthy way helps balance the negative outlook. Basically, you learn that having fun is part of life, too. And there's nothing more positive than that. I think it's the *Talmud* that says that when you die you will be held accountable for every elicit pleasure you could have enjoyed but didn't.

Fear of dysfunctionality. This is sort of a paradox. As codependents we are so dysfunctional. Yet we are sometimes *terrified* by dysfunctionality. For example, some of us are so afraid of dysfunctionality that we refuse to face the dysfunctionality of our past. In psychology, I learned that it's called **Denial**. I start looking into my past, at my OG Family, I initially refused, insisted that there was nothing wrong with the way I was brought up. I exhibited the **"I Know"** disease: *I know I didn't have the perfect family or perfect friends or perfect environment but nobody does, so my problems can't be coming from there.* And in trying to deny my past dysfunctionality I become married to my present dysfunctionality: the headaches, depression, nervous tics, drinking, overeating, gambling, shopping, working, silent treatment, drugs...Jesus, whatever.

My point here is this: Don't be afraid of dysfunctionality. The entire *world* is dysfunctional. The purpose of it is that you learn from dysfunctionality. So, accept it. Accept that part of ourselves. Get into your own recovery. And learn from it. And in the meantime, enjoy life. Play a little.

Just think of what happens to a relationship, when what you bring to it, is tainted by a negative attitude, rigidity, and fear of dysfunctionality.

After the honeymoon wears off, the negative attitude makes you a burden; **W**here's **T**he **F**un (WTF), the joy? Rigidity kills creativity, so how does the relationship stay fresh and spontaneous? And fear of dysfunctionality makes you super critical, so afraid of doing something dysfunctional, something wrong. Ever live with a super-critical person? It's fucking rough.

As for rigidity, as codependents we are like robots. No mystery here. Our feelings are frozen. Our values are frozen. So how could we be anything but frozen? Learn to play, and you relearn spontaneity. By the way, you cannot be rigid and spontaneous at the same time.

If you are not familiar with the concept of the Inner Child, it's very simple. It is you as a child still living inside yourself. He or she has all the healthy things that ever happened to you, all the pleasant nostalgia. And he or she also has all the unhealthy: neglect; abuse; unresolved anger, fear, and frustration; depression and anxiety...The theory is, and it seems to work, that if you work through the unhealthy, own your history and process it through writing your inventory and discussing it with trusted people, you will nurture the inner you until you heal the unhealthy, settle with it, come to peace with it. Then the healthy, the good, can come bubbling to the surface, to your conscious thought and feeling.

SOME EXERCISES
In my research, I ran into workbooks and things to do, like actual assignments. Good codependents like assignments. I hated assignments, but I had nothing to lose, nothing else was working for me. I think I hated assignments because it meant I had to admit my life had become completely unmanageable and I could not fix it on my own. Some Caretakers, codependents, *love* assignments. Probably because of the structure we're all addicted to. So here are some of the assignments I thought resonated with me and had a positive effect.

No recipe ever baked itself (Cliché). Right? In other words, you can read all the books you want, but if you don't practice what you read and learn, it won't do you any good. So, I wanted to make an effort to do these assignments. I'm not going to try to explain how they work. But I did learn a few things about myself. I got to meet another part of myself, one I have tucked away and probably hidden in the closet. I did definitely experience feelings, both positive and negative. I felt things like anxiety and anger, clarity and understanding. As I completed different exercises, I also felt things like love and trust, and I definitely laughed my ass off on a few things. I noticed with many of these exercises, had to do with: **Control**.

I needed to learn how to let go, and stop trying to control everything. Because the simple fact is you can't control very much of anything, let alone everything. My Dad tried to teach me this for years.

First assignment: If you're the type of person who makes their bed every morning and tries to keep everything perfect, I want you to stop that for the next seven days. One week. Leave the bed unmade. Leave the dishes in the sink. Leave the computer on after you use it. If you read a book, leave it out, don't put back on the shelf, whatever. And if you're generally the opposite, the messy type, then for the next seven days make your bed, clean the dishes, tidy your mess. I said try it for one week. Seven days. See if you last *twenty minutes.* See how you feel after just twenty minutes.

Second assignment: If you're the type of person who's always on time for everything, I want you to be late for all your appointments for the next week. And if you're the type who's always late, do the opposite. Now, with this one, aside from watching your own reactions, watch the people around you. Some people aren't going to like it when you're not as predictable as you were. They won't like it when you change even for a week. I'll tell you two things about this one. **First**, there's a little principle, a little advice, for people who want to change their circumstances but feel they can't. They're told to change themselves. You see, if you change yourself, your circumstances have to change. Think about it. We are each like a brick in a wall. Shift that brick and the entire wall has to shift. **Second**, many people in your life particularly those who like to *"push your buttons"* can predict your behavior. So, consider the implications of you making a change. Even for one week.

Third assignment: Over the next week, take at least one hour and do nothing. Absolutely Nothing. No TV. No phone. No radio. no Internet, no books, no movies. Nothing. Just sit and be. This one was so fucking rough. We are so movement oriented that it might not be easy. These were all my tools to try and satiate the pain, or loss, or anxiety, whatever I was feeling. They were my escape. But to get back to the assignment, take an hour this week and do nothing. Get to know yourself.

Call in sick to work and go to a movie. Get some friends together and have a sleep over. Or just watch TV. I mean, really watch it. Ever see us codependents watch TV? We watch while we do something else: cleaning, cooking, looking at Facebook, watching YouTube...Just sit and watch TV for once and get into the show. Enjoy it. Or get a friend and take a walk. Just walk and talk. Who knows? If you really get into it, you might just start skipping along the way. Try it. **Dare To Be Different (cliché).**

ACCESS THE INNER CHILD

There is so much on Inner Child work, I mean books and books, it really is a critical part of recovery and I am listing some activities that worked for me, that started my Inner Child activations. These activities were critical in my recovery and discovery. The key is to approach these activities with a sense of curiosity, openness, and non-judgment. Allow yourself to fully embrace your inner child and the joy, wonder, and authenticity it brings. It worked for me, and I promise it will work for you. I listed a few ideas below:

   1. Photo Exploration: Look through old photo albums or childhood pictures. Reflect on the memories and emotions they evoke. Allow yourself to fully immerse in the experiences captured in those images. This one is wild, because I looked at my childhood photo and there was one in particular where I could look at the picture and identified how sensitive and creative of a little boy I was.

   2. Storytelling: Write or tell stories about your childhood, focusing on joyful or significant moments. Use descriptive language to bring those memories to life and reconnect with the feelings associated with them. There is this fantastic movie called 3000 Years of longing, starring Idris Elba and Tilda Swinton about Storytelling that is absolutely brilliant. Idris Character is a Djinn that tells the most amazing stories the entire movie. That is what Storytelling is.

   3. Music and Dance: Create a playlist of songs from your childhood or songs that evoke nostalgia. Sing and Dance freely and joyfully to the music, allowing your body to move and express itself without inhibition. My Wife loved this one. When she wants to get in touch with her Inner Child, she will go to a club with her friends and she will literally be the only on the dance floor, just dancing and singing away. She loves it; she totally let's your inner child dance free. It's beautiful to watch and even better for her and how she feels.

   4. Toy Play: Engage in play with toys or objects that remind you of your childhood. Play with dolls, action figures, or building blocks, and let your imagination run wild. Create scenarios and immerse yourself in the world of play. If you have young children or grandchildren, a young niece or nephew, please allow yourself to be completely present and sit on the floor and play toys with them. Something magical will happen to you. I promise.

5. **Outdoor Play:** Spend time in nature engaging in playful activities like swinging on swings, climbing trees, blowing bubbles, or having a picnic. Reconnect with the sense of wonder and adventure you experienced as a child. Blowing bubbles with my grandson, and laughing, and catching the bubbles with him, I was right there in step with him. Magical!

6. **Revisit Childhood Hobbies:** Revisit hobbies or activities you enjoyed as a child, such as painting, coloring, playing a musical instrument, or participating in sports. Allow yourself to engage in these activities purely for the joy they bring.

7. **Dialogue with Your Inner Child:** Engage in a written or spoken dialogue with your inner child. Ask your inner child questions, express love and understanding, and offer support and reassurance. Listen to the responses that arise from within. This one was initially difficult until I had my grandson. He truly helped me gain access to my Inner Child. When I talked to him, and asked questions, I imagined talking to my younger sensitive self. It's truly been magical how this specific practice works.

8. **Dress-Up or Costume Play:** Put on costumes or dress up in clothes that make you feel playful and childlike. Allow yourself to embody different characters or personas and embrace the sense of fun and imagination. If you have a young child or a niece or a nephew., do this with them, your inner child will love it. They won't judge you they will engage with you and you can interact safely back.

9. **Playful Exploration:** Visit a local playground, amusement park, or carnival. Engage in activities like swinging, sliding, or playing games. Embrace the thrill and joy of these experiences. My grandson and me could not get enough of the playground or the splash park, I just loved joining in, again, I just looked at him as if I was looking at myself. And I asked myself how much I enjoyed playing and exploring.

10. **Letter to Your Younger Self:** Write a heartfelt letter to your younger self, offering words of encouragement, compassion, and guidance. Share wisdom and reassurance that your inner child may have needed to hear. This one is powerful and because of this, I had the most needed and most powerful dream that I will never forget. Messages received loud and clear, and it created another Turning point. I decided to express my dream as a poem.

THE BULL AND THE CHILD

The following is a dream I had when I felt like I had no hope, this was the only medium I felt I could use to express how profound and beautiful this message was to me. It was an absolute gift to me. For, the first time in my dreams I was able to see my younger self, to hold him, to love him, to protect him, and to tell him, that we are going to be OK.

In the realm of dreams, where imagination soars,
I found myself on a ranch, surrounded by doors,
Inside a bright shed, with windows to the light,
A scene unfolded, surreal and filled with insight.

Through the windows, rays of sunshine danced,
Yet, confined within, a sense of longing enhanced,
The door stood firm, keeping me within those walls,
As I yearned for freedom, for adventures calls.

And then, a sound, faint at first, but clear,
The echo of hooves, a presence drawing near,
I turned my gaze towards the door so strong,
And there, before me, stood a bull, bold and long.

Its massive form commanded attention and awe,
With majestic horns and eyes so gentle, I saw,
A wounded boy, held tenderly in its embrace,
A sight that left me breathless, frozen in place.

The bull approached, its steps slow and sure,
With each stride, my heart's rhythm did endure,
Its eyes, like liquid pools of warm brown hue,
Pierced through my soul, as if they always knew.

A silent connection, a message unspoken,
The bull's gaze held me, my spirit awoken,
And with a gruff yet gentle sound, it conveyed,
A plea, an invitation, for me to come and aid.

Without hesitation, I ran to the bull's side,
Past the threshold, where shackles once tried,
To hold me captive within those walls of fear,
But now, released, I embraced the boy near.

Upon closer inspection, a revelation found,

This wounded boy, my younger self, unbound,
Battered and bruised, but with a resilient light,
He whispered, "I'm okay, together we'll make it right."

With the bull's guidance, we walked the path,
A journey of healing, of reconciling the past,
The ranch, a symbol of growth and transformation,
As I nurtured my younger self with love and dedication.

Through the fields we ventured, hand in hand,
Healing wounds, embracing the grains of sand,
Together, we faced trials, and let go of the pain,
Knowing that in unity, we could truly regain.

The bull, our steadfast companion and guide,
Led us through valleys, where shadows subsided,
And as we emerged, stronger and more whole,
I realized the bull's purpose, its divine role.

For in that dream, a profound truth I found,
That love can mend what's broken, turn things around,
And though the boy was once wounded and frail,
Through the bull's intervention, his spirit did prevail.

In the realm of dreams, a journey was paved,
A reunion of selves, a wounded soul saved,
And as I awakened from that vivid dream's embrace,
I carried its message, love's transformative grace.

BALANCE

Embrace the Yin and Yang: The concept of Yin and Yang is central to the I-Ching. Embrace the understanding that self-love and freedom involve finding **balance** between **opposing forces within yourself**. Embody both Yin (receptive, nurturing) and Yang (active, assertive) qualities, recognizing the importance of integrating and harmonizing these energies within your journey.

In this chapter, though I talked a lot about play, what I am also trying to bring up is balance during this process. Balance is the real gift of recovery. There is a great book that puts things in perspective very well: *Everything You Need for Life You Learned In Kindergarten*. The book tells you basically to do your work but don't forget to enjoy, to celebrate, especially the little pleasures in life. So many of us codependents are afraid to relax, are afraid that if we can't control and organize everything, we'll never get anything done. But I'll let you in on a little secret. The more you learn to balance work with play, the more work you'll get done. In my own case, I find that by separating the two and giving each its due, I even enjoy the work. I have read so many beautiful and insightful quotes on balance that really helped me see its importance and its efficiency.

Here are a few:

"Balance is not something you find; it's something you create."

"Finding balance is not about standing still, but about continuously adjusting and rebalancing."

"Balance is the key to everything. What we do, think, say, eat, feel, they all require awareness, and through this awareness, we can grow."

"Balance is not about spending equal time on everything; it is about spending the right time on the right things."

"In seeking balance in life, we must learn to sway with the winds of change while remaining rooted in our core values."

"Balance is the foundation of a fulfilling life. It allows us to navigate the challenges and cherish the joys with grace and stability."

"Balance is the key that unlocks the doors to personal peace, contentment, and success."

"True balance comes from within, from understanding and honoring your own needs while also embracing the world around you."

CHAPTER 4

CODEPENDENCY ON RELATIONSHIPS

> *"Codependency is not love. It's a form of self-love, that sabotages true love."*
> — ***Yvonne Pierre***

THE FACE OF CODEPENDENCY

At this point, I'd like to share some true stories with you to put a better face on codependency. I hope this sharing makes it easier for you to recognize it when you see it especially in your own life. I'd also like you to see how it creates unhealthy relationships, and how you can change that.

Of course, I protect the confidentiality of all involved; I don't use names and have changed some of the circumstances. And, with these stories, I diverge from what actually happened in the end to consider various ways the situation could have played out. As I go through these stories, I'm going to use the terms and concepts we discussed before. The more you're exposed to them, the better you'll understand them and be able to work with them.

CODEPENDENCY EQUALS CONTROL
In relationships, codependency manifests itself as control. You see, the great majority of us are only comfortable with what is familiar to us, with our *normals*. For example, as we said, our OG Families taught us to be shocked by racially mixed, or ethnically mixed, or culturally mixed couples. These couples frightened us. Or, to put it in terms that make our Inner Child tremble, they were *scary*. The same thing with gay couples. And now we have another phenomenon in society. Older people, particularly widows and widowers, are living together without being married. It's an economic phenomenon. In these particular relationships, if the parties marry, they'll lose pension benefits or Social Security benefits. They get more money and they need it to survive if they stay

single. So, they live together. Openly. And that would have been unheard of a generation ago. Do you see how we are now crossing, what, five generations of what not used to be socially acceptable to absolute acceptability. Each generation is definitely fighting for it, but everyone's *normals* are changing or influenced collectively. (Ironically, many of those who are living like that now were the ones who were most shocked by the phenomenon of mixed couples when they were younger.)

We are uncomfortable with the unfamiliar and unknown. And we are afraid of the uncomfortable as afraid of that now as we were afraid of the chaos in our families when we were children. Follow the patterns as they developed. In our families, we naturally wanted our basic needs met: Security, Love, Safety, Life Skills, a sense of Identity, and Intimacy. But our families were codependent, dysfunctional. We were shamed and abused physically or emotionally and exposed to all sorts of other insanity and chaos. The chaos terrified us. So, we developed our defense mechanisms to cope, to make some sense of the situation or at least give us the ***illusion of control.*** Remember, we were only very young children when all this happened. And what were our main defenses? We became ***Isolators***, ***Fantasizers***, and/or ***Caretakers***. I became a Caretaker, with a dash of an Isolator, and a Splash of a Fantasizer. Fuck chaos, but this became my Identity. Ok, once again, as I said before and now, I am going to repeat myself for emphasis, in my studies and research, I discovered that I was all these different labels, I felt relief, I could describe to myself for the first time, what and who I am, my current "**Identity**", in all my glorious dysfunction. It was fucking awesome; it was absolutely glorious. I finally had an understanding and a starting point. I began to discover what my "**normals**" were. I could finally put a stake in the ground and peel back the layers, tear down, and rebuild. My dopamine levels went through the roof, my new drug of choice started to become understanding ME! How cool is that? I wanted to know honestly for the first time "**Who I am**"? What is it that I want and need? What do I want to be when I grow up at age 50? Yep, can you believe this shit? I am trying to figure myself out, after half my life has been lived. Who the fuck does that? Seriously? I do!

These roles were an attempt to control "the chaos." And these roles became my *normal*. So now, as adults, those are the roles we carry into our relationships. In short, for so many of us in our adult relationships, we look for the normal that was a given in our childhood: chaos, insanity. And we apply the normal we learned and use those roles to try and control it. We do it in business, with our spouses, our parents, our lovers, our children, and our friends. The pattern repeats itself.

And the pattern is usually a two-way street. For example, we say to someone, in effect, *I'll love you if you love me back.* But that's not really love. It's business, it is an exchange. And what we normally exchange are our needs, the roles we play. Deep inside our consciousness, we are probably not even aware of it, our Inner Child is saying that if I can play my role, I'm in control. So, we don't have intimacy in our relationships. We have control. When you grow up in dysfunctionality, you are out of control, so you try to find control wherever you can. It's called: **SURVIVAL**.

Let's call it a: CASE STUDY
This particular story happened to involve a male and female, but it applies just as well to female-female, male-male, child-parent or to the relationship between a person and an institution. Remember, institutions often substitute for people in relationships.

In this case, we start with a young man. His father was a severe and violent alcoholic. He often beat his son. The father was also a contractor and the son worked for him. The son was almost like the father's slave. The father would also call the son names, tell him he was a bum, was no good, even that he wished the son had never been born. The son did the natural thing; he turned to his mother for help. But the mother was in denial, in fact she was submissive, about the father's behavior; pretending it wasn't so bad was probably the only way she could cope and survive, married to such a man. So, she told the son that what he felt just wasn't true, the father wasn't so bad. See, Mommy was just as scared of Dad as the son was, so she pretended that none of it was happening, that it wasn't real. That's a common survival technique. In this case it severely confused the son, taught him not to trust his own feelings, as though they just weren't valid or important.

Now remember, this is happening to a child. So, he is not only being abused emotionally and physically, he now thinks, in plain words, that maybe he's crazy. Maybe there's something wrong with him, since he's the only one reacting about the father. That is **SHAME**, plain and simple, the feeling that there is something fundamentally wrong with you, that you are **BAD**.

The boy grew up to be a lonely young man. So, his natural role was an **Isolator**. He was angry, frustrated, afraid, and ashamed. But he still wanted his father's love, the love we all want, so he tried his best to please his Dad to no avail. In high school, the boy finally found something to take away his emotional pain, to numb his feelings: alcohol. When he drinks, he doesn't feel anything. But it wears off and he has to repeat the cycle: bad feelings...drink to numb them...alcohol wears off...feelings return...drink to numb them...He was mummifying himself. Side note: mummys don't feel anything (numb).

By the time he left high school, he really didn't like who he was, really didn't think much of himself, he really didn't care, in plain words, whether he lived or died. Add to the fact that he still wanted his Dads attention and approval, and he comes to the conclusion that he knows a way to get it finally: join the army and volunteer for a War. Maybe he'll get killed, but so what. He'll come back a hero dead or alive. And Dad will have to pay attention. Finally.

Unfortunately, as he saw it, the army found out he could type. So instead of sending him to War, they send him to the mid-west as a clerk in boot camp. And somewhere in his mind here's how he sees that: *My Dad rejected me. My family rejected me. Everybody rejected me. And now even the army rejects me.* He's not even good enough, worthy enough, to get killed for his country. How does he cope? Alcohol. Numbs himself again.

Now, let's leave him for a while. Let's go to the other half of the story. There's a woman who grew up as the oldest of the eight children in her family. Her mother was so busy having children that she didn't have time to take care of them. She left that to the older daughter. Which gave the daughter her role in life. Miss Goody-Two-Shoes. Miss Fantastic, Mother's Little Helper. In short: Caretaker. And caretakers are what can be called professional victims. See, the daughter, as we said before about caretakers, goes straight from 3 to 33, skipping her entire childhood in the process. She works at home taking care of her siblings. She works at school to get good marks. She works so hard she's always tired, always exhausted, and, though she has a smile on her face, she's also always resentful and angry though she's not totally aware of it. She thinks she's angry from the normal frustrations that go along with all the jobs she assigns herself. But she's really resentful about her normal, about her caretaker role. It's like that song again: "Yes, I'm the Great Pretender." And when she leaves high school as a young woman, she becomes a teacher. But that's certainly no surprise. Her whole life is taking care of kids and that's what teachers do. If she hadn't become a teacher, she probably would have been a nurse in a pediatric ward or some other child caretaker.

Now our hero and heroine come together. You see, once upon a time, they met when he was home on leave. He, still the little child looking for a parent who will pay attention to him, She, the perennial mother. They have a whirlwind fantasy relationship; the fantasy is that they think they are in love when all they're doing is exchanging needs. Within months, they're married. Within six-and-a-half years she has four children; she's basically exchanged one house full of kids for another. In reality she has five children; her husband finally has the "parent" he wanted and will never let go. What they have is a functional and a dysfunctional relationship.

Soon she's chronically exhausted again. But that gives her an excuse to stop having sex with him, which is OK because she's so frustrated and angry and resentful again that she has no appetite for sex with her husband. In fact, the few times he tries to approach her, she does things like clean, till three in the morning, hoping he'll fall asleep before she gets to bed. Which, though disappointing to him, is also basically OK, because he has what he really wanted in the relationship: a mother. All he needs to convince himself that this relationship is really OK, really safe for him, is to put a few more tethers on her so she'll never get away. He will tell her what to wear; He will watch where she goes; and he will make sure that, God forbid, she never talks to any other men. They might steal Mommy away. The wife doesn't like it, but she accepts these tethers he puts on her, because by now she is actually afraid of him.

You see, what has developed in this marriage is a mixture of two classic types of dysfunctional relationships. One is a master-slave relationship. The other since he is really like her child, what I learned, is called an incestuous relationship.

What happened was that one-day when she was about thirty, her kids were all finally off to school, Just grade school. And yet she suffered a premature case of empty-nest syndrome. There was no one to take care of during the day. She could no longer use her caretaker role to block out her feelings. And she became depressed. She found herself sitting on the side of the bed in the morning and pondering, even obsessing, *is this all there is to life? There's got to be more!* But she was intelligent, so she started to fill the time by reading and following some informative shows on TV and Internet. She begins getting a sense of what's making her tick, her motivations. She even starts going to some local meetings and groups, all in secret, of course, because she knows how jealous her husband is. Soon she takes a bold step: therapy. Which she pays for in secret, by siphoning off a little house money here and there. Inevitably she faces a moment of truth. She's learned that her marriage is not a healthy one and she knows that she can't improve things unless she starts by sharing this realization with her husband.

In truth, the wife did share the information. And she got the expected reaction. The husband was very nervous and very upset. What he said in effect was, *I had everything set up perfectly. I work. You take care of the kids. We have each other. Nobody else to interfere. And now you're ruining it!* She was changing. And she wasn't, in his mind, supposed to change.

Now I'd like to diverge and give you some possible outcomes, sort of a composite picture from other real cases that show how things can turn out in these situations.

First, there's the possibility that after he gets over his initial shock, he too, will agree to treatment maybe only because he's so afraid of losing her. But if they both at least try to keep an open mind in therapy, they'll probably make progress, one step at a time, until they see the unhealthiness in their relationship and work to change that into something healthy. You see, many people are afraid of what they'll find out in therapy and about themselves, or their relationships. Yet the reality is that many find their problems are very average, if painful to live with and face; that they can be corrected with patience and sincere work, an open mind and effort; and that their depression and anxiety and negative compulsions diminish as the problems are faced. When it comes to relationships, some resist facing their problems because they're afraid to let go of a relationship. *What if I really did marry the wrong person?* The short answer to all of this is that there is a saying common to all good therapies: *Trust the process.* Do your work, whatever it is, counseling, Twelve Steps, meditation, prayer...or a combination of these and other types of therapy and trust the process. *When you are ready* the process will take you to where you are supposed to be.

But to get back to our couple, maybe they work on their problems together and develop a healthy relationship.

But let's say the husband can't face the change. He will try to bring things back to the way they were before. And remember he is an Isolator. If he is a *passive* isolator, he'll begin to pout, then threaten: *If you don't come back to the way things were before I'll hurt myself maybe even commit suicide.* If he is an *aggressive* isolator, he can become truly insane and dangerous. You've heard the term *"Restraining Order."* You've heard of all kinds of situations where aggressive isolators have actually killed people rather than let them go, or see them change. That, too, is a possible outcome.

And then there are the kids. They're caught in the middle either way. And being kids they, too, will resent the change, at least at first. And guess who they'll blame? Dad? No. They'll blame Mom. She, after all, is the one upsetting the apple cart. You see, she, too, as well as Dad, was responsible for creating a fantasy in the kids' mind: *Everything is OK in this family, everything is terrific, and it will never change and Dad and I will always be together. The* kids will need their own work to adjust to the change, because Mom's change is making them deal with reality now, deal with their own unhealthy *"stuff."* So basically, the kids are scared to death. Scared of what Dad will do. They'll walk on eggshells around him, taking whatever reaction they get from him just so he doesn't go off the deep end. And scared of the internal changes Mom's actions have triggered in them. And they'll let Mom know it, blaming her, complaining to her, but guess what? That's also a very healthy reaction because the fact that they communicate with Mom shows that they trust her, that they know that, no matter what, she will not abandon them, and they can talk to her.

So, there are some possible scenarios. Needless to say, it will take a lot of courage for the woman, as her own person, as a wife, and as a mother, to continue on the path of healthy change, which we call recovery.

This story is very true to my own story, with exception of War, of course, but hopefully makes for good story. I am just trying to layout a real-life scenario when we are not willing to do as I have been talking about. Without complete admission, this has been my painful outcome. And I have taken my whole family down with me. Its fucking painful, and it will not change, unless we change. Recovery is important, and it is very real. This why I am writing this fucking book, in the hopes that someone can catch it soon enough and find peace, happiness, and freedom. Mostly me.

1 + 1 = 3

In all of the above stories about me, and many you hear about and read about and see on TV and in the movies, and in social media. You literally have one codependent living for another and sometimes the other just feeding off it. The problem is that codependents do not know how to have healthy relationships. So, they migrate into situations like those above.

The problem is that we think we come together as two halves to make a whole. We think that's how it should be. So romantic! Sorry, but that's just unhealthy. A relationship should be two *whole* people coming together to form something more by their interaction. They add to each other, they do not take from each other. One of my favorite **relationship math equations** is that **1 + 1 = 3**. You are two separate humans that love each other and bring your own unique qualities and when 2 whole people do that, the 3 in the equation is a whole healthy relationship, so;

Healthy Partner + Healthy Partner = Healthy Relationship

How do I think you should get into a good relationship? Remember when we said to play, doing something healthy, and learning to play. Socialize like this. Remember the family systems we described as being Society and Media? Play is socialization. Learn socialization and you learn healthy intimacy. It's the exact opposite of going out to *"pick somebody up"* or get *"picked up."* Or, going on tinder, grindr, and every other app where men and women just want to fuck, even boys and girls, just want to have sex, if I'm being honest.

Socialization is centuries old and it works. It is also fun. Why can't we be more old fashioned and get to know a person through honest socialization and play and date. Maybe, 6 or 12 people go out to a park and have some food and play a game or whatever. No deals. No contracts. Nobody belongs to anybody else. Through socialization, some people will migrate into your life and become friends. Some will become significant others. And maybe later one will become your primary relationship. Maybe. When it's supposed to happen. And you can learn to be yourself in the meantime. Like the old Carly Simon lyrics, when her lover is pressing her to marry: *I've never learned to be just me yet, by myself.* Sadly, the lyrics end with her giving in, like a good codependent: *he wants to marry me. We'll marry.*

I feel if you are a whole person nothing in this world will become the center of your life but you. YOU are the center of your life. Which does not mean that your life itself can't be centered on healthy things. And when I say nothing else is the center of your life, I also mean institutions like church, I lived in Utah a long time and I have seen so many partners make that their center.

You see, if you accept yourself as the center of your life, then you have to work. Work on your issues. Work to make yourself a whole person. Then you learn to give people space and let them have a life of their own. Parents, friends, spouses, acquaintances, have lives of their own, even your children have lives of their own.

That's called giving up control, giving up codependency. You don't need to control anybody else. You don't need to organize them or try to run their lives. Work on yourself, take care of yourself, if you do that, you're saying goodbye to codependency and all the unhealthy things that go with it. In fact, it has been my experience that, if you work on yourself, if you take care of yourself, *everything else* falls into place.

And I am just learning this now. To be brutally honest, I am just at the beginning of seeking a healthy relationship with my kids, with my grandkids, and even my Wife. I am just learning to be the center of my own life. And, I have had to accept the consequence of my actions, hence all the stories above and this damn book I'm writing. So, **PLEASE** catch it before I did, but if you are starting now, that's ok too, better **NOW** than **NEVER**.

CHAPTER 5

ROLES THAT CODEPENDENTS PLAY

"To be codependent means we sacrifice our power to others. We give others the responsibility for our feelings and well-being."
— **Melody Beattie**

THE POWER OF ROLES

The goal is to turn your codependency into a healthy lifestyle. One thing I noticed, or another way of looking at it, is we all play our own Roles within our Family Systems. It's like a survival technique. I could not reconcile *why all* of our roles have such a strong hold on us. I wanted to answer the question that I've asked myself so many times: *If I know these roles are so unhealthy, why don't I just stop playing them?* There are two basic reasons: **Time and Motivation.**

First, we adopted or programmed ourselves into our roles since childhood. How long ago was that for you? Twenty, thirty, forty years? For some it's even longer. As we said, these roles have become our normal, and change is a very uncomfortable, very scary, thing for us.

Second: Motivation. We adopted our roles for the most powerful reason of all: **Survival**. And this brings into play two other concepts: **Abandonment and Loyalty**. I'll go into more detail on these later, but for now here's a brief description of the process. As a child, to be abandoned by our OG Families equates to fear of death, nothing less. *If I lose my family, who will take care of me?* To avoid being abandoned, we decide so often on an *unconscious* level, to give our family, our religion, our culture or whatever our **Loyalty**. This is why, if I play these roles, they will accept me. *If they accept me, I won't be abandoned. I will survive.* Remember, we referred to our roles as Survival Techniques.

If you doubt that abandonment by our OG Family, which equates simply to death for a child, talk to some foster parents. One couple I know told me of two separate incidents, one with a little girl and another with a boy they had living with them. In both cases, when the children realized that they would not be returning to their biological family, they began asking questions like, *Do you think when I get bigger I'll be able to cook for myself?* Or, *how will I know how to take care of a house? How will I know how to go to work?* What the social workers in these cases explained is that the children were feeling separation anxiety and were really asking, *Will I survive?* And the workers told the couple that it is a common phenomenon. That's how powerful an issue of abandonment is with children.

You've been playing your codependent roles virtually all your life and for the most powerful of motivations. It's the only "character" you know. It's the only way you functioned. Do we really have to ask why our roles have such a powerful hold on us? Going back to my own experience, when I was a teenager, I had to be the perfect student, perfect Mormon, perfect son, loyal son. But, as a good codependent, it took me *30 years* to finally make the decision to just accept me for me. 30 years for me to finally face the questions that evolved during that period, from my unconscious to my conscious, that went from being vague thoughts to real fears: *What will I do? How will I function? What will people think? Where will I go?* And on and on.

Codependency traps us. We become afraid to change. When we think about change, we think things like; *OK, I want you to work the whole thing out for me first, give me all the answers, and then I'll make a decision, make the change.* But it doesn't work that way. So, we stay loyal to people, places, things, relationships, organizations, and lifestyles that just don't deserve our loyalty. We remain loyal to our roles. And the longer we live our roles, the more they begin to manifest themselves in other ways.

CODEPENDENT ROLES IN RELATIONSHIPS: OPPOSITES ATTRACT
If we live our roles long enough, they manifest themselves in other ways by *"growing"* into something else, more complex roles. In codependency, there are six of these other roles in particular that we talk about in pairs, or sets. They are:

- Chemically Dependent/Chief Enabler,
- Family Hero/Family Scapegoat, and
- Lost Child/Mascot

The first pairing: Chemically Dependent and Chief Enabler. When we talk about the Chemically Dependent, we are not just talking about alcohol and drugs. You can become drunk on your emotions, on behaviors, on many things other than drugs or alcohol.

I call the Chemically Dependent type person the **Total Child**. The **Total Shame-Based Child**; they do not like who they are or who they think they are. Their insecurity basically leaves them a mess inside, and to hide what they have become, on the outside, very rigid, very judgmental, and very hard on themselves and others. In other words, in many ways, they are like babies. They want what they want when they want it or they're going to make somebody pay. I'm sure you recognize the issue.

As a baby exercises its control through its behavior, the Chemically Dependent type also tries to control. They try to manipulate people into being who they want them to be, to play roles. If people do what they want, they feel safe, but only for a brief time. Their shame predominates, basically takes over again, and so they turn to their chemical dependency. In the case of substance abuse dependency, like alcohol and drugs, what the Chemically Dependent type does is use the substance to numb the feeling of shame. Or, as I put it, very simply, they *numb* themselves. Temporarily. Because when the effect of the abused substance wears off, they're back to the cycle: Shame, Chemical Abuse, Numbing, Shame...

Chemically Dependent types naturally find Enablers, getting closest to what we call the *Chief* Enabler. This could be the spouse of an alcoholic. That spouse is always complaining, always trying to change the other person, but always accepting of the alcoholism in the end. It's as though the Chief Enabler is the consummate Caretaker, addicted to fixing, or going through the motions of trying to fix the other, the Chemically Dependent. Like the Chemically Dependent, the Chief Enabler is also very rigid, and, again, the issue is control. **Big-Time control.** Chief Enablers usually never play. They never have any fun. They're always analyzing. And so, they're very resentful. Of the two, in fact, as sick as the Chemically Dependent type is, the Enabler is much sicker. At least the Dependent takes a break once in a while and gets drunk, and/or high, to get some relief. Enablers don't take breaks; they break down as in nervous breakdown. So, both of these types pay a heavy price for trying to control other people.

Second pairing: Family Hero and Family Scapegoat. Their main issue is Attention. Each seeks it in his or her own way. The Hero gets it by always doing what the family wants, never mind what the Hero really wants. These are called the Pedestal Children. They always come through for everybody else, so everybody puts them on a pedestal. I joke that when they die, they put statues of the Heroes up in the park. But what happens to statues? Pigeons come and crap on them. And that's the problem for the Hero. They get crapped on. They're never happy, because they're not doing what *they* want. They're some of the loneliest people in the world. And if they wise up and try to shed their role of Hero, guess what? Nobody likes them anymore. They fall from grace. The Hero is not allowed to have a life of his or her own. You see this all the time in war hero movies. They sacrifice themselves for their country, they are actually Heros, but in the end, there country craps on them.

In my own history, I was *eighteen/nineteen* when I served a Mormon mission in southern Italy, Sicily. I loved it, but when I arrived to sell and share God, I realized that I had not even finished reading the Bible or any Mormon religious text in its entirety for that matter. So, I am in a country of which I have had only 2 months to learn a language. And, no, I still could not speak Italian. I am in a home with 3 other missionaries that have only been in Italy 4 months before me, of which they could barely speak Italian. I barely knew how to cook, or clean for that matter in house full of strangers thousands of miles away, excited to be in Italy for sure, but then I had to ask some fundamental questions of myself that I should have asked years before. Why did I go on a Mormon mission? Is this what I truly believe? Was this truly my choice? First let me tell you that I have zero regrets, Italy was transformative for me, beautiful, and enlightening. Maybe I was guided to go because that is exactly what I needed, but I did go because others wanted me to go, I was expected to go, I was taught at a very young age to go, so at the time, I did not realize that I did not do it for me. So, in my naïveté, I went. I am incredibly grateful for it, but at some point, you have to make your own decisions. I didn't realize it at the time, but I wasn't doing it for me. In my family systems, having a missionary in the family was a great honor. It was expected in my family. My whole family was so proud, I am in Italy, serving a religious mission, preaching the doctrine of Christ, almost heroic. And being on this Mormon mission actually put me on small, but imaginary pedestal. I remember what that felt like. I loved it, so I decided to be the best at my craft, so I committed to reading everything and praying and asking God if what I am doing is right. Years later after being home and starting a family, I departed from the Mormon church. Wow, I cannot explain, the blowback I received when I was vocal about my departure. I had those on my mission many years later say, *"Why, you were one of the good ones?"* What in the fuck does that even mean? I remember being a teenager up to my young adult married family life. And, having small kids, I constantly felt this underlying deep conflict that I could not explain. I was very lonely, very unhappy, deep down. But yet, on the surface, I was very happy, I have 3 beautiful children, a stunning and giving wife, a home, a job, I had it all. But this oxymoron of conflict that I am happy, I really am, but buried so fucking deep is this small soul sucking horcrux telling me that I am not really happy, that it is fake, and a lie. It's the only way I can describe it. Because there was this fear, uncertainty, and doubt (FUD) attached to me deep down.

And when I finally changed and started doing what I wanted...It was as though I had disgraced and betrayed myself, and any level of "my Hero" status. Did you ever see [Mission Impossible]() with Tom Cruise when the Russian scientist says, "Dimitri, every hero needs a villain!" It stuck with me and then in a moment of clarity, fleeting, but still a moment, I wanted to be my own hero. This makes sense. In my first moment of self-awareness, I realized I wanted to save myself, from myself. Are you fucking kidding me? Where do I start? There is an amazing scene in a subsequent [Mission]() [Impossible]() where Alec Baldwin's character, now director of IMF is talking to Ethan hunt (Tom Cruise), he said he moved laterally from CIA to IMF because of Ethan hunt, because Ethan absolutely cares for *"the One."* Meaning every single person matters and he sacrificed himself to always save at least the one person in trouble. That's what made him so powerful, driven. But in caring for the one, he also saved the many. The blueprint begins to morph in my mind. *"The One is **You**", "The One is **Me**."*

It also takes quite a while for Heroes to realize what they're doing to themselves. I talked to this one woman once and she told me how angry she was. Her sister had said to her one day that the family didn't worry about anything happening to them, because if it did, they knew she'd take care of it. It was an off-the-cuff comment. But it was like the straw that broke the camel's back. The woman finally realized that she was the family Hero. And she didn't like it. She was resentful and angry and sad.

And she had been that way for a long time. She had started playing her Hero role *forty years* before!

The Scapegoat, on the other hand, gets attention in negative ways. Sometimes they actively get into trouble: drinking, drugs, unwanted pregnancies...Sometimes it's more of a passive thing, like being the sick one or the one who takes the blame when things go wrong. It's like that baseball pitcher Mitch Williams. The *"Wild Thing."* Hero one day, Scapegoat the next. His unorthodox style was OK to the team when he was drawing crowds and selling tickets. But when they lost the World Series, It was his fault. Or like David Beckham, who is a superstar footballer for Manchester United. He is invited to play for the England National Team to win the World Cup for England. England fans and his coach are placing their entire World Cup wining chances all on David Beckham, yes he plays phenomenal but in one of qualifying matches he gets brutally fouled and responds in kind. Barely even touching the opposite player, the opposite player fakes a huge foul and David Beckham receives a red card and is ejected from the Game. England looses and they are out of the World Cup. Now the ridiculous part, the referee absolutely maid a shitty call, the coach blames all World Cup chances on David Beckham, all of England blames Beckham and these supposed fans that loved this soccer Hero and everything he accomplished to that point, lost their shit, constant Booing, death threats to him and his family, and shaming for years. There are 10 other players on the field. It's called a team for a reason. The coach was absolutely ridiculous. Anyway, he was this country Hero and now they hated him. He totally got crapped on. Bullshit!

Or take the case of when I was in Rehab. There was this girl that received constant visits and calls from her mother. In talking to her I asked if she had other siblings, She did, two other sisters. But, as she put it, they were perfect, never got into trouble. I was like thinking, maybe her Mom needs to spend more time with other kids and let the girl I met to develop and grow on her own. I felt bad for the other girls as if they didn't need help or even attention from their mother. But they did need her. I mean look at the message that mother was sending: *If you want my undivided attention, use drugs and alcohol and go into a rehab.*

Maybe the scariest thing about Scapegoats, as with Heroes and the other roles, is that they don't even realize what they're doing. It's like they become permanently Sick. *"Sick"* has become their normal. They get to go into hospitals regularly, and in the hospitals; they get taken care of, get all the warm fuzzies, and even get free shit for all the attention they want. Problem is, they have to trade their lives for it.

The third pairing; Lost Child and Mascot, are perhaps the saddest cases of all. Their issue is Identity. They didn't get it in their family systems so they look for it someplace else. Anyplace else. The Lost Child type drifts through life basically asking other people to tell him or her who they are. Very sad. And very dangerous. They're like walking, talking, living, gullible targets.

Especially targets for movements and cults. They'll become whatever anybody else wants them to be just so they can fit in somewhere. They are also targets for schemes. They are constantly being scammed. These are the types that buy the Brooklyn Bridge from some Hustler. Exaggeration I know. But, you get the point. There are a lot of Lost Children out there.

You have seen them and you read about them. When you ask them something like, *"What do you want to do tonight?"* You get, *"I don't know, whatever you want to do, I guess."* They'll see what movie you want to see, eat whatever you want to eat, go wherever you want to go. An epitome of a Lost Child is a prostitute. The pimp gives him or her an identity; they do what the pimp wants at any cost. When Lost Children hit the mental health system, they're actually relieved. Some doctor finally gives them an identity, a label, even though it's only something like *schizophrenic*. On the street, Lost Children latch onto one person today, bunch of people tomorrow, and then a different group the next day, and then someone else after that. In short, the Lost Child is a chameleon.

Where the lost Child is a passive type, the Mascot is aggressive. They, too, want to fit in. They, too, want to please. And they're all over you trying to show it. Sometimes they're funny, the constant comedian until you realize how sad they are. When they join a group, an organization, they stand out; there are six jobs to do, they volunteer for all six. *I'll do it! I'll do it! I'll do it! I want to please you, please everybody, I want you to like me!* Sometimes they make good sales people and politicians. But whatever form they come in; they are tough people to be around. They eventually exhaust you.

Deep down inside, the Mascot is just like the Lost Child. Empty. Sad. Lonely. They have no idea who they are. They run around and do everything for everybody and make everybody happy and then maybe everybody will love them. In relationships, you *hear* them constantly: *Are you mad at me? Are you sure? Are you sure? Do you still love me? Do you still love me? Are you sure? Are you sure? Are you sure? I used to say all this in my mind but never had the courage to say it out loud. So overcompensated by working harder, buying more gifts, when I really should have started confronting these emotions. Thing is, I had no idea how to do it. I was programmed differently.* Sad, but after a while, you feel like swatting them away like a fly. They are so *needy,* so *intense and* sometimes so *belligerent* when they don't get the reaction they want, that you just want to avoid them. You see them coming down the street, you head the other way. Because the Mascot is relentless and you just can't give them what they want.

BACK TO THE REFRAIN: CHANGE!

The good news for all of us trapped in roles is that we can shed them. The word again is Change. Which is what these following **Six Stages of Recovery** are all about. But before we can get into them, we still have to come to grips with a few other things.

First, we have to know, to realize, and to be aware of what we've been doing. Just keep in mind that knowing alone isn't enough. Don't get trapped by the **"I Know"** disease. Also, keep in mind that when you realize what role or roles you've been playing, it's usually painful. Very painful. For example, take an extreme case. Take the prostitute who realizes just what he or she has done with his or her life up to that point. Add to that the feeling they will have when they realize *why* they did what they did: they were Lost Children. That's not easy to accept. It's not easy for any of us to accept the codependent roles we've been playing. We feel foolish. Silly. Hopeless. Shamed. Embarrassed. You name it. Some of us feel like giving up when we realize how sick we've been acting. Which is why we said before, we have to accept and embrace our personal histories: **Knowledge and Acceptance**. But don't get stuck there. Continue with the process. Trust the process. It's leading you away from the sickening feelings to the positive feelings of peace and joy. It's no accident that the New Testament of the Bible has parables like the Lost Sheep and the Prodigal Son. There's a powerful message in them.

After you begin accepting your past, explore the issues in more detail. Let's go back to the two mentioned in this chapter. **Abandonment**. Just as when you were a child and you were afraid and scared almost *to* *death*, you might say that your Family Systems might leave you or reject you, you are afraid as an adult that other people might leave you. It's a carryover from one stage of your life to another. Deep down inside you're saying to yourself that if you make other people angry, if they leave you, you will become nobody, have no identity. You are afraid of changing your relationships with others because you do not have a healthy relationship with *yourself*.

And the other issue: **Loyalty**. To me, it's even bigger than Abandonment. I still have a hard time personally, breaking old loyalties. Let me share this little bit with you. When I talk about my own issues, I felt disloyal, I still feel disloyal. I love my family. I'm sure they love me. But when I talk about our dysfunctionality, which every family has, I still feel disloyal. If I were to give a lecture and start talking about my family and one of my family walked in, I would probably freeze: *What will they think? Have I betrayed them?* You see, the old *"deal"* we made still has a hold on us: *I will be loyal to you so that you will accept me.*

How many examples can I give you? Look at the work force today, legions of older workers laid off after twenty, thirty, forty years of *loyal* service because their companies *"downsized."* They know what downsized usually means: somebody younger was later hired because they work cheaper and have lighter benefits packages. So, the old, loyal workers walk around in a daze. They identified with their companies. They feel abandoned. Like Lost Children.

Or look at relationships in your own experience. How many marriages have you seen that were really over, even though both parties still hung on? Ask them why and what would they say? *He needs me* or *She needs me.* Loyalty.

I have never in all my years met a dumb codependent. If I asked you now to sit down and make a list of all the negative people, places, and things in your life, you could do it with no trouble. You know who and what they are. And even with people and things that are basically positive like your spouse, your child, your job, you could list unhealthy situations and patterns. You know what they are. But, as we said, knowing is not enough. We have to change. We have to start by *learning* how to change. It might help to get started by remembering these few phrases about Loyalty: *Loyal to people who do not deserve my loyalty. Loyal to people who hurt me. Loyal to people who are destructive to me.*

CHAPTER 6

SIX STAGES TO RECOVERY

> *"The journey of a thousand miles begins with one step."*
> — *Laozi*

> *"When I let go of what I am, I become what I might be."*
> — *Laozi*

Preparing for Recovery

Before you get into your recovery process, you should prepare yourself to avoid some common pitfalls. I can share some thoughts on these, because, like most people, I experienced them all myself in my own recovery. We'll talk about them in more detail later in the book, but for now, briefly:

Don't try to intellectualize the process. As good codependents, we have a tendency to obsess: How does the process work? Therapists, Performance Coaches, Psychologists and rehabs, at all levels have a saying: **Just trust the process.** It works. We say that because we're not exactly sure how it works for each individual just as we're not sure why certain medications work for different individuals, If, you try to work out your recovery in your head, you're probably just going to short-circuit your brain and wind up a little crazier than when you started. With recovery, there seems to be a time when you just have to let the intellect go and get into the process and experience it. In other words, don't try to figure it out. Just do it.

Don't try to organize the process. Just tell me what to do, tell me what books to read, what videos to watch, what podcasts to listen to, and I'll go home and work hard and settle it all by midnight. But recovery is not only a process. It is an ongoing process. It lifts you from the depression and anxiety and unmanageability of codependency to higher levels, keeping you growing throughout your lifetime, just as physical exercise helps keep you healthy if you keep doing it. There are no timetables. You're not competing with anybody else. You go at your own pace. And, if you think about it, that's the way it should be, because your issues and your experiences are unique to you. Your recovery will happen at its own time and in its own way. There is a saying about this: ***Show up for your own recovery!*** I want you to fight for yourself! I want you to invest in yourself! You show up by working the process and not worrying about the results. New saying: ***Show up for yourself!***

Many of us worry anyway, especially if we are feeling the pain of depression and anxiety. We want some assurance that the program will work, and the sooner the better. If that's the case with you, all I can say is do your best to minimize the worry; in other words, don't start worrying about your worrying. Concentrate on working the program as much as you can.

Don't get stuck in the Victim Game. As you work on your issues, there's a tendency to start blaming people in your past for what is happening in your life now. That's a phase that you need to experience. You have to come to a lot of painful realizations about other people, as well as yourself. You have to feel the anger and rage and other feelings those realizations release. Fine. But don't get stuck there. Your attitude going into recovery should be that you will face your issues in due time, heal the hurts, and use the experience to improve your life now. In short, you will learn from the past, not get trapped in it. That is the point: Learn from it!

Don't let your expectations SHAME you. Shame is the feeling that there's something fundamentally wrong with you. It is a major cause of depression, anxiety, addictions, and all sorts of other crazy behavior. In recovery, you realize things like being Loyal to people, places, things, institutions, ideas, whatever, that these things might be unhealthy for me.

Approaching the Six Stages
With that as a backdrop, I would like to introduce you to my Six Stages of Recovery. They are not really mine; all of these have already existed throughout time. All I am doing is reorganizing it into what I find is simpler. I did this for me. It makes sense to me. And, this is just a general description of what they are and what they aren't. I'll give you the formal introduction to them in the next section.

First off, I want to tell you that this is not an *"Event."* Not a *"Magic Bullet."* Not a miracle pill. Not something you do once and then you're cured. It's not like when you were a kid and thought of going to the gym, and thought something like, I'll go and get in shape and have this great body and then I can stop. And when you got older you realized it doesn't work that way, that staying in shape is an ongoing process. Recovery is an ongoing process. The process of learning: **How to Change**.

Of the Six Stages, the first four are for you to work on yourself. It's not until Stage Five that you do OG Family work (OG being Original Gangsta Family, or Family-of-Origin), and Stage Six is where you confront your Inner Child. Again, notice that...these are Stages Five and Six, not One and Two. There is a reason for this. Sometimes in recovery work, we use an analogy. OG Family work, the fifth Stage, is like surgery. To have surgery, you have to be healthy enough to handle the trauma and the Pain, even the discomfort; you need preparation. The first four Stages are the preparation. After surgery, you have recovery. And that is Stages Five and Six. It is an ongoing process of life, of learning and nurturing and developing the healthy you.

THE SIX STAGES
My Six Stages to Recovery and Freedom are:
1. Self-Knowledge/Self-Awareness
2. Developing A Support System or Recovery Family
3. Self-Parenting or Family Reconstruction
4. Developing A Positive Attitude
5. OG Family Work
(OG meaning: Original Family or Family- of-Origin)
6. Inner Child Work

Note, that the last two come with the word *"Work."* The first four, well, work is implied. This will be an ongoing process in which you come to realizations about yourself and then incorporate those realizations into your life. In the Fifth Stage you discover that the foundation, the pattern, discovery of your entire personality, that this was programmed in the first eleven years of your life. You get to spend the next eighty years or so working on them. In Stage Six you discover the child within you, learn how to nurture it, and learn how to build a very powerful relationship with the two most beautiful parts of you, your **Inner Child** and your **Adult Self**. *It's like bringing into balance your **emotional side, the child**, and your **rational side, the adult**.* You see, there are still issues from your childhood very much active inside of you. They create feelings that are often not logical within the context of your life now. Let me give you an example.

Let say a man named John was born by Caesarean section. His mother almost died on the operating table. As a result, he had to be taken from her, separated from her, in the hospital, so they could work on saving her life. She was in a coma for a while, so he didn't get to see his Mom, be held by her, feel her, be fed by her, for maybe the first weeks of his life. Extreme example, I know, but you get it.

The adult part of John understands what happened, and there are basically three ways he can respond. **First is denial**. He can shrug the whole thing off, as so many people try to do, and insist that something that happened so long ago, has nothing to do with his life now.

Second, he can fall **victim** to the "**I Know**" **disease**. He can say, yes, he knows what happened, and, yes, he believes, as most psychologists and therapists now do, that the events in his infancy do have an effect on him as an adult. The danger is that he might stop there. He might say something like, since he knows what happened and he knows it can have an effect, he simply has to keep reminding himself of that, and that alone will be enough to negate the effect. It's similar to when you hear people say things like, Yeah, we all have trauma in our past. Just get over it. In other words, if you work it out in your head, that's enough.

The problem is, it's not enough. You can't work out your emotions entirely in your head. And what you're dealing with, from your infancy, is emotional. The Inner Child was wounded. This beautiful baby expected to have a mother. She wasn't there; it's not her fault, regardless of the reason. So, the Inner Child feels abandoned and angry about it. Children are like little sponges when it comes to emotions. We absorb feelings and then spend our adult lives living them out. Because John felt abandoned, he often feels afraid that he'll be abandoned in present relationships. Worse, he often expects to be abandoned; that's the pattern he knows from his earliest, most primal, experience. So, guess what? John often attracts people in his adult life who abandon him. It's Crazy. The mind and emotion run so deep, it is amazing, when you think about it. But the cool part is, that if at a primal level, I get programmed this way, then we are powerful enough to deprogram and then reprogram ourselves, if that is something we want.

Third option in dealing with the facts of John's life is that he can **identify** them and **work** on them. **Work on them!** Get in touch with the events. **Get in touch with the feelings around them.** Process the feelings by sharing and writing those histories and other therapies. Basically, go over them and through them until they lose their power over him. And please note, when we do this, we are not negating the power of using our intellect. The first stage of recovery is learning, self-knowledge/self-awareness. It's just that we don't stop there. We don't ask our intellect alone to handle something it's just not equipped for.

Total Child/Total Adult
Without recovery, as we touched on before, our feelings get frozen. Instead of a balance **between our Inner Child and present Adult** we tend to let one or the other take over. It works something like this. Our past emotions have such a hold on us that we literally become children emotionally. Our life becomes unmanageable because we function on the principle of the needs of the Baby. We demand things: I want, I want, I want...We carry this attitude in to our relationships, friendships, marriage, work...We look for what we never got as a child. Of course, those around us can't give that to us. So we exhaust them, drive them away, in one form or another. Even if they stay with us physically, they withdraw in other ways. The basic problem is that, functioning as a child; I will have no sense of personal responsibility. I have become the **Total Child**.

But many of us go to the opposite end, the **Total Adult**. We go to all sorts of extremes to deny our feelings. We try to dominate them with our intellect; we analyze everything. Or we take in our minds at least the moral *"high ground"* on everything. We become cynical. We criticize; look for what's wrong in everything. We try to fix people, even when they don't ask to be fixed. We become responsible to a fault. We are always on duty. We wake up in the morning, we don't yawn and stretch, we start organizing stuff in our heads. You see, we are so ashamed and so afraid of our emotions, our past, that we try to bury them. We try to disown our Inner Child by becoming the Total Adult. Which is impossible.

Stage 1: SELF Knowledge/SELF Awareness
Working the First Stage
Know Yourself and Your Enemy: Sun Tzu emphasizes the importance of self-awareness and understanding your opponent. In the context of addiction, knowing yourself means recognizing your triggers, vulnerabilities, and patterns of behavior. Understanding the nature of addiction as your "enemy" involves studying its effects, recognizing its power, and gaining knowledge about the recovery process.

Self-Awareness and Understanding: The Kabbalistic tradition emphasizes the importance of self-reflection and self-awareness. Engage in introspective practices such as meditation, contemplation, or journaling to gain insight into your thoughts, emotions, and behaviors. Seek to understand yourself on a deeper level, exploring both your strengths and areas for growth. **(See Chapter 12, Self-Awareness) There are many ideas on how to become more SELF-AWARE**

Notice that we describe codependents as people with frozen feelings. I laugh when I read the quote in one codependency book, to the effect that codependents feelings are so frozen they have freezer burn. Our head, our intellect, doesn't freeze, so that is where we begin in stage one.

Notice, too, that while becoming the **Total Adult**, we get too wrapped up in the intellect; we create all sorts of insanity and unmanageability in our lives. Stage one is a place to be skeptical; in fact, it is so good to develop a healthy skepticism. We accept the fact that we are afraid, that, we do not trust, because we have been hurt. We have put people, and doctrines and organizations and other things, up on pedestals, and they did not live up to our expectations. They did not cure my unmanageability. They did not make me feel better, feel healthier. They did not bring me peace. So, now hopefully, I have to **Prove it!** I have **Attitude**, finally. That's part of the learning process in Stage One. We question this program. Good. Because then you can really see what the program does for you. You don't have to take anybody else's word for it and pretend to be feeling something that you are not.

Also in Stage One, you are not being asked to do anything but listen, observe, and learn in any way you can. You don't have to stand up in a group and start talking. You don't have to do anything you are not comfortable with. If part of this stage is for you are going to Twelve Step lectures or Adult Children or other groups, nobody will even ask your name. That is important for codependents because it gives us a sense of control. We have been out of control so often that it's scary. So, in Stage One you control your own participation.

But what does Stage One look like? How do you do it? How long does it take? To answer the last point, it takes as long as you need. As for what it looks like, it might involve you reading, listening, watching; there are tons of books available, talks, videos, movies, documentaries, podcasts. You might want to attend lectures, conventions, or focus groups like Twelve Steps, Adult Children of Alcoholics, or Codependents Anonymous. There are also tons of other groups. You might want to enter therapy or professional coaching. You might want to meditate. You might want to do all of these and more. But please remember that it is suggested, some group work. Attending groups and listening, because you will want to build a support system as you go along. You will want to build a recovery network at some point with people you trust and like. Brad Pitt stated publicly that it was working with a group of twelve guys, and just listening that really opened up his view on his addictions and loneliness.

Also today, many people go to a general group, we're not just talking about substance rehab here, but general lecture groups as well and they hear the information and they start saying things to themselves like, Hey! He's talking about MY mother or father or brother or husband or child or whatever. They realize that we've all had similar experiences, similar trauma. Our issues are similar. We are not alone. And they get to talking to other people after the lectures. They begin socializing in a very safe, very discreet manner. In fact, many of them get into the process more over a cup of coffee with a newfound friend than they do in the lectures themselves. This is why I love to go to cafés and coffee shops around the world. It seems to be safe and calm place for people to discreetly open up and talk. To put it another way, you hear things that others are talking about and eventually you will get around to it yourself.

A couple of other very basic principles about Stage One and recovery in general is, don't trust your life to another human being unless you feel totally safe, totally comfortable with that person. Do not put anybody up on a pedestal. Including therapists. They are not gods. Therapists are just human beings like you: on their own journey, doing their own searching and learning. If you don't think one is helping you, find another, if they can't handle that, fuck'em.

In Stage One you work on yourself and you grow. The process works automatically. So, get all the information you need, take your time, find things out, ask questions...But remember: **do it on a safe level.**

Stage 2: Developing a Support System

This is where you start to make a transition from your first stage. In other words, you continue doing much of the same work, but on a different level, in a different way. For example, you learn to let go of control a bit. This does not mean that you give up your safety. It means that you start to connect with a support group, what we call the Recovery Family, so that you can start to share and process your own work. Who will be in the group? That depends on you, on who you feel comfortable with. It's your network.

You connect with other people who are going through the same process with you. Why? It's a very basic principle: You are not an island, not alone. The minute you left your mother's womb you became part of a set of family systems, your OG Family and peer groups. In Stage Two you are going to develop and connect with a healthy family, healthy in the sense that it will be open to let you grow, and will depend on you as well to help others in the family grow **Safely**.

You will also learn something extremely important by connecting with a Recovery Family. When you interact, both listen to others' stories and issues and experiences and share yours, you will learn that you are not the Eighth Wonder of the World or something fucking weird, you are not unique in your trauma and your issues, not crazy. You will gain **PERSPECTIVE**.

For example, In my Rehab, a young man sits, depressed and anxious, in middle of the room, surrounded by 35 addicts in recovery. He has a terrible secret. Our therapist, she intuits that he is ready to escape the room, and she is maybe 90 pounds wet, she wraps her body around his leg, loving and supporting him, helping him to finally share this horrible secret, and all 35 of us, supporting him, and loving him, wanting him to also share and let go of something so painful; His horrible secret was **Death of his best friend**, he believed that he killed his best friend. Oh My God, I will never forget the courage it took for him to say it and start to accept it out loud. He stood up and he wanted to leave, but our therapist just clung to his leg and lovingly said, you can do it. We all supported him, telling him he could do it. It was so powerful, a loving intuitive therapist and 35 male addicts in a circle with him in the middle, all of us energetically routing for him to let go and heal. I will never forget what that kind of support felt like. I will never forget what courage looked like. And guess what? Him sharing with all the tears and fears that go with it prompted others in the group to open up and confess their own secrets. The relief that my friend had that day was biblical, you could see it on his face and in his body, you could feel it from his soul, he really was floating on a pink cloud for days, weeks even. It was and is still beautiful. My point is, you are not alone, it might look a little different for you, but it's still the same. There is power in numbers, radically honest numbers, with no judgment, just love.

But you will never know that, you will never experience that, if you isolate yourself. Can you also do one-on-one therapy? Yes, of course you can. But, like I said there is great spiritual power in numbers, and in your own Recovery Family. The key to the second stage of recovery is building your own Recovery Family, your own network. Get creative, you're an addict. Addicts are so clever and creative. Look how clever and creative you get when you want and need drugs and alcohol. So, apply that creativity and cleverness to recovery, now that you want, desire, and need freedom, and love.

The Pitfalls

For us codependents, there are potentially two major pitfalls to individual therapy. First, we are, by our codependent nature, or conditioning, extremely manipulative. And we're good at it. So, we'll try to take the therapist hostage, or anyone for that matter. We will try and mold him or her into what we want them to be.

The other pitfall is that we'll do the therapy and get all this information and then...What? What will we do with it? So, like I read this book, <u>Adult Children of Alcoholics</u>, I realized that a lot of it pertained to me and that this was the way I was brought up, and then I ran back to my family with the book under my arm to share my realization with them: Look what I found out! Our family is dysfunctional! We are a disaster! But there's a way out! Guess what? That experience was a disaster. They wanted to have me committed to another rehab, or another therapist, or even better, go back to Church!

The dynamics of that second pitfall are simple, basic. I'm doing what every child tries to do. I want my family to understand. I want them to come on board. I want them to give me all the emotional things I never got from them. In other words, I am repeating the dysfunctionality of my childhood. I am going to the wrong places to get what I need for the growth in my life.

Can I make it more simple? There was this dude in rehab, he talked about how he just crashed, and he had been admitted to the hospital for depression. He got out and went into individual therapy. He learned a lot about what had put him in the hospital, the issues that had brought his depression on. Some of those issues had to do with two very close friends he had known since high school. So close, in fact, they had often been called the Three Musketeers, if you saw one, you saw the other two. He realized there was a lot of emotion unresolved among them. Old hurts. Disappointments. One of the disappointments even had to do with the way they had handled his breakdown; they had basically denied he was hurting, right up until the time he went into the hospital. Well, he took his newfound knowledge and ran to them to share it. He believed it would help their relationship, bring them closer. Guess what? These issues were really his issues, not theirs. And even if they had agreed on the issues, they weren't ready to face them. Plain and simple.

As a child, I don't have much choice about my OG family or who I hang with. I'm born or sent into an environment, like school, where some sort of relationships will naturally develop. But as an adult I can choose my surrogate OG Family. In recovery, I can include people in those families who are on the same path as me.

Fake it Until You Make It
I kinda like the "Fake it" phrase. It's my advice for that crucial part of Stage Two: networking. Group work. You'll resist it for a number of reasons, some of them even valid. It's natural to say things to yourself like, I don't want to get involved with a group of addicts, nut cases, and crazy-ass people. How do I know I'll have anything in common with a particular group? What goes on in these meetings? If they relate to Adult Children and other works on addictions, aren't they just for drunks and addicts? And so on.

But the people in the groups are just like you and me. People in therapy are just like you and me. Do you know, for example, that psychologists and psychiatrists do their own therapy regularly? They have their own therapists, own groups. And the typical people in any group will be just like you, fed up with the depression and anxiety and other craziness in their lives. Wanting something better. Willing to work for it.

And the groups aren't just for substance abusers. I had a good friend of mine that attended rehab for PTSD. He didn't drink or drug. But his PTSD was so unmanageable that this program helped him. It really did. He sat in a room full of drug addicts and alcoholics, working twelve steps. This was his group, his network. No Judgment!

I want to be extremely clear. I am absolutely borrowing and stealing from AA, NA, Twelve Steps, and Adult Children of Alcoholics, Buddhism, Kabbalah, Chinese I-Ching, The DAO, and so many more. All I am doing is borrowing the knowledge that these sources provide through their own hard efforts. I am not borrowing their classifications, their particular issues. Our fear of group work has to do with that little stubborn part of us that doesn't want to let go of control, doesn't really want to take a risk, take that leap of faith. Remember a very, very, very important thing: **Codependent groups are not CONFRONTATIONAL.**

You are not expected to start pouring out your heart or challenge anyone or be challenged. Yes, you will experience dynamics. But you do it **SAFELY**.

I remember in rehab, always in group therapy, there was a particular person that would get up every week and share a story, always the same story...It got to the point where, when she was just a sentence or two into it, everybody in the room could have finished the story, we had heard it so often. But we listened, week after week. For some reason, it was important for her to repeat it, and the group provided an ear, we listened.

In groups, you accept people for where they are. Just as they accept you for where you are. Some say things to test the group: Will they really accept me after this? Some are just stuck on particular points trying to work them out, trying to process them. It's not for anyone in the group to decide when the process is finished for anyone else.

Dynamics. You might just sit and listen. You might be prompted to share, slowly at first. You might sit there for a while wondering what good it's doing you. Which is why you stick with it for a while, give it a chance, fake it...To go back to the beginning of this chapter, don't try to organize it or figure it out. Just show up for your own recovery, make the investment, and observe. Connecting with other people works. It might work on principle, something like, wherever two or more of you are gathered...Who knows? But it seems that when you connect with people working toward the same goal, something great happens. I am a first-hand witness of this, over and over again.

It's just like deciding to go to a gym to workout. You're not happy with how you look, how you feel. You wonder what it's like to be in good shape. You watch Movies and social media posts of all these fit people, these beautiful and gorgeous people, so you get interested, you get hooked. Then you try a gym. You don't like one gym, because it's too busy and it feels more like a club to pick up people. So, you try another and maybe another. Finally, you connect where you're most comfortable. It's time to get in shape, to look great and to feel great. BTW, physical exercise should be in everyone's toolbox. It's a great way to release and pass any urges of addiction, or any emotional challenges you might be suffering through.

Now something to remember, now that you are committed and excited, you decide to run to the bar where your buddies are, you start explaining the benefits of getting in shape and telling them that they need to do the same as you, but they aren't interested in getting in shape, you went there looking for their approval. Also, you don't want a personal trainer who will give you a hernia by shouting at you to add more weight to your workout while you're already straining. It's the same in recovery. Nobody is in charge of you. You will be around people who are just like you. Again, you discover that you're not crazy, you are not the Eighth Wonder of the World of Emotional Wrecks. You discover that we codependents like to be classified, it gives us a sense of identity, and we don't need classifications, other than that you are a human. Everything else, all your issues, can be dealt with.

Let me cap it this way: **FEELING SAFE IS ONE OF THE MOST IMPORTANT PARTS OF RECOVERY**. Follow your own pace to wherever your heart leads you. But give it an honest shot.

My Celebrity Recovery Family
This is how I got creative with my support family. People just like me who had to overcome something so painful and so hard but had to experience it publicly. I can't imagine! Seriously, HEROS to me. Anyway, here are a few of these powerful people that had a huge influence on my recovery:

Tom Hardy – said; *"there had to be better way, that he was afraid of losing control of the one thing he could control."* That to always keep helping and talking to those that needed help, because somewhere in between the insanity and the chaos, a word of motivation or wisdom works its way through, the concern of care will break through to instigate change.

Emenim - Overdosed and came back and wrote songs to not be afraid and follow him. He showed you a path. A path that worked for him.

Keith Urban - Keith overcame with the support and love of his wife and family. I can't tell what that meant to me. She stood by him. Healthy Family.

Robert Downey, Jr. - I followed Robert his whole life, and court cases when he said to the judge, *"I just don't know"*, he said, *"when I did drugs, it was like putting a shotgun in my mouth and loving the taste."* In some strange way, this actually helped me, I understood how that felt, so I accepted it.

Russell Brand - his books, his story, and actions are legendary, there are no words. He has plenty of words to say and I love it.

Brad Pitt - His battle of loneliness and how he found a men's group, as well as Bradly Cooper, leading him to sobriety. But taking a year and half off to get sober. I needed to hear that.

Colin Farrell - the poem he wrote to his kids and how much he loved them and his deep fatherly apology was so profound.

Bradly Cooper - Jesus Christ, **Star is Born** the movie. Damn

Mathew Perry - his book, donating his house as a rehab, I mean who does that? Awesome!

Anthony Hopkins - 45 of years of sobriety, and he said on Jimmy Kimmel, *"You just have to get up each day and keep going!"* So simple and profound!

Every one of these celebrities, publicly showed how they overcame their addictions by writing music, creating books, and making movies, showing me TV. But all of this after they said some really important and vulnerable things in public, these experiences spoke directly to me, at the right time and right place to help me recover. To See things differently, to know that I am not alone. So yes, I turned all of those sincere words and beautiful creations that impressed me so much into and important part of my recovery.

I am not going to lie, when I started alcohol and drugs and pills and every combination thereof, I loved it. I absolutely loved it. But that is what got me hooked, so hooked. It was great at the time, because I finally found relief, I could numb, and I experienced a fake sense of peace. And that's the lie. It really is a lonely, very dangerous place to be. And I chased the drugs and alcohol and codependency for way too long. Like way too Long.

In the next section, we'll continue with the stages of recovery. As a prelude, I want to give you an assignment. I want you to start getting out of your head and into your gut. Before going to the next chapter, sit down and think about what you would have liked your family to be, from the time you were born till you were eleven years old. Write out this description of your Fantasy Family.

I don't care if you can't write well. We're not interested in grammar here. Write it out so you can understand it. And it's a fantasy. Anything you want. Maybe you had no biological family that you knew. That's OK. Create one. Maybe you never had brothers and sisters but wanted some. Good. Create them. Describe them. Tell them what you'd like to do with them. Maybe your Dad was a laborer and you wanted him to be a doctor, or vice- versa. Make it any way you want. That's the only rule: **Make it any way you want.**

Now, as good codependents, you're saying, that's silly. I promise I'll give you a good reason for it. A reason approved by traditional therapy, if that makes you feel better. I'll give you the reason at the beginning of the next chapter. I promise.

(Now, also as good codependents, a bunch of you will immediately turn to the next section to judge whether or not it's really worth it. That's OK. And yes, you can read the next section even if you don't do the assignment.)

Stage 3: Self Parenting
Meeting your own Needs

Why did I tell you to write about your Fantasy Family? Because it will show you your wish list straight from your own heart. The roots of our codependency are in the dysfunctionality of our OG Family, especially the first ten years of our lives. So, when we recreate that family as a Fantasy Family, we are really identifying what we wanted from that family but didn't get. Since we didn't get it, it is still a need. So, we are really making a list of our unfulfilled needs. In regard to relationships, we often sabotage them by unreasonably expecting them to fulfill these needs. As we go through this chapter, I will give you examples of such needs, and we are going to do something very important in recovery based on that list.

Also, getting into fantasy gets us out of our heads and into our guts, into our feelings. We resist that for a number of reasons, which we already discussed. But let's list some again as reminders. We are afraid to get out of our heads and into our guts because:

- Our head is our Control Tower and we are afraid to let go of control;
- Our feelings are too painful to face;
- We are not used to dealing with feelings, we have blocked them and denied them and shut them out for so long; in fact, some of us wouldn't know a genuine feeling if we tripped over one;
- We are afraid of the unknown; we have some very strong hints that we have pent-up feelings, but we're just not sure how big and ugly these "demons" are.

But getting into our feelings tells us what we want, what we need, what we have needed for a long time. Then we can work toward getting those needs met. Getting them met is called Parenting. The process of Stage Three is called Self-Parenting; we will get our own needs met. In short, we will begin to take responsibility for our own lives. We will stop frustrating ourselves and stop carrying unrealistic expectations into our relationships.

Failure to take Responsibility: The consequences

We already know the consequences of abdicating our responsibility to get our own needs met. Codependency, along with the depression and anxiety and the other many insanities that goes with it. To pull from Buddhism, please keep one basic principal in mind: **To get your needs met, look inside of yourself, and go back to the beginning.**

We have a very, very, very hard time understanding that. When we are children, we have friends, and we think, if only they would do this, or do that, or treat me this way, I would be happy; then we become teenagers and think, if only I had a boyfriend or girlfriend, I would be happy. And it goes on through the stages of our lives. If only I had someone to marry...if only I had kids...if only I had a better job...if only I had more money...if only I had...If only I had...And we get things and they don't make us happy, don't cure our addictions or our depressions. So, we think, well, if only I really had it made, like a famous actress or ball player or business mogul or...Yet we hear the stories of actresses and ball players and moguls all the time; money, fame, and all the other external things just don't make them happy. AND WE STILL DON'T GET IT! We keep looking outside of ourselves.

More often than not, we keep turning to other people. We are looking to be parented and to have our needs met. And when they do not meet our needs, we feel shamed like there's something wrong with us. And we start feeling sorry for ourselves. And we get angry at them. And while we're beating them up, we also beat ourselves up. Soon our bad feelings overshadow everything else. We have just enough energy to get up each morning, go to work, come home, eat, go to bed, and start it over again the next morning. That is, of course, unless your bad feelings turn into clinical depression and you get dysfunctional for a while until you can be medicated or hospitalized back to functionality. BTW, I did the medicated thing, and it about killed me. If it is something you need, then by all means, while you are working on yourself, but if you don't need it, don't get it.

It reminds me of a saying, back in my 80s: **LIFE'S A BITCH AND THEN YOU DIE!** Wonderful, isn't it? You function, you survive, and then you die. And you wonder why you're depressed? And guess what? There's a bonus! You get to pass the pattern on to your kids. They see the way you live. We have this phrase, I'm coping. Your kids see how you cope. That's how they'll try to cope. It's a shame. We're all coping. When we should be living. That's what happens when you don't get your needs met.

Stage Three, Step One
Writing out your fantasy family is like Step One of the third stage of recovery. Let me give you some examples. I was talking to a woman who started doing these exercises, she was like, "*I don't believe this,*" she said. "*I started the assignment and I'm sitting here crying like a baby.*" I said,

"Congratulations!" She said, *"But I don't like it. I have all this sadness coming up."* What was she learning? That she had feelings she had hidden. That she wasn't used to dealing with these feelings. I said to her, to just continue, trust the process. That's how you get the feelings up and out. That's how you find out what you wanted and never got.

In my own experience, when I started reconstructing my mother in my fantasy family, I was totally amazed at what came up. My Mom is high energy and intense, and her love language was food and providing for her family. I love my mother, there is nothing she would not do for me to help me. In fact, I was spoiled as a child when it came to food, everyday home cooked meals. In many ways she probably enabled me. But my Mom, hardcore German, born during a war, had to leave everything. She had twins and then 11 months later my sister and then 2 years later my youngest sister. A young mother with 4 kids all under the age of 4 and my Dad is starting a new business. I can only imagine the insanity for her. I get it, now that I am a father of 3 and a grandfather of 2. But growing up, there were things, as a young I child could not reconcile. There were zero intentions of hurting my feelings. We all do the best we can do in our family systems. Again, this is part of my journey of learning and discovery. I was a sensitive kid that required maybe a different method of support and motivation, or encouragement. There was absolutely a lot of positive as well, but like I said before, you tend to focus on the negative and not the positive. You see, I would have never realized any of this had I not started these exercises to see things from a different perspective. Seriously, this shit works. I have absolutely no judgment on my Mother, she is amazing and she absolutely loves me unconditionally.

Now take this to the next step. What do I do with all this knowledge? I choose, in my present life, to meet those needs. You avoid the things you need to avoid; stay closer to those things that make you happy.

These are choices I make to have my needs met. Self-Parenting. Setting boundaries. So, what was the end result of all that functionality and dysfunctionality in my early life? It became my teacher. By practicing the Six Stages of Recovery, my dysfunctionality became my teacher:

THAT'S ALL THAT DYSFUNCTIONALITY IS:
YOUR TEACHER

Surrogates
But let's go further still. In my real childhood I wanted to express my thoughts and Ideas at the dinner table, Like in my surrogate Italian families.

Doing my fantasy family, and really diving into this exercise, I mean truly thinking about this fantasy family, I also realized a few more things. That I had carried my childhood experience into my adult life. I didn't really bond with other women very well, unless it had something to do with business. I couldn't, for example, just go out and have a cup of coffee with a friend and talk about movies, sports, the weather, or whatever. When I started going to bars, before I drank, I thought it was so strange how everyone would order drinks and just talk. It made no sense to me. And if I decided to talk about something, I'd have to talk about work. I couldn't even offer an opinion about anything. I had to be intellectual. I was intellectualizing my life. Living inside my head. Instead of just having fun. Instead of just playing once in a while.

Now, knowing all that, I had a choice. I could continue that way, in semi-isolation and disappointment. Or I could change it.

It's funny, because when I look back initially, I never really thought I had surrogates in my life. But, when I served an Italian mission, I was drawn to these special Italian Mamas in my life. I would call them, and they would call me. I lived in many cities over those 2 years and I had 4 Italian mothers. They were beautiful, lovely, giving, passionate, and caring. Also, they were the most amazing cooks. Again, cooking for them was also their love language, so I was also naturally drawn to this. These lovely women, played surrogate mothers in my life and I played a surrogate son to them. I loved their food so much! I loved the individual effort they made specifically for me as I lived thousands of miles away from my family system.

My third mama would make the most amazing Italian dishes and she would sit across the table, just me and her, and she would stare at me and I would ask *"Mama, what's wrong?"* And you know what she said? *"Nothing Carlo, I just love to watch you eat!"* I would then ask her, where her children were. She said, tongue and cheek, *"they are all bastards, they don't love my food like you do!"* I adored her! I loved it! She would call me every evening and ask if I was hungry and I would say. *"Si, Mama! I'll be right over!"*

My first Mama was feeding me one night, and in the middle of me enjoying this delicious food, she asked if I had written my Mama. I told her not yet! She immediately took my food away, hit me in the back of the head, and called me a bastard son for not writing. It was beautiful. She then got me pen and paper, I wrote my mother, she gave me an envelope, and I finished the letter, and put it in the envelope, filled out the address. She then took the letter, because she said she would mail it, and then she gave me my food back, and with a big smile said: *"Buon Appetito!"* OMG, I loved it. She absolutely cared!

My second Mama was absolutely beautiful, every time I came to her house, she would stand right in front of me, and she would hold my face in her lovely hands and look into my eyes, and then slap me across the cheek, and say: *"Carlo, you are too skinny!"* and then she would feed me. I was about 170 lbs. back then, at the beginning of my Mormon Mission. Then a little over year later I was able to go back and see her, but at that time I had gained over 45 lbs. I walked into her house, she would stand again in front of me again, all 5' 2" of pure sweetness, she held my face in her wonderful hands again, and looked me in the eyes, and then slapped me across the cheek again, and said: *"Carlo, now you look good!"* OMG, I lapped it all up.

My point is, surrogates can play an invaluable role in your life or you can play that role for others. These surrogates did not take away the love I have for my mother. They helped me see something in me that I needed and wanted. I know I have played that role many times, my regret is, I wish I knew then what I know now.

Ask for what you want, then Do What You Want
Aside from using surrogates, just plain ask for what you want from people and then do what you want, take your own action, to get your needs met. We find that so difficult. This has been almost impossible for me; ask any of my friends or family. I do not ask. This is why I bring this up. This is about taking charge and asking for what you need. And I am talking about Healthy needs!

Parent yourself and get your own needs met. Ask. Do NOT wait for someone in shining armor or a hot dress to come along. Usually when they do show up, the armor is tarnished, and/or the dress is torn. Don't leave it in anyone else's hands but your own. I think you know what I mean.

Get off the crazy codependent game. Stop looking for external relationships to make you complete and happy. You hear it in songs: You are my life! You are my all! You are my everything! There beautiful songs, but ultimately create Codependency.

The only relationship you should worry about is the one with yourself. All the others flow from that. You are your life. You are your everything. If you believe in a Higher Power, it's just you and that power. Everything else flows from that. Take care of yourself and everything else will fall into place. Even healthy relationships.

In the next chapter, we are going to cover, Affirmation principles. We're going to go back to the "Fake it, till You Make It" idea. As a prelude, here are two more assignments.

First, for the next seven nights, before you go to bed, look into a mirror, into your own eyes, and tell yourself you are special, you are beautiful, and you love yourself just the way you are. I am telling you, this was hard for me. When I was using, my eyes were flat, no sparkle, glazed over, but when I was not abusing, I could look in the mirror and finally see these deep blue marbles sparkling with life. Then if you are really going for it, blow yourself a kiss in the mirror, and say, *"I love you, you are all right!"* You can be cool about it, go ahead and be gangsta about it, 2 fingers to your lips and a nod of the head. I don't care, just do it. Look directly at yourself in the mirror, blow yourself a kiss and tell yourself *"Love you!"* If you try it, it's called an affirmation. It's quite an experience. And you don't have to let anybody else know what you're doing. Just close the door and have some privacy. You're allowed.

Second, write a love letter to yourself. Then mail it. Don't write and email it, or a text message, because it comes back to you instantly. It will not have the same effect. Seriously, Think of it. In three days or so you'll get a love letter in the mail. Some of us have wanted one all our lives. Now you can get one. There's a point to that, too, something many people experience when they do it. We'll talk about that. But forget looking for big, psychological reasons. Just do it to have fun, to affirm yourself.

Remember my old saying from the 80s I told you about:
LIFE'S A BITCH THEN YOU DIE

We should replace this 80s saying with:
IT'S NEVER TOO LATE TO HAVE A HAPPY CHILDHOOD

Stage 4: Develop PMA

Positive Mental Attitude (PMA), Affirmations, Strengthening your Adult-Self. For those of you who did the exercise with the mirror, many, if not most, probably found it uncomfortable. Why? Why is it uncomfortable to give ourselves a little affirmation? Basically, because we're not used to it. Remember when we talked about our "**defaults**," our stress behaviors, we used the analogy of the computer. We have been programmed, and bought into the programming, of accepting the negative about ourselves, and about life in general. To take the analogy further, it's as though we have our own custom "**programming.**" I call them programs. The cynical programs. The critical programs. The negative programs. When you do affirmations, what you're doing is challenging the message within your programming. And they won't simply go away. They resist the change, the reprogramming. The old message is in conflict with the new. And it's that conflict that makes you feel uncomfortable.

My advice to you is to work on yourself first. Strengthen your adult-self first. Make the **Adult** strong before you work on the **Child**. Think of it. If a simple affirmation makes you uncomfortable and causes you internal conflict, what do you think tackling major issues will do to you? It will most likely cause you to relapse into your defaults, your stress behaviors, your addictions, and all the depression and anxiety and other insanity that go with them. You will identify your issues, but you will not be coming from a healthy perspective, and you will not have the strength to deal with them. You'll wind up blaming people, carrying resentment and anger and rage and all sorts of other powerful negative feelings into your present life, when the only purpose to identifying your issues is to learn from them, heal them, and make your life more peaceful and happier. I write this, because, I promise you, this is important. Because I fell into my defaults so many times and with so much pain, I honestly wasn't ready.

If you still doubt the strength of the old programming, consider a few other things. Some of you couldn't even try the simple affirmation exercise. We use the excuse that it's silly or it's too basic, I can skip it. Then what's the harm in trying a simple silly or basic exercise? It would only take a minute. What do you have to lose? The real reason for the resistance is that it is threatening. Giving a simple affirmation to ourselves is threatening.

The old programs are negative. For example, if you go through a typical day, a pretty nice day, with no particular problems, then you have a problem, say, from 7pm to 8pm that night; I guarantee that you'll talk about it the next day. You will focus on that hour. You will forget the other twenty-three. Or take another example. What attracts crowds, the healthy, positive things in our lives? No. It's usually the bizarre, the crazy, the murders, its tragedies and mayhem that attract us. Just look at a news broadcast. We broadcast tragedies. We do it in mass media. And we do it in our personal lives. In my own experience I try to resist being drawn to the negative. And it takes effort.

As a last example, I go back to my grammar school experience. Back in the 70's, if you misbehaved, and in this one example I did not misbehave, we were at a school assembly and a student was constantly hitting and kicking me from behind, I finally told him to knock it off. I was maybe 7 or 8 years of age, when the principle came over, grabbed me by my hair and dragged me along the floor across the entire teacher and student body. I did not do anything fucking wrong. Insane right, how do you reconcile something like that at a young age? He **Shamed** me for no fucking reason. I did not deal with that trauma until I started doing my exercises, I had forgotten about it, but my Inner Child never forgot and it came out in different ways my entire life. It sucked, because this dysfunctional adult, who is supposed to be wise and helpful, forced me to believe that **"I am a bad boy."** Funny thing now is that in my exercises, I literally wrote the experience down, felt what I needed to feel, and simply wrote. **FUCK HIM!**

There was this study done at a school, where they took a class and changed its entire profile. As it was graduating from one grade to the next, they told the new teacher that the better students were the slower learners and vice versa, that the well-behaved children were the problems and vice versa. And guess what? The kids began to act as the teacher expected. In terms of our analogy, what they basically did was create "a program" of the children, and then everybody listened to that programming and acted accordingly, until it finally affected the children themselves, which, I hated that they even did this experiment. But you get the point.

So, what we need to do as part of strengthening our adult selves is to challenge the old programming. But I have another secret to share with you. The old programming, the old messages we carry inside about ourselves, will not go away. They have been part of our history and the core of our lives for a long time. What we need to do is create new programs about ourselves and play them louder and longer than the old ones. It's an old concept. It's called brainwashing. You play the new programs long enough and loud enough and they and their positive message will take over.

And here's something really cool to consider. Most of you know already that no matter what your history is, you have done the best you can, you are a good person, and you can change and grow. That belief will respond very quickly to your affirmations. Of course, there will be things, old messages and programs, that won't be so easy to overcome. That's OK too, part of the process of Recovery. Remind yourself again please: Recovery is an ongoing PROCESS. For those stubborn messages, you can use another approach; the old **Fake it, till you Make it!**

But before we get into some affirmation techniques, let's look at three principles that make affirmations effective.

Three Basic Principles
These are very simple.

First, an affirmation is a totally positive statement. For example, a major issue in my own life is guilt. I do not approach it by saying I am not guilty. That still carries the negative concept of guilt. I should approach it on a positive level with something like I am an innocent, gentle, and beautiful person. What an affirmation does is accentuate the positive.

Second: Repetition. Don't look for magic. If you start right now saying affirmations, will your whole attitude change overnight? It doesn't work that way. And I'll let you in on a secret. It might get worse before it gets better. There was this one counselor who advises that getting into issues and affirmations is like trying to clean out a garbage pile. Left alone, the pile stinks. But it stinks even more when you stir it up and start to get to the bottom. The stink, the negative feelings, come from the conflict of your old programming with the new. But repetition will overcome that. To finish the analogy of the garbage pile, keep cleaning and soon the odor is gone. Stick with your affirmations. The same counselor used to give a formula for effective change. He would advise you to do the positive things Regularly, Over A Long Period of Time, and With Respect.

Third, one of the most powerful ways of doing affirmations is through the subconscious. We'll explore this more when we cover techniques of affirmations, but basically why we work through the subconscious, is because it's our defenses, our walls. We are open and vulnerable in the subconscious, particularly when we are asleep. Because when we are sleeping, we are totally open to hearing and receiving messages.

Now let's look at a few proven techniques for affirmations, and I'll give you examples of how different people have used them effectively.

Affirmation Techniques - SELF Statements

The first technique I want to share is the one I already suggested: Tell yourself you are a good and beautiful person. Say it before you go to bed and when you wake up every morning. If you want to have some fun with it, look at yourself in the mirror when you say it and give your mirror image a kiss. What's it going to take, a minute or two? If it makes you uncomfortable at first, if you have a hard time believing the message, fake it. Fake it till you Make it. Because soon you will start to believe it.

No matter what comes up to challenge this message that you are, in fact, a good and beautiful person whether that challenge comes from things you've done or things you were told about yourself, you know your own circumstances. You know that you've tried your best, and you know that you were created exactly as you were supposed to be. You are looking for Progress not Perfection (cliché).

And to show you how effective this affirmation technique can be, I read examples of two schoolteachers. One is a first-grade teacher. She tried an experiment. Every morning she would have her students go to a mirror and say, *"you're special, you're beautiful, and I love you."* At first, the kids would do things like run to the mirror and say it fast and run back to their seats, or they would cover their eyes when they said it. They were very uncomfortable. But she had them stick with it. And she said that after about six months. There was a profound change. Now they would almost fight to get to the mirror, and some of them really hammed it up. It was actually hard to get them away from the mirror. They went from shyness to feeling good about themselves, all because of this simple affirmation.

Another teacher, in contrast to most of the other teachers she worked with, believed in affirming the positive with children. She focused on the positive, even when the children made mistakes. Her constant message was that her kids, her students, were good and lovable and beautiful. She believed that kids are impressionistic and would absolutely respond to affirmations. Her whole philosophy of life revolved around affirmation. And this is how she conducted all her classrooms. As she reflected, many of those children grew up feeling positive and reported back to her over the years thanking her for being, not only their favorite teacher, but they affirmed to her that the positivity left a huge impression on their lives.

Even my daughter told me about an experience with my grandson. He was 4 years old; he got him self-ready for school, did it himself, and he looked at his Mom and said Mom, "I am going to have a great day!" He said this at the age of 4! Awesome, consequently he had a great day. The power of children and affirmations is huge. We can learn a lot from our children. Why, because they are a mirror and a reflection of us.

Affirmations are positive statements that can help shift your mindset, build self-confidence, and promote a more optimistic outlook on life. There are various affirmation techniques you can use to incorporate affirmations into your daily routine.

Here are some different types of affirmation techniques:

    1. Mirror Affirmations: Stand in front of a mirror, look yourself in the eyes, and say positive affirmations out loud. Speaking directly to yourself in the mirror can reinforce the message and make it more powerful.

    2. Written Affirmations: Write down your affirmations in a journal or on sticky notes and place them where you can see them regularly. This could be on your bathroom mirror, computer monitor, or fridge.

    3. Visualization Affirmations: Close your eyes and visualize yourself embodying the qualities or achievements mentioned in your affirmations. Imagine yourself living your best life and achieving your goals.

    4. Affirmation Meditation: Incorporate affirmations into your meditation practice. Repeat positive statements silently or aloud during your meditation sessions to enhance their impact.

    5. Affirmation Recordings: Record yourself saying affirmations and listen to the recording regularly. Hearing your own voice delivering positive messages can be empowering.

    6. Affirmation Cards: Create or buy affirmation cards with different positive statements. Shuffle the deck daily and pick a card randomly to focus on that particular affirmation for the day.

7. Affirmation Walks: Take a walk outside and use the time to repeat affirmations in your mind. Being in nature and moving your body can enhance the effectiveness of affirmations.

8. Group Affirmations: Practice affirmations with a group of friends or in a support group. Sharing positive statements collectively can create a sense of community and support.

9. Affirmation Challenges: Set a 30-day affirmation challenge for yourself. Repeat specific affirmations consistently for a month to see how it positively affects your mindset.

10. Affirmation Visualization Board: Create a vision board with images and words representing your goals and desires. Include positive affirmations related to the images to reinforce your intentions.

11. Affirmation Apps: Use smartphone apps that provide daily affirmations and reminders to help you stay focused on positivity throughout the day.

12. Affirmation Journaling: Write affirmations in a dedicated journal, and also reflect on how you feel after repeating them regularly.

13. Affirmation Affixation: Write affirmations on sticky notes and stick them to places you frequent, like your desk, bathroom mirror, or car dashboard.

14. Affirmation Breathing: Practice deep breathing while repeating affirmations. Inhale positivity and exhale any negative thoughts or doubts.

15. Affirmation Gratitude: Combine affirmations with expressions of gratitude. For example, "I am grateful for my health and well-being."

Remember that the key to effective affirmations is repetition and belief in the positive statements you are making. Choose affirmations that resonate with you personally and genuinely feel uplifting. By integrating these affirmation techniques into your daily routine, you can cultivate a more positive and empowered mindset.

In Summary: Be Creative!
Be as creative as you want with your affirmations. Have fun with them. Make personal cards that you carry with you and check during the day. Play your personal affirmations while driving, not the subliminal ones, I don't want you to fall asleep at the wheel. I bet you can find some with the voice of Mathew McConaughey. Then just do it and let the results show for themselves.

You can also make affirmations part of the events in your life. In some cultures, affirmations are used in the connection of mind, body, and spirit and in developing close relationships. For example, in certain Chinese philosophies, people in relationships have exercises they do with each other in which they physically and even sexually say good morning and good night to each other, and join in different forms of prayer.

When you're working on affirmations, you are investing in yourself. You are programming positive stuff inside of you. You will look at life more positively. Your environment, your programs, your time for self...They are all simple things, just as a hammer or saw or chisel are simple tools. Affirmations are the simple tools you use to replace the old, negative messages about yourself with the new and the positive.

OG Family Exercises

OK. For those of you who are dying to get to your *"issues"* and Inner Child, we have come to the Fifth Stage of Recovery. Next chapter is dedicated to Inner Child work. I have included a few more resources just before **Chapter Five**. Please stick with me, don't skip; these mirrors were critical to helping me do inner child work. But I'm going to warn you again: Make sure you work on the first four before you tackle five and six. And just reading about the first four isn't working on them.

To me Recovery has been an absolute mind fuck, make sure you don't get stuck in your head, this is absolutely a process, so work it, what else do you have to lose, how is your life working for you so far? If you are this far into the book, I'm impressed. Again, It's a process! A constant process! In a subsequent chapter I have an explanation of Kung Fu? **"Supreme skill from hard work." *"Practice. Preparation. Endless repetition. Until your mind is weary, and your bones ache. Until you're too tired to sweat. Too wasted to breathe."*** *I promise if you do this, it will sink in, and you will change, evolve, and you will start to feel moments of relief and happiness. Keep working and repeating, and those moments will turn into hours, then days, then weeks, then months, then years and then you will have your whole life ahead of you. You will literally take each step, in gratitude and love and you might want to help one other person achieve what you so courageously achieved. That's just simply fucking awesome!!! It just is!*
So, AFTER you;
        1. Develop self-knowledge and self-awareness;
        2. Build a healthy support system;
        3. Learn how to parent yourself; and
        4. Learn how to affirm yourself;

You can start looking at your OG Family through a simple exercise. Sit down with a paper and pencil, say a prayer to your Higher Power, if you believe in one, and write your personal history from as far back as you can remember. No matter what comes to you, write it down. Positive and/or negative, no matter what, write it down. Don't ask anyone to help you. Don't ask brothers or sisters or friends or other family members what they remember. You are dealing with your perceptions, not theirs. You see, if there were eight children in your family, or ten, and I asked each of you to write your perceptions of the family, I will get eight to ten different versions of events. Everyone has their own perceptions, their own experience. What is important is that you see what your own perceptions are. This is where I discovered _The Seven Essene mirrors of Self_ as interpreted by Greg Braden. I had a difficult time looking back and seeing or even wanting to see my issues, trauma, challenges, and who knows what else. The mirrors helped me look at myself through seven different mirrors. These mirrors became a wonderful tool and reference in my self- discovery. I cannot stress enough how important this chapter is and a critical part of the process, it's the thing that helped me get too the core of so much pain and to let go. But you really have to go into it prepared. I did not go into it very prepared the first couple of times. And the tornado and vortex of absolute pure emotional mayhem took a toll on me and anyone around me. It was awful, ultimately good that it came out but so fucking inelegant and ugly. These steps or stages especially the self- parenting part when shit comes up and out is to protect you and those around you. **So fucking important.**

The Seven Essene Mirrors of Self

Greg Braden has discussed the concept of the "Seven Essene Mirrors of Self" in his book "Walking Between the Worlds: The Science of Compassion." These mirrors are based on the ancient Essene teachings and offer insights into how to foster personal growth and relationships with others by looking into different mirrors. By understanding what they are, life and life's challenges seem to make so much more sense. Here is a brief description and applications of the Seven Essene Mirrors:

1. Mystery of the First Mirror – Mirror of the Moment

This is the mirror we are all familiar with. We have all been there, someone says or does something (we like or don't like, it doesn't matter), and it may be mirroring an action or word within you or some action or word you need to learn at this very moment.

2. Mystery of the Second Mirror - Mirror of that which is Judged This is the mirror that we have the most trouble with. The thing(s) that we judge will present themselves to us over and over again, until we realize that it will keep happening again and again until we understand, that it is the charge we are placing on the people, situations, words, etc. Let me explain further. Take something you really judge let's say dishonest people (addicts). You have put a charge on it, then I can pretty much guarantee you will have many dishonest people that show up in your life. Another one is erratic drivers. The charge I placed on it was with undignified language and an occasional hand gesture to the car or individual driving the car. Until I came to the realization that it was a judgment call and to get into a place of non-judgment you can bet, I had this happen over and over and over again. Yes, it is possible to get to that place of non- judgment. The second mirror is all about allowing within yourself, another possibility of thought action and feeling that you do not allow within yourself. In other words, they have a right to do exactly what they want, BUT you have the right to not react.

3. Mystery of the Third Mirror - Mirror of Relationships
The Mirror of That Which is Lost, Given Away, or Taken Away. Any relationship can be a momentary one that happens as quick as a flash or as long as lifelong friend(s) or partner(s). This is the mirror, which tells us that we see something in another individual that we don't see in ourselves or there is a void in ourselves. As this part *"awakens"* in us, many times, the relationship(s), is completed or the void is filled. The relationship happened just for the simple reason of *"awakening"* some part of us. Other times, after we reclaim that part, the relationship will need to be redefined and continue with the context of the redefinition or it will discontinue because it is finished.

4. Mystery of the Fourth Mirror - Mirror of the Most Forgotten Love
This is the mirror of compulsive/addictive behaviors, The Mirror of the Most Forgotten Love. I want you to just take a minute here and spend some time figuring out your compulsive/addictive behaviors. Everyone has them. I used to think I didn't have an addiction; I thought addictions were drinking, drugs, alcohol, gambling, etc. I spent some time and I identified my addictions. For me, it was trying to be perfect. Trying to fix everyone's lives, or food, or control. Now, figure yours out. Next think about what you have missed out on because of addiction/compulsion. What I *"lost"* was being able to be myself. I lost time for myself. I lost me. Through missing out on being myself, I was missing out on life. What do I love most? Life and Living. This is a very interesting Mirror. You can think of the alcoholic: he loves his family and what does he end up losing but that which he loves the most, his family. Braden says that your greatest fear may be re-defined as your most forgotten love. Addiction/compulsion may be re-defined as a behavior pattern, which, in its extreme, will provide the opportunity to experience exactly opposite of that which you most desire in your life. The addiction/compulsion is your way of providing yourself the opportunity to experience your greatest fears (most forgotten loves), in degrees, as you drive

from your life the very things that you hold most dear, until the fear is either resolved or manifested.

5. Mystery of the Fifth Mirror - Mirror of the Mother/Father

This mirror has an exercise. Take out a piece of paper. List on the top, mother figure then father figure. Under each put a + and a -. (If you did not have a Mom or Dad, put down your childhood caretakers. Under each heading, list all the positives and negatives about each as you saw them before you were 12 years old. (Again, not through an adult's eyes, but a child's eyes). If you don't have any positives or any negatives, that is fine. Use phrases or key words. Do this before you read on, do not read on until you do this. Now I'll write down what the Essenes have to say about this list. Your earth 'Father/Mother' holds and reflects your expectations and beliefs of your relationship with your heavenly father/mother. (Spirit is energy or whatever you call the higher essence/power). The way that you see your 'mother' and 'father' probably have very little to do with the person that you call 'Dad' or 'Mom'. Through their lives, your father and mother have loved you so much that each has held a reflection of how you see, or have seen your relationship with heaven and earth. Sit and think about this mirror awhile. _This mirror was the most profound for me. My father larger than life, a genius, caregiver, suffered a war, hunger. He became a figure I could not live up to. He is my idol and it's been my greatest honor and pleasure to work with him and be his son. My mother is a person that you cannot keep up with. I always said that most mothers try and keep up with their kids, for me, I can't even begin to keep up with the energy she carries. She knows one speed and confronts all of it head on. Both have traits that I believed I felt so short._

6. Mystery of the Sixth Mirror - Mirror of the Dark Side of the Soul

The best way to describe this mirror is to tell you what the Essenes have to say. *"You are not capable of entering the Dark Side of the Soul until you have amassed all the tools necessary to move through this experience, with grace. And trust, you will allow your 'experience' to push you over the edge and leave you to find your way out, ALONE!"* This is your opportunity to demonstrate your mastery of who you have become. The Dark side of the Soul is your way of re-defining your perception of one, or some combination, of the Universal Fears of Abandonment, Separation, Self-Worth, Trust, Etc.

7. Mystery of the Seventh Mirror - Mirror of Self

In this mirror, we want you to set up a report card. Put on it: Physical, Mental, Emotional, and Social. Then give yourself a grade in each. Starting with fail, average, above average, excellent. After you do this, read the next passage. Don't cheat now! *"Your view of yourself in anything other than perfection will reveal your greatest doubt (least trust) in the ONE. The view that others hold of you in anything other than perfection will reveal their greatest doubt (least trust) in the ONE."* It also gives you a good connection to look at yourself and really 'get it', that you were made in his perfection. Do you think that God (your higher essence/power create junk? HELL NO!).

> *We Humans, have the ability, the capacity, and the power to change, create, build, to do anything and be anyone we want, if we choose!!!*

These Seven Essene Mirrors offered me a framework for self-reflection, self-awareness, and personal growth, enabling me to deepen my understanding of myself, my relationships, and my connection to the world around me. I love what I put in about these mirrors, please use as a reference in that there is further detail within each mirror I just love. And it helped. I swear to God.

Also, don't beat yourself up if you don't remember much, initially I had a lot of blanks. In rehab and in random conversations, I kept hearing they have blanks in their lives, periods for which they don't remember much. I learned that It's OK. It just meant that I was not supposed to remember them at this time. The things I do remember are the things I was ready to work on. That's all. And that's why this next chapter is so important. I cannot stress this enough.

Stage 5: The OG Family
Approaching the Process
AFTER you work on the first four Stages of Recovery, you are ready to **BEGIN** looking at your inner issues, which I call OG Family work. I see this as the Fifth Stage of Recovery.

Note the emphasis on the two words, "after" and "begin." I compared the process of recovering from codependency to surgery. If you have surgery, you must be strong enough for it, or you will not survive the operation. So, you "prep" for it. You make yourself strong enough to survive the operation. Recovery is very similar. The first four stages prep you for the fifth and sixth, the actual surgery and healing. Also, I say BEGIN to work on OG family issues because the work is not an event. It is a process. It is ongoing.

Further, before you approach the work, you must have the right attitude, a positive attitude. You are doing OG Family work to learn from your past and move on in your growth process. If you approach it with a negative attitude, you will only hurt yourself more than you have ever been hurt.

You will fall into the Blame Game, the Victim Game, blaming others for how you are now. You will become obsessed with the people whom you perceive as having hurt you. You will become obsessed with your issues. You will, in many ways, become your issues. I mentioned before that you sometimes meet people who are like this. You say Hello, and they start telling you about their issues. They have no life, no focus, other than their issues. So, as you begin your OG Family work, keep the basic principle in mind that the only reason you are doing the work is to learn from it. You are a grown ass adult now! You can think, you can feel, you obviously know how to make a decision, that's why you are here. So, Change your world, make different decisions, you obviously know how. You are gorgeous and capable and beautiful; don't let anyone tell you any different. If the people around you don't believe you, well then, **Fuck'em**.

It helps to keep in mind that even the most dysfunctional situations in your life can become your teachers. For example, in my own life, I suffered from depression, panic attacks, full synaptic shutdowns, I went to rehab, and severe detox from cold turkey withdrawals, I mean I was doing like 4-30s of Oxys every 6 to 8 hours. 120mg snorted is just fucking dumb. (OMG, I do not recommend that kind of special Hell for anyone). And there were a few times too many, which was few times too many, that were so dangerous, so stupid, so awful, but I did it again and again. I honestly died twice, the second time for just over 2 minutes. Shit, Damn, Hell, who the fuck does that? I mean, are you fucking kidding me? Nope! I did it! Over and over again.

As painful as all these experiences were, I now realize that it actually planted the seeds of my recovery. It is part of my personal history. I accepted it, I learned from it and use it to grow even today. Fuck, it's another reason for writing this book. In fact, I think I am going to add a chapter of what it is like to be on drugs and what it does to your body during your highs & lows, and then I should write what it does to you when you decide to go off and what withdrawals feel like and what that does to your body. Maybe if people knew the consequences before trying anything so toxic they would think twice, three times, hell maybe ever four times before going into absolute insanity and pure chaos.

Further, let's go back yet again to the word "process." OG Family work takes time. Don't think that what you read in the next few pages is something you can do by midnight tonight! I see too much of that. Hell, I know, I tried it so many times. We get into recovery and we get very intense, very impatient. We want everything to happen and fall into place FAST, especially if it was depression or anxiety or other intense pain that led us to this process. But, again, recovery is not an event, not a *"magic bullet"* cure that happens overnight. Remember the fundamental principle that we joke about. **It says that basically we learn all of our patterns and foundations in the first ten years of our lives.** Then we spend the next eighty years working on them. We joke about it, but it's no joke. That's about how it works. That does not mean that you stay sick and unhappy and depressed and anxious as you go through a lengthy process. Basically, the process will bring you peace of mind and freedom from the negative, true freedom from what's holding you back from becoming your best self- loving self.

Finally, I use a Twelve Step model in my OG Family work, so from time to time I'll be referring very briefly to some of the Steps.

Your Perceptions, Your Issues
When you do your OG Family work, you are basically looking back at your childhood, and then beyond, for two reasons. **First**, to identify your patterns, foundations, and issues. **Second**, to give yourself permission to heal. The second point, as we already touched on, is so important. Many of us, if not all of us, need feedback about our thoughts and feelings. We need to have them validated. Then we can move on from there to the process of healing. Since no one has given us that feedback, that permission, we must give it to ourselves. If you are not going to give yourself permission, then I will give you permission. Sincerely, listen and read my words, I AM GIVING YOU PERMISSION TO HEAL until you give it to yourself. Sincerely. Feel ME!!!

And when you look back at your patterns, foundations, and issues, you are dealing with what you remember about your childhood—with your perceptions. These are your perceptions. And there are some basic things to keep in mind as you go through the process.

First, as I mentioned in the last chapter, don't ask anyone else about their perceptions of your family. If I take eight siblings and ask them for their perceptions of their family, I will get eight different stories. Every child perceives the family differently. Let me share an example. A man I know viewed his mother as being controlling, smothering, possessive, and manipulative. His perception was that she did not give him his own space and distance when he was growing up. His cousin, on the other hand, viewed the same mother quite differently. The cousin came from an alcoholic home. Her father was a violent alcoholic, her mother an extremely angry person. The cousin did not experience any attention, warmth, or affection at home. So, whenever she came to her cousin's house, she loved it, because her cousin's mother, in her smothering way, gave her all the attention she craved. To the cousin, his mother was the epitome of nurturing. That was her perception. And when she hears her cousin complain about his mother, even today, she basically tells him he's crazy, his mother was the salt of the earth. Different perceptions.

Second, it is common for people approaching OG Family work to start doubting themselves, doubting their memories. They follow this by thinking that if they can't be sure their memories are accurate, their work won't be valid. Forget that. It doesn't make any difference if your perceptions are accurate or real. They are real for you. They are what has been driving you into and keeping you in your codependency. So, it is them that you have to deal with.

Third, people complain that they don't remember very much, and they think that this will lessen the effect of their work. Forget that, too. You remember what you are supposed to remember, when you are supposed to remember it. End of discussion. Your mind will only show you what you are ready to handle. What you are ready to process. It's like a ladder you have to step on to the first step before you can step to the next step. Or like an onion, if you have to peel back the first layer, before you can get to next layer, each layer accepting and taking away the stink of pain, depression, anxiety, and more to process so you can finally reach the core or the top of the ladder.

And in regard to the last point, let's go over something again. In doing your OG family work, you will be resurrecting FEELINGS. And I mean, really unpleasant feelings, like guilt, shame, depression, anxiety, sadness, anger...But remember that this time they are not being resurrected so they can hang onto you indefinitely and fuck up your life. This time, you are bringing them up to process them and throw them out, so you can heal.

*I will say it again and again, the beginning of this process is called an **Inventory**. It is your personal history. This process is truly the beginning of healing, it's in the 12 steps for a reason. I swear to God, 12 Steps got it from Buddhism, Daoism, the Kabbalah, the Chinese I-Ching, and/or all the above. Because each one of these beautiful rich and ancient teachings say the same thing. This is your starting point, it's a proven* *method, and technique, in any program you choose to implement. Just fucking do it!*

Inventory and Journaling Techniques
As I asked you to do at the end of the last chapter, you should write your inventory. Start by finding a quiet place. Block out the time. And remind yourself that the only reason you are doing this work is to learn from it and grow and move on. It is a spiritual exercise. Spiritual does not mean religious. Spiritual meaning is related to growth, your own personal growth. Remember (Security, Unconditional Love, Safety, Intimacy, Identity) these are spiritual traits.

If you believe in a higher power, say a prayer to that power to guide you. If you don't believe in one, tell your own mind to open your heart and your memory, just by telling yourself, you will **ACTIVATE** what's necessary inside of you to come out. Then write down everything you remember from your first consciousness in life up to the age of ten or twelve. A good cut-off for this first segment is the end of grammar school. But there are no hard and fast rules regarding this. **Activation** is big now; it will become more powerful than you can imagine. My chapter on Affirmations and PMAs is all about activating what is already inside you.

It doesn't make any difference if it comes out in order, chronologically. Your grammar and penmanship don't have to be perfect. In fact, my handwriting is literally chicken scratch. My father, God rest his beautiful soul, would tell me this as a young child. This would really upset me. He never meant to hurt me, it wasn't malicious, such a small thing but to a sensitive child it had a profound effect on me that I could not reconcile for years. Anyway, this is much more than some kind of test. Ignore any blocks or blanks, what you don't remember, don't worry about it.

If it feels uncomfortable, ignore that too, and work through the feelings (you might have to pull some tools out of your personal tool box to work through feelings so that you can continue). Also, don't censor what you write. Write what you remember. Good codependents like us tend to drive ourselves crazy with worries like the ones I just mentioned. They are not important in this exercise. Which is not to say that the exercise is not important, that it will not resurrect strong feelings.

That's the first part of the technique. Write your history down. Don't try to think it, because then you will try to analyze it. If you do this properly, you will be doing what the Twelve Step Program refers to as a *"fearless moral inventory."* And remember, when you write your perceptions down, you are actually bringing them up and getting them out of yourself. You're starting to peel back the layers.

Share your inventory with Safe People

This is why **Stage Two** of the recovery process is so important. If you really did that stage, you have some people you feel safe with, that you can now share your inventory with. Sharing means you will read it to them. In good group work, you will also hear their stories. The first time I did this was in Rehab in southern Florida with 35 strangers. I wish I would have learned all these steps sooner then and had been able to execute on what I learned after 10 years of hard-core addiction, relapse, and recovery, but it is just that, that lead me to this moment of being able to see the path, the steps, the stages, and executing on this steps, and ultimately peeling back all the layers of the onion, the OG Family work leads to ultimate self-love.

The idea and goal, is, that after some weeks, you might have a network of several people maybe six or seven who are committed die-hards, like you, that stuck with it; Your *"die-hard"* group feels comfortable enough together to share their inventories. Taking turns reading them. This is important for two reasons:

First, the act of reading is an act of opening up, of releasing feelings, which is a key to the healing process.

Second, reading to a group and then listening to their stories demonstrates to you that your problems and issues are not so unique. Sharing with a safe group gives you perspective. But, more important, sharing with your group is like sharing with your family, your Recovery Family, which is a healthy family. You will be allowed to express your feelings without criticism and without **Judgment (God I hate Judgment)**. You will experience unconditional acceptance and love. Your perceptions will be validated. In short, you will get from your Recovery Family the things you sought but never received from your OG Family. And this is a crucial part of the healing process as well. Basically, did you ever walk away from a family issue asking, *"Is it me? Am I crazy? Doesn't anybody else here see the dysfunctionality I am experiencing?"* With your Recovery Family, you will be working with other people who will give you the answers: It is not you, you are not crazy for feeling what you are feeling, and they see the dysfunctionality you have seen in your own experience.

My personal experience; the first time I did this was in Rehab, so worth it, so much freedom in knowing that I could express my perceptions, my feelings and my trauma to a group of strangers but awkwardly enough my Recovery family, and they did not judge me. When I go home, I did not have this recovery family, so I created my own microcosm of a fictional recovery family. (I would write down my inventory and express my inventory one at a time to individual family members without them knowing.) I would use the testimonials and videos of celebrities that have experienced and endured the same thing I was going through and made them part of my Recovery Family. I would watch interview after interview hanging onto every word and listen so intently to see how they overcame their addictions. These celebrities ended up become my idols and my inspiration. I can't even imagine to already being in the public eye, famous, and then to be judged and criticized for their addictions only to show everyone that they did what they had to do to recover. And because of their fame, they had a huge impact on me. Their stories, their books, their movies, their TV shows started to show what healing looked like and how hard it was but that it was possible. So that was my Recovery Family. What I am saying is, look outside the box, break the norm, be creative, you can create whatever Recovery Family you want. Maybe it's a family of animals; maybe it's a family of stuffed animals. I don't fucking know; only you know. But please, just do it.

If you are not in a Twelve Step program and do not feel comfortable sharing the negative parts of your inventory with even your Recovery Family, you should find a good therapist, a good coach, but one who is trained in this type of technique. The reason is that you must feel comfortable with the process, otherwise it will only add to your negative feelings. I cannot emphasize this enough. You only do what is comfortable for you. If you can, as you do your inventory, dig up some photographs of that time in your life. Photos are often an uncensored record of you and your family. They tell a lot about you and your experience.

Composing Lists for Journaling
After writing and sharing your inventory, I want you to compose three lists from it. The **first** *is a list of all the negative persons, places, and things in that part of your life.* The **second** *is a list of the issues you experienced during that period.* For example, some of them might be fear, abuse,

abandonment, guilt, and shame. **By the way, guilt and shame, which we'll get into, are two entirely different things.** I have subsequent chapters understanding the importance of guilt vs. shame. It was so important when I learned the difference, it was a huge turning point for me and how to look at all decisions I had made and will make, it changed everything for me. Because for the first time I realized I was not a bad person (which is the definition of shame). The **third** *list covers the positive persons, places, and things during that period of your life.*

Just coming this far in the process, you might begin to experience something different. You might have been looking at your childhood as all negative, but you'll realize that there were positive influences as well. You will be gaining a sense of balance, which is part of the recovery process. You will even have positive feelings about the negative people, places, and things in your life. In fact, some of these may appear on both your positive and negative list. For example, one person related that he had several negative perceptions and issues regarding his father. He had basically felt abandoned by his father. But in composing the lists, he also realized several positive things that he hadn't considered before. His father had worked hard for the family, and in his own way had expressed his love for his son.

But to proceed with the process, once you have your lists, you can start journaling, which is, basically, letter writing. I do this I by opening two separate notebooks. I call them simply my positive book and negative book. Start by going to your negative list and writing a letter in the negative book to each person, place, and thing on that list.

DO NOT MAIL THESE LETTERS!!!
Let me repeat: Do not mail these letters. Don't give them to people. They are not about other people. They are about you! What you are doing by writing is giving the child within you permission to express your feelings, to release your feelings and eventually let them go.

You might want to share these letters initially, **Don't**! I experienced the power of this at rehab when my family came to visit me and they had to all write me letters. The reason we could do this exercise directly, is because they participated in my recovery, openly and honestly. It was a very healthy, but scary as hell experience for all of us. This type of confrontation was done under the guidance of a therapist.

There are other principals involved in this exercise as well. I Write the negative letters first. And always follow your negative letters with positive ones. For example, if you write a negative letter to your mother, you put it into your negative journal, thereby releasing it from inside of you. You then immediately go to your positive journal and write another letter to your mother.

But what if you can't feel anything positive just then? Fake it. Till you make it. Just write something like, "Dear Mom, I love you." And sign it. Why? Two reasons. **First**, you always want to end on a positive note, leave the positive for yourself. **Second**, the purpose of the exercise is to heal.

Sometimes we have experienced terrible things at the hands of other people: incest, rape, emotional abuse...How can we write something positive to them? A positive letter in those cases might say something like, *"What you did was terrible, but it taught me to be strong."* It's like the old biblical passage about loving our enemies. I used to have a very hard time with that until I explored it further. It doesn't say that you have to like your enemies or what they did. It doesn't say that you have to associate with them. It just says love them. **Love Them; Pray for Them; Let Them Go**. The hardest thing for us to do is to let go of people, places, and things. This exercise will help you let go of the negative...and hold onto the positive.

You can even use this method in everyday situations. Say you have a fight with your spouse. You can journal the negative and the positive. Let go of the negative. Keep the positive. What you are experiencing is the fact that because of a fight or disagreement you do not throw out the positive with the negative. You have undoubtedly seen this yourself. A couple gets into an argument and they caught up in it. They react, It turns into a shouting match, and they start bringing up everything negative that happened over the past twenty years. Then they're beating each other to death with the negative. Yes, they have issues. We all have issues. But the trick is remembering the positive and keeping the positive while getting rid of the negative.

And remember...I asked that you keep separate journals: positive and negative, I'm going to show you something else to do, to emphasize getting rid of the one and keeping the other.

And to go back for a second, I'd like to repeat that clearing out the negative might lead to some deep positive feelings you didn't even know existed. People in therapy often experience this as they work on their issues, get rid of old, negative, mental and emotional baggage. Life in general starts looking brighter, and they actually report feeling positive, nostalgic feelings that they never experienced before about past events. It's like, brush away the dirt and see the diamond shine.

You also apply the negative/positive journaling technique to your list of issues. For example, look at addiction. You can write in your negative journal all the unhealthy things that addiction did to you. But, in your positive journal, you can also write the healthy things that the addiction led you to, like recovery and discovering my inner strengths, like learning to set boundaries and limits. In the process, you are allowing your negative issues to become your teacher, and you are identifying the positive things you got from these issues. You are training to look at life through the eyes of learning so that you can heal and make peace. If you don't, then what you do, is carry the negative around with you. For example, say your mother is deceased and you still have negative issues that affect you involving her. What you are actually doing is giving a dead person control of your present life, just as though she is still alive inside of you.

As for your positive list, it's obvious what to do with it. Write a positive letter in your journal to each person, place, and thing on the list. That's for you to keep as well. I believe we have certain spiritual messengers sent into our lives when they are supposed to be there to help us cope and learn. Before moving on in the process to an interesting *"therapy,"* You can have some of the same people, places, and things on both your positive and negative lists. You still write them one of each type of letter. And the following *"therapy"* will show you what to do next.

Cemetery and Fire Therapy
Cemeteries are very therapeutic places, which is why we recommend the next step in the journaling process: Cemetery Therapy. Cemeteries are ending places, places where you say good-bye. They are very clear, very concrete. They are also a very good place to get rid of your negative letters, as follows.

First, take all of your negative letters and refer back to your second stage of recovery. Go to your Recovery Family and have someone, or various people, act as surrogates. Read them the letters. Release them and let them go.

Second, take the letters and bury them or burn them. This is the *"cemetery/fire"* aspect. One person I know actually has what she calls her recovery graveyard in her back yard. When she's done with a negative letter, she takes it there and buries it. Once in a while, she even puts a flower there just like visiting a grave, to remind herself that the negative that is buried is gone. Other people burn the letters. The point is to go through a concrete act of letting go.

Now, a word to good codependents that own a computer. Don't back up the negative letters on your hard drive so you can go back to them, just in case. There is no, *"just in case."* **There is just letting go!** Is it the end of the process? Will all your issues suddenly die? No, in fact, you might repeat your inventory later. It depends on you. But, if you do repeat it, each time you will have a different insight and let more of the negative go.

Finally, I want to reference the Ninth Step of the Twelve Step Program. It says that in everything you do in life make sure that you don't injure yourself or anyone else. As applied specifically to journaling, this means that the process is not about beating yourself or others up. Which is why we say do not share your negative letters, do not verbally throw up in anybody's face. Don't print out a bunch of negative letters and then make Thanksgiving dinner, and place each letter on a corresponding family members plate. The purpose of journaling is to heal. Recovery is not about punishing. It is about letting go. It's interesting how in my own life, I saw how I carried around so much emotional baggage, most of the time, not even knowing it. And, when I became self-aware enough to recognize it, it was so hard to let go.

In fact, in my case, I am not an angry person at all, but when I started to deep dive into this emotional baggage, I started to see real fear, and real anger, and real pain. I was so resentful, and I numbed it all with drugs. And I didn't have a clue. I understand today that it will be an ongoing process, and that I peeled back the layers and I have been releasing it as it shows up, I can start to reduce the shame, and experience freedom one day at a time. This is a good practice, as I have already said. If you have a fight with your spouse, your significant other, or your children or your friends, you can process it through journaling, through a negative and positive letter. The negative helps you get it out of your system. The positive reminds you of the things you love about the other party. Then you can go deal with them over the issue in a balanced way.

YOUR POSITIVE LETTERS
Now what do you do with your positive letters? You have three options.

First, for letters involving people, if those people are alive then sharing could be a healthy situation, and then you can share the letters with them. But remember, there are times when even a positive letter can open a Pandora's Box. Especially when it comes to old relationships. You might be working on making amends and settling things, but the other party might not be ready for that. And that's OK, they don't have to be. The important thing is that you do it for you so you can heal things inside of yourself.

Second, if a person who is the subject of a letter is dead, you can go to the cemetery, visit their grave, maybe bring them some flowers, and read the letter to them. This is a very therapeutic, very powerful exercise.

Third, you can use your positive letters as affirmation letters, as I already mentioned. Use them as something you can refer back to, to realize and appreciate all of the positive things in your life and all of the positive things you are learning through recovery. The bottom line is that it is extremely important that we use this process for growth and healing. Keep taking "a fearless moral inventory." You don't do an inventory to make yourself sicker. You do it to make yourself healthy.

IN SUMMARY
The whole idea of journaling, of doing your inventory of positive and negative, helps you learn your personal history. So many of us would like to forget parts of our histories, or discard them outright. We can't do that. All that you can do is embrace your history. And then learn from it. Learn what it teaches you about yourself. About why you act the way you act, why you are attracted to certain types of people and relationships even when they are not healthy for you. Learn about the things that you just have to accept and let go, and what things, what issues, you need to still work on.

Ok, now, I will say this one more time: Do not attempt journaling or your other OG Family work until you have completed the first four steps of recovery, until you have stabilized your situation, especially any addictions or other codependent behaviors. Otherwise, you might resurrect feelings that will only activate these behaviors, and whatever family work you've done to that point you will only have to do over again. I feel that if people try to do too much family work too soon, it only backfires. Sadly, and frustratingly, in my experience, many therapists, psychiatrists, and psychologists do not even understand this principle; do not understand the depth of the relationship between addiction relapse and premature OG Family work. When you activate issues when you are not prepared to face them, you also activate relapse into addictions and other negative behaviors.

My observation is that we want to dive right into our issues, our family work, because we want to eradicate the dysfunctionality in our lives, we want to settle all of our issues. Yet, as I said before, we will all have issues to work on fourteen days after we're dead, and dysfunctionality will always be with us. Dysfunctionality is part of life.

But once you go through the first four stages of recovery, and then into the fifth, you have a sound basis for the last, which we call Inner Child work. The rest of this book is about that work. It will cover some things you can do alone, and some that you should only do under the guidance of a professional therapist. Later I talk about a core concept, the concept of **Shame**, which I believe is at the heart of many of our depressions and anxieties and other problems and which is also something very different from Guilt. And I will try to demonstrate how Inner Child work, in healing the child within and developing the adult you are now, is something that we do as an ongoing process, this process called, **the growth of life**.

Stage 6: The Inner Child
Final Stage of Recovery Process
As noted, before many of us codependents coming into treatment or recovery are in such emotional pain that we want to dive into our deep issues so we can get the quick *"cure."* And so much has been publicized about the "**Inner Child**" that we think the quickest way to our issues is to get in touch with the child within. But my own approach, I'll say it again, is that Inner Child work is the Sixth Stage, the final stage, of the recovery process. It must not be done until the other five; the *first* five have been covered. Why? Because in getting in touch with your Inner Child you are naturally getting in touch with the part of your life in which you were a child, your past. And you simply don't know what you will find when you start diving into your past.

For example, we've all heard of cases of people who go into therapy and, after long months of work, suddenly remember trauma that they had repressed. We read the news stories about Your Inner Child people who suddenly remember that they were sexually abused by an authority figure years before. Or people who suddenly recall long-forgotten episodes of incest, emotional abuse, physical abuse, and abandonment...All sorts of issues and events. Sometimes the things remembered are such major traumas that we can't believe they actually happened, because we can't believe that the alleged victim could possibly have forgot them. But repression forgetting is a basic defense mechanism of the human mind. If what we experienced was too overwhelming, too painful to accept, our minds simply block it out until we are ready to face it again. But even without major trauma, most, if not all, of us will uncover significant issues that developed over periods of time in our lives; for example, feelings of abandonment, neglect, and shame.

In fact, many psychiatrists and psychologists think it might be easier to deal with major trauma than with more subtle forms of abuse. Think about it. The victim of major trauma, once the trauma is identified, knows that he or she was abused. Those of us victimized in more subtle ways, by chronic emotional abuse, for example, aren't as clearly aware of what our root problems are. In either case, we might have such powerful feelings about our issues, those words, like anger and frustration just aren't adequate to express what we feel. We discover that our Inner Child is full *of rage* and *bitterness*. We might also come to the realization that this is where our current depression and anxiety and addictions and other unhealthy behaviors stem from.

When you reach that point, if you don't have a way of processing what you are discovering, you could very well become so embittered that you *become* your issues, as we discussed before. You get caught up in the Blame Game so much, are so driven by a desire for revenge against the people you think are responsible for your problems your "victims," as we called them that the issues become your whole life. Or you are driven to numb yourself against the feelings you are resurrecting by falling back into your addictions: alcohol, drugs, sex, and eating disorders, whatever. You also have to remember that what you "uncover", in diving into your Inner Child are your *perceptions*. Even though these perceptions are real enough to you, they are holding you in your current codependency, they might not, in fact, be completely accurate. Which again is why you need a healthy environment in which to process your perceptions.

It all goes back to the basic principle: the only reason you get in touch with your Inner Child issues is **to learn** from them. The only way you can learn from them is:

First, to feel the feelings that come along with them, which means that you cannot fall back into your addictions, which are merely ways of avoiding your feelings.

Second, to learn from your issues, you must be able to sort them out, to process them, in a healthy environment. You get the healthy environment and the protection from relapsing into addictions through the first five stages of the recovery process. Then, and only then, are you ready for Inner Child work.

Simple Definition of Inner Child
You might find the following definition of Inner Child to be helpful in this stage of recovery. Think of your Inner Child as the emotional part of you, as opposed to your intellectual part, which may be referred to as the Adult you. It's not that one is not "good" and that the other is "bad." The idea is to bring them into balance. You'll see this definition in more detail, as we get deeper into the Inner Child stage.

Getting in touch
Getting in touch with, or exploring, your Inner Child is often referred to as Relapse Prevention Work. It helps identify your codependent patterns and where they came from in your childhood, and it prepares you to face the feelings you are literally resurrecting by exploring your past without escaping into your addictions. It prepares you to deal with your triggers, patterns, issues, and feelings.

There are several ways you can proceed with Inner Child work. Some of them we already mentioned: individual therapy; group therapy; the Twelve Step program, particularly inventorying or journaling. Usually, we use a combination of methods. I had this one therapist describe it to me like this; each method is like going over the same ground, but with a different lens for a different effect. What I would like to do at this point is describe one other method, the GeneSchematic. Very powerful, it will tell you so much about your generational history. You don't just learn a little about your history or family and then go off and do them alone or with friends. You do them under the guidance of a trained therapist or counselor.

All of the methods will teach you a lot about yourself, but the key lessons will be the patterns you picked up in the earliest stages of your life and the fact that those patterns *are still affecting you today!* I'll give you an example in a moment, but first I want to go back to one of the codependent diseases: the *I Know* disease. You see, at this point, some of you are saying, "I know, I know. I know what happened in my childhood. I don't have to look at it again. What's the point?" The point is that knowing alone doesn't help you. If it did, you wouldn't be reading this fucking book. You wouldn't be suffering from codependency and the depression and anxiety and addictions that come with it. If you want to get emotionally healthy and experience the serenity and happiness that goes with that, you have to *work* with your self-knowledge. Use it for something. Which is what this Sixth Stage is all about.

There is this great dialogue from the TV Series <u>Billions</u> between Wendy Rhoads (Maggie Siff) and Rebecca Cantu (Nina Arianda). Wendy is a licensed medical therapist and Rebecca, the CEO of her own company. They are talking in a bar after using heavy equipment to play, digging up the earth, destroying cars, trying to play and get present from the stresses of the everyday grind. I know, the things billionaires and millionaires do, however, what Wendy says to Rebecca, about Rebecca, is so appropriate:

> **Wendy**: *"You had to be totally present to deal with it. Got me right out of my head."*
> **Rebecca**: *"I figured it would work better than a day spa."*
> **Wendy**: *"Thank you for taking the time."*
> **Rebecca**: *"I needed the reset too, though I probably don't have to tell you what I need. You already know in what—5 minutes with someone?"*
> **Wendy**: *"Truth?"*
> **Rebecca**: *"Yes!"*
> **Wendy**: *"I'd Love to work with you, but you don't need much that you don't already give yourself. That's what sets you apart. Most people let their childhood bullshit run them. You use yours to propel you. And not in a way that you're hiding from it, either, and its gonna bite you. You synthesize it. Like you do information about companies. Well, I'm doing what I'm meant to be doing, too."*

See, you start to see that your childhood can help you for good if you embrace it and synthesize it, not run from it. Use it like a CEO does, gathering information and then process it for advantage, for good, for profit. Like an investment in yourself.

The following example I'll share with you is very simple. It involves a young woman who recently got married. Now that the honeymoon part of the relationship is over, she finds that she doesn't trust her husband, and she often gets very angry at him. Yet he really hasn't done anything she can identify as the cause of her resentment. When the problem gets bad enough and she begins working on it in therapy, she discovers that in her family history, her personal history, her father and brothers and other men in her early life either abandoned her or hurt her in some way. Maybe they were there for her physically, but not emotionally. For her, that became a *"normal,"* a pattern she expects to be repeated. So now, years later, she is taking out her anger and resentment on her husband, expecting him to hurt her, too, and reacting to it *in advance*. That's the Inner Child. The emotional part of us. The angry, frustrated part. When it's out of balance. To get the Inner Child back into balance with the Inner Adult, the rational part of us, we use the methods described above. Again, to focus on the Gene Schematic, which will give you a visual presentation of certain recurrent issues on paper.

The Gene Schematic

Today a Gene Schematic refers to a diagram illustrating a person's family members, how they are related and their medical history. I want to extend the Gene Schematic as a family history diagram, including not only medical history, but, emotional history, and individual historical issues. These are generational behaviors that we inherited by years of programming of which I discussed earlier. To compose one, you would sit down with a trained counselor and basically construct a family tree, focusing on recurring issues for as far back as you could go. I did not do this with a therapist, I just did it myself. But there is value with doing it with a trained therapist. Some people who do this get a powerful awakening, a realization that many of the same issues recur in their families for generations, like alcohol abuse, abandonment, physical abuse, emotional abuse, and so on. This was so true for me! Take the case of a young child who ends up in foster care because of certain neglect and abuse issues. His biological father is not in the picture; he left the marriage, abandoning wife and child, shortly after the child was born. The mother has substance abuse issues and was attracted to a live-in boyfriend who then abused both her and the child.

Here is the cool part (not the abuse and substance abuse parts), but the ability to recognize this inherited pattern that a Gene Schematic can demonstrate. A Gene Schematic was constructed for the child, it was discovered that the same patterns had been repeated in the mother's family for as far back as the local social agency had records. For example, the grandmother had ongoing substance abuse issues. Her husband too, had abandoned her after childbirth. And it was likely that the same pattern had occurred with the great-grandmother as well. In short, the family had been actively involved with the same issues and same agency involvement for generations. So, we now can identify that all of us are subject to our generational issues and literally inherit those issues as the same patterns that get passed down from generation to generation.

The purpose of constructing the Gene Schematic in this case is to focus the efforts of counselors, and later of the child himself as he gets into therapy, on the particular issues that recur with this family. It is *one* tool that can be used with many others in the child's eventual recovery process, which would probably not begin to take effect until the child grew into an adult who could understand the events in his life.

CHAPTER 7

SHAME, SHAME, & more SHAME!

"Shame is a soul eating emotion."
— *C.G. Jung*

"Shame is the lie someone told you about yourself."
— *Anais Nin*

As you get more into your self-discovery or recovery, you will realize that the biggest and most major issue of all codependents is **Shame**. Understand what shame is. It is the belief that there is something wrong with you, that you are bad. Contrast this to guilt, in which the essential element is the belief that you did something wrong or did something bad. There is a huge difference in your actions being wrong, or unhealthy, and the belief that you are somehow defective, right down to your core. When you do something, you know you should have not done, you can correct your behavior. But when you believe that you are fundamentally flawed, how do you correct that? And once you come to believe that there is something wrong with you, doesn't it seem only logical that depression, anxiety, and all sorts of other codependent symptoms will follow? For example, you will find yourself in unhealthy relationships, trying to get the approval and acceptance of another person, just so you can feel good about yourself, no matter what the relationship costs you. Or you will find yourself caught up in addiction trying to numb the chronic bad feeling that is deep in your heart and gut.

In my own life, my own experiences, I would say, **First**, that shame is the major issue in 95% of everything that happens in my life, in all our lives. **Second**, shame is an issue that involves power, ownership, and boundaries, which is where I will focus on addressing methods of shame reduction. Notice I say "reduction," not elimination. You cannot eliminate shame in life. From the time of birth, we participate in what I call the Shame Process, a normal, if certainly not pleasant, part of life. There's an old saying that if you put two human beings together in the same room, you will eventually have shame issues. Why? Because, We are human! Shame, like dysfunctionality, is part of the human condition. In recovery, we attempt to learn from our shame issues and reduce them to where they no longer plague us. Otherwise, the ongoing feeling of shame we carry traumatizes and paralyzes us, though most of us don't appreciate the depth of the problem.

Our shame comes from two places: **Original Shame** and **Traumatic Shame**. Where they build (Compound) on each other, until they reach critical mass, then they become **Toxic Shame**, causing all sorts of problems in our lives.

ORIGINAL SHAME
Original Shame messages are usually subtle, especially because they happen to you as a child. They tell you indirectly that there's something wrong with you. For example, you want to go out and play with Johnny, but your Mom tells you not to hang around with him. The unspoken message is that there's something wrong with you for not picking better friends and not realizing on your own that there's something wrong with the ones you have. Or you ask your Dad to read a story, but he says no. He doesn't explain that he's tired, so you get the message that there's something wrong with you for asking. You feel shamed, whether you know it or not. Other subtle shame messages come in the form of telling you not to go out and play because you might get hurt, or basically not to do other normal things because somebody just doesn't like it. They are subtle because they are not necessarily intended to make you feel bad. They might even be given with the best intentions, because the person telling them to you actually believes that the normal things you want are bad for you. All of us have had such messages from the first authority figures in our lives. Which is why we say they are part of life, inevitable. The problem is that we receive a steady stream of them as we grow older, and they eventually make us feel that there is something wrong with us. We become what psychologists call "Shame Based." **Shame becomes our Normal.**

TRAUMATIC SHAME
This, simply, is shame that comes from certain events in your life. For example, a sexually abused child is a shamed child. Deprivation and poverty can be long-term "events" that generate shame. One of the events that many people describe is always being the last to be chosen in a game when they were children, or the one who never had a date in high school. All of these generate shame, to a greater or lesser degree, but enough so that the feeling of shame certainly sinks in.

EXPECTATIONS

To further explore both forms of shame, let's look at the core of shame itself: **Expectation**. When we are born, and as we are little children growing up, we have expectations. You expect your family, whatever your OG Family is, to love you, like you, feed you, clothe you, and nurture you, teach you. All normal and natural expectations. They are also very concrete expectations. When my family doesn't meet my expectations, I feel ashamed. For example, you want to experience unconditional love from your family, but there are days when they make you feel like you were a mistake, when they wish you had never been born. Some parents, in anger, actually tell their children this from time to time. So instead of receiving unconditional love, I'm being abandoned and emotionally abused and receiving all sorts of other negative messages.

I've labeled this "the Shame Game." The game happens when it's played in different dimensions, so to speak. You see, the family also has expectations of you. Like, children should be seen but not heard; they expect you to be quiet when they want you to be quiet. They put that demand on you. You see, in reality, expectations are demands.

Your family also expects-demands-what? Ask different people and hear what demands were put on them: to always get good grades, to become a doctor, or to take over the family business, or always mind your manners. Expectations. Demands. And when you don't meet them, the family let's you know you let them down, there's something wrong with you, maybe even that they are ashamed of you.

Now, for those of you falling into the "I Know" game at this point, I want to assure you that I also know. I know that my family had its expectations of me and made its demands on me for reasons. They wanted me to survive, and thrive, and be kind, and be accepted, and all sorts of other good things. But, despite the intentions of those making demands on me, the process still resulted in shame. And the Shame Game expanded, as we grew older. As we had more contact with our environment, we realized that our neighbors had expectations of us. Our religious systems had expectations of us. Social Media now has expectations of us. If we didn't meet the first, we would not be accepted. We would be ostracized. If we didn't meet the second, God would surely punish us. Third, if we don't look a certain way or are successful a certain way, that we would brand ourselves as bad or even worse inadequate.

I heard this story about a woman that was born through caesarean section. Her mother almost died in the process. As a child, she had an aunt who would watch her sometimes while her mother was at work. Whenever the child misbehaved, the aunt had a way of controlling her. She would scold the child, *"you almost killed your mother once, do you want to kill her now with your misbehavior?"* OMG, I can't stand shit like this. She was only four or five years old and had that indictment laid on her, that she almost killed her own mother! WTF!!! To understand the impact of something like that, and of all shame messages, consider life through the eyes of a child. A child doesn't think in terms of adult logic. The child doesn't say, *"Oh, yeah, auntie. I understand. You're just saying that because you need to calm me down."* Children don't function that way. A child functions in a **child's mind, an emotional mind.** So, whatever the adult says, the child believes.

To the child, it's almost as though God is saying it. To the child, what the adult says becomes what is supposed to be, the child's normal. If you want to get a feel for this, stand over the crib of a baby and try to imagine what that infant sees. To the infant, you are mammoth, a giant. As far as the child is concerned, you are the Higher Power. Whatever you say becomes reality for the child. It's sad sometimes, but we adults play all kinds of expectation games, shame games, with children without even knowing the impact we are having. I remember once going into a restaurant with my wife. A man came in with his two-year-old son. He had the boy placed in a highchair and then proceeded, and I love this, he was talking to him about how he should behave in a restaurant. *"Don't make any noise. Don't play with your food. Mind your manners."* OMG, he is two years old, It took all of about five minutes for this precious boy to dump something on the floor. And the father started screaming, *"Didn't I just tell you!"* Dude, he is two! The Shame Game. The kid just did something totally natural for a two-year old, and the father is yelling at him. In public no less, the child gets a shamed message of: I am **BAD**. Keep doing that to your boy and eventually you'll see him/her with a Tattoo: **Born to be Bad!** I have nothing against tattoos, I promise. But tattoos can be very telling about a person, and what they have experienced.

Anyway, the message will have sunk in. Now think about this. We also said that society, the neighborhood, our peers, religion, media; all put all sorts of expectations on us. Here's the scary part. Some of those expectations clash and conflict. Your family insists that you always behave the way they want. Your friends insist on something else. Or your family raises you in their religious tradition and expects you to follow it to the letter. But they don't practice what they preach. Then there is Social Media, so powerful and influential, showing you it should be completely different, Confusing, Right? How does a child cope? How did we cope? How did I cope? We became good little codependents. When we were with our family, we followed the family's rules. When we were with our friends, we followed their rules, a different set of rules. Then comes Social Media and we are in the metaphorical closet, developing a whole new set of rules for our future. We became little chameleons. And we feel guilty about it. We felt as though we were violating one group or the other, and that made us feel bad about ourselves, whether or not we knew it. The feeling was there. The feeling is shame. So later in life, shame becomes our mask. Under it are the other issues: guilt, fear, abuse, abandonment, dependency, and the list goes on.

COMPOUND SHAME

Ok, So, now we are leaving childhood with our mask and our hidden issues, and what happens to us? We have more expectations dumped on us. For example, I get a job; the job has expectations of me. If I don't live up to them, I'm terrified I might get fired. And I get into a relationship and that comes with expectations. As a codependent, I probably get into a relationship with someone who has expectations like, *"If you really love me, then you will do this."* The *"this"* is basically clean up my mess for me or act in a way that lets me keep playing my own codependent role. So as children, we have our **Original Shame** and **Traumatic Shame** and we know how to play the **Shame Game** and we carry it all into adulthood. All the systems we get into come with expectations. All have the potential to shame us. And we're conditioned toward **SHAME**.

Even in recovery we play the shame game. We put expectations on ourselves: have to make so much progress in so much time, or else I failed. And others put expectations on us. I've seen sponsors in AA/NA programs tell people that they have to work that program just such a way or the sponsors will quit working with them. So, what happens? The person slips up a bit and they learn a new game: **Deception**. Tell the sponsor what he wants to hear. The white lie. Which also creates shame. And adds to the addiction itself.

Codependents are good at deception. Why not? We learned it when trying to balance the expectations of our families against those of our peers when we were kids. And we continued learning it as we entered other systems of recovery, in therapy, in working whatever program we get into.

Holy Shit! Seriously, when I finally was able to pull back and see the total picture of SHAME! OMG, I was so angry and grateful that I could finally see it. Because now I knew I could do something about it. But the rage I felt when I could see how all encompassing **Shame IS**. I believe it's the most important thing we have to stop as a son, as a father, as a grandfather, as a friend, as a boss, as a partner, as a human. We have to fucking stop this kind of behavior. Because it does compound. Welcome to the SHAME wars.

THE SHAME WARS
I call this whole process of compounding shame, The Shame Wars. I have expectations of you and everybody else and every system I participate in, and I have expectations of me. For example, as mentioned before, we get into recovery and all of a sudden; we want our families to participate. We *expect* them to participate, to *want to* participate. After all, we have suddenly found *"Truth"*, we have *"seen the light"*, the reason for all of our family problems. All they have to do is get on board and all our dysfunctionality will be gone, we will heal, and we will all live happily ever after as the perfect family. By approaching the family this way, all you are doing is shaming them, telling them what's *wrong* with them. As a result, they react by shaming you, by countering with what's wrong with you and the things in the past that you did wrong. The Shame Game. The Shame Wars. You are trying to do their inventory for them, and they defend themselves by trying to do your inventory for you. You are shaming one another. You are, in simple terms, BEATING THE SHIT OUT OF EACH OTHER.

I look at my own experience. When I was attending church, I didn't like or understand all of the rules. I knew deep down I could never be happy living by all of them, so I went around trying to get the Church to change for me. What I was saying, in effect, was, *"I have these expectations of you. You have to meet them. You have to change so I can be happy."* It was easier for me to try to change the Church than to change myself If that sounds crazy, think about it for a minute. How many of us do the same thing? *"If only my family would change..."*, *"If only my job would change..."*, *"If only my friends would change..."* And on and on and on. Now, if we all expect everything to change for us, guess what? We have a major problem. It's called Chaos. Because the changes we all want don't jibe, they don't sync up, there is no balance. So, in the end we are all going to be disappointed all over again. We are going to be shamed. And when the shame Wars start, we get into the **victim game**, **blaming** everybody else for what's wrong in our own lives. *"I drink because of you." "I use drugs because of you." "You made my childhood miserable, so my adulthood is miserable because of you."*

You want to hear something funny, it wasn't then, but it is now too me. I was absolute in **Denial** and the **"I know"** disease and **"The Blame Game."** I was always looking for a reason to abuse crack, smack, and cognac. I remember my wife had said something too me in the kitchen, I think. And I fucking cracked, I jumped in my truck, hit up my drug dealer got and 8-Ball of cocaine, and fifth of whatever liquor and just got numb and lost it. Looking back, I don't think she said anything wrong or bad, I really believe the only she said was: *"Hey Karl, how are you feeling?"* Seriously, no shit. I was so miserable in my shame I could not hear her love and concern when it was literally staring me in the face in all its beauty and unconditional love. OMG, horrible, those are the moments I regret the most. I still have that pain, because it runs so deep. I just hurt the person I love the most by leaving and abusing drugs and alcohol. Are you fucking kidding me? who does that? I did!

This is a nice sequel and look into classic codependent relationship (my relationship): the alcoholic and his/her spouse. Alcoholics play the shame game because they want their spouses to understand their drinking and clean up their mess for them. The spouses, on the other hand, get to call the alcoholics assholes every time they come home drunk, and get to blame the alcoholic for everything wrong in life.

But let me suss this out for you. I heard a call on some podcast; a woman called and said she had a problem: her husband was sick. He was an alcoholic. She said that for *nine years* she had been waiting for him to change, to just do something simple, like take her and the kids on a Sunday picnic. But every Saturday he would get drunk and wake up Sunday sick and hung over. He had neither the interest nor the ability to take them on a picnic, for *nine years. The* podcast told the woman the truth: that she was the sick one. She did not like that! He told her, if you want to go on a picnic with the kids, get up and go. Stop blaming the husband for making your life miserable because he's a drunk and won't take you on a picnic. Of course, if she did that, she'd have to get into other issues with her marriage and how miserable she was in that situation. And she might have to make a choice: change it or continue to live in misery. And a change that big is terrifying. So, she was marking time for nine years by basically playing the shame game with her alcoholic husband. My wife is and was such a saint to help me and stick by me for so long, but honestly, she should have dusted my ass years ago, she absolutely deserved so much more.

To site a religious example, many attendees get to the point of complaining more and more. *If only the church/patrons would change...* And one day, I heard a therapist say, "did you ever stop to think that this might be *your* issue? I mean, the Church is pretty clear on its rules: *Here's the rule. If you don't like it, you change.* And she was right. Dead right. It was so clear. The Church had laid out its rules in black and white hundreds, even thousands of years ago. Yet patrons run around saying, *"Me change? No, you change!"* We see it in all relationships and all situations. When problems come along, things we don't like, we have a tendency to get into a shame exchange, an insanity exchange, the Shame Wars. *Everything would be all right with me if only you would change.* It's so common, because, as we said before, shame is part of life. It is normal. The trick is to learn a technique that we are going to get into a little later: **Shame reduction. If we don't reduce our shame, our shame truly becomes TOXIC.**

Ok, here is a thought, I look at shame like cutting someone or being cut. Think about it this way, every time you shame an individual, your kids, your partners, your friend, it's like you are taking a knife and cutting them. Seriously, and every time you get shamed you are getting cut. You get cut, you bleed, and then you have to fix the cut depending how deep, big ones require stitches, small ones require a Band-Aid. Then it scars. You shame, you cut, you bleed, put a Band-Aid on it. You scar, Overtime, you are going to look like a fucking metaphorical Frankenstein's monster, because, since birth we are getting thousands and thousands of cuts. SHAMED. If you knew that every time you shamed someone that you would be cut. I promise you, you would stop. So, Stop it! And another thing, Shame compounds so if you do not start to reduce your shame, you are going to keep opening up the same cuts, each time more painful until the scars are so noticeable that it has taken on a whole next level of shame. TOXIC SHAME.

TOXIC SHAME
How about some math, I love math, I used to hate math:

ORIGINAL SHAME + COMPOUNDED SHAME = TOXIC SHAME

In other words, if you don't learn shame reduction, shame will grow until it ruins your life with depression, anxiety, addictions...with codependency and all the signs and symptoms that come with it.

Let me give you an example. It involves a woman I know, her father had sexually abused her when she was a child. She went through 3 marriages. Three. And when she was finally in her 50's she was able to talk about it. She had finally come to understand that;

1. *She held inside a furious rage against her father;*
2. *That rage had created a terrible sense of shame in her; and*
3. *The shame had become so toxic, until she actually became her own issues, and lived those issues every day of her life.*

When she was three, she had the natural expectations we all have of our fathers. When he didn't meet them, she transferred those expectations onto three husbands. And when they couldn't meet her expectations, she beat the hell out of them and finally left them, one by one. And it wasn't until she was in her 50's that she realized that the issues were HERS.

Was her father, right? NO! Was she hurt and traumatized? YES. But, FOR WHATEVER REASON, she had not dealt with the shame and so it grew and compounded until she became the **Shame**, which she then projected onto three husbands, and who knows what type of men they were, what her inner child attracted, maybe they deserved it, maybe they were the opposite of her father. You get my point. Even for those three husbands, there was something in their past that attracted this toxicity. They also have Shame, they found a mirror in her and that is why the initial attraction existed. Relationships help us see the **Mirror** of what we lost, or gave away, or was taken, or became our most forgotten Love (Essene Mirrors).

TOXIC PEOPLE, PLACES, & THINGS
Ok, here are couple parables. The **first parable** is about two people relocating to a new town. To get to the town, they had to cross a bridge

where an old toll taker worked. As the first person drove up to the tollbooth, she told the man that she was relocating to the town and asked what it was like. *"Well,"* he said, *"If you don't mind my asking, what was your old town like?"* *"Well,"* she said, *"It was actually pleasant. Nice people. Friendly. Like family."* The old man smiled and told her, *"Then you should like this place. It's just like that."* The woman passed on and the next driver pulled up. She, too, told the toll man she was relocating and asked what the town was like. He asked her the same question about her old town. *"It was nasty,"* she said. *"Couldn't get along with the people. Very unfriendly. Very cold."* The old man shook his head. *"Sorry to tell you"*, he said. *"But I'm afraid that's just what you'll find here."*

The **second parable** is similar. It comes from eastern tradition. It has to do with a man who went on a trip through the forest. Towards evening, as he was getting tired, he thought to himself, *"wouldn't it be nice to find a nice grassy knoll where I could sleep tonight?"* Sure enough, around the next bend, he saw just such a knoll. *"Wouldn't it be nice if there was a stream nearby so I could wash and get a cool drink?"* Sure enough, he heard the gurgling of water and saw a stream just through the woods. Just as he was bedding down for the night he reflected, *"That was strange. First, I wish for a knoll and it appears. Then I wish for a stream and find one. This place is spooky. I wonder if there are any ghosts here?"* And guess what he saw? I think you get the point. Sometimes we create our own reality. And sometimes we get caught up in the negative so much that we create a negative reality for ourselves. Let me explain this in terms of shame, I use the analogy of people, places, and things becoming toxic to us. The more we associate with them, the more shamed we get, and the more we create our own negativity.

For example, while in rehab, I listened to so many people that have issues with their parents. Of course they do, its ok, but it's not ok, Instead of looking at their childhoods, learning from them, and moving on, they create their parents as victims or scapegoats. We touched on it earlier: *"I am depressed because of what you did to me when I was a child,"* or *"I am an addict because of you,"* or *"I am dysfunctional because of you."* Then they add, *"If only you would have changed..."* Or *"If only you would change now!"* So, guess what these people find when they get together with their parents, or, in the case of parents who are dead, with the memory of them? They find shame. At toxic levels., They can't learn from the past, embrace it, accept it, and detach with LOVE. They can't, as we say, *"love them, pray for them, let them be who they are."* So, their parents remain toxic to them. And they remain toxic to their parents.

One of the most powerful displays of shame and shame reductions, and healing was one of my favorite movies, <u>Good Will Hunting</u>. This is the dialogue between Sean (Robin Williams, therapist) and Will (Matt Damon, abused genius student);

> **Sean:** My father was an alcoholic. Mean fuckin' drunk. He'd come home hammered, looking to whale on somebody. So, I'd provoke him, so he wouldn't go after my mother and little brother. Interesting nights were when he wore his rings.
> **Will:** He used to just put a belt, a stick, and a wrench on the table. Just say, "Choose."
> **Sean:** Well, I gotta go with the belt there.
> **Will:** I used to go with the wrench.
> **Sean:** Why the wrench?
> **Will:** Cause fuck him, that's why.
> **Sean:** Your foster father?
> **Will:** Yeah.
> *[pause]*
> **Will:** So, uh, what is it, like, Will has an attachment disorder? Is it all that stuff?
> *[Sean nods]*
> **Will:** Fear of abandonment? Is that why I broke up with Skylar?
> **Sean:** I didn't know you had.
> **Will:** Yeah, I did.
> **Sean:** You wanna talk about it?
> **Will:** No.
> **Sean:** Hey, Will? I don't know a lot. You see this? All this shit?
> *[Holds up the file, and drops it on his desk]*
> **Sean:** It's not your fault.
> **Will:** *[Will shrugs]* Yeah, I know that. *[Will averts his eyes to the floor]*
> **Sean:** Look at me son.
> *[Will locks eyes with Sean]*
> **Sean:** It's not your fault.
> **Will:** *[Will nods]* I know.
> **Sean:** No. It's not your fault.
> **Will:** I know
> **Sean:** No, no, you don't. It's not your fault.
> *[Sean moves closer to Will]*
> **Sean:** Hmm?
> **Will:** I know.
> *[Will stands up, trying to keep distance]*
> **Sean:** It's not your fault.
> **Will:** Alright.
> **Sean:** It's not your fault.
> *[Will closes his eyes, he's fighting for control]*

Sean: It's not your fault. **Will:** Don't fuck with me. *[Will shoves Sean back]*
Will: Don't fuck with me, Sean, not you! **Sean:** It's not your fault. It's not your fault. *[Will breaks into sobs. They hug]*
Sean: Fuck them, ok?

In short, toxic people, places, and things are those that activate shame feelings in you. The guy at work who holds a grudge for something you did years ago is toxic to you. You are toxic to someone else when you are the grudge holder. A bar is toxic to an alcoholic. Your past can be toxic. Anything you do not learn from and make peace with becomes toxic. That's just a fact of life even though we are just learning it.

And you can carry your toxic patterns into your present. For example, I go to the airport to leave for work, check-in, go through security, get to my gate, and then find out my flight is canceled due to airplane safety issues. Now from personal experience, this is where everyone loses their shit and literally become stupid. First class is at the counter demanding the plane not be canceled "funny right" or demand they get first class on next plane but they have to get home no matter what, but there is no first class. Everyone is losing it. OMG, people, the plane is not safe to fly! So now what do we do? We curse the airline, curse the counter people, shame them, and shame ourselves in the process. But the fact is, the plane's canceled. It happens. Yet this simple event becomes the trigger to activate shame patterns; I take it all personally. I create insanity around it. And it's all very needless. Which leaves us with a choice. We can continue to victimize ourselves with our old codependent, shame patterns. Or we can learn to change them, tackle Shame as one of our **CORE ISSUES**, head-on.

Means of Change

Earlier I said that Daoism, Buddhism and Kabbalah encourage and teach us Means of Change for overcoming codependent issues, and I'd like to elaborate how;

1. Mindfulness of yourself, gentle admittance of the problem, whatever it is;
2. Developing an awareness of the extent of the problem, self- reflection to find root cause;
3. Action and inaction, letting go and doing healthy tasks to do to overcome the problem. Turn into wisdom. Let go, be Free!

I cannot emphasize the third point enough. If you have experience with therapy, you might also have experienced the problem that many of us who have tried therapy alone have encountered: we get all this self-knowledge, but we don't know what to do with it. We go into therapy because of depression, anxiety, and/or addictions and all sorts of other codependent behaviors and symptoms, but we find that the knowledge we gain doesn't do much on its own to alleviate our problems. We need to act on this hard-earned self-knowledge and self-awareness. This is how you attack and reduce Shame head-on.

From all these methodologies, teachings, and all the other approaches we spoke of, individual therapy, group work, inventorying, etc., you will hear two basic principles. **First**, every time you get stuck blaming somebody else for your present situation, the **Blame Game**, all you are doing is avoiding your own issues. Yes, maybe they did you wrong, serious wrong. But you are in the present now. Are you going to face your experience, learn from it, and move on? Or are you going to stay stuck? **Second**, there are three things you will need to learn and absorb in order to deal with shame. Let's call them, The Big Three: ***Boundaries, Acceptance, Love.***

Now notice. I have not used the words *"eliminate"* or *"get rid of"* or anything like them in speaking about shame. I already said that shame and insanity and dysfunctionality are part of life, part of each of our lives, not just life in general. So, when we speak of the Means of Change in regard to shame, when we talk about the Big Three, and all the other concepts we covered, as well as others we will cover in the final chapters, we are not talking about eliminating shame in our lives. We are talking about another concept, as introduced in the next chapter: ***Shame Reduction.***

Bringing our Past into our Future
Are we trying to bring the past into the future and make it manifest again? If so, this is a very difficult way to try to allow ourselves to experience the new. And yet, it is a normal way for most of us, for we are security minded entities and choose not to give up something old when there is a danger that something new may not replace it, or be as good.

It is the fear of the unknown that we all face, and, there may be a number of things, which could be adapted or changed in order to allow the new to come in. We must stop and examine the totality of our attempt, and then see whether or not there are additional areas that can be causing our problems.

Sometimes, there are many things along our path that we would choose not to experience, had delays and frustrations not been laid before us. We would avoid many of the lessons that we need to grow. Therefore, complications can be of an inner soul growth nature for us, although creating a frustration in the outer sense. It is only through these tactics, sometimes, that we can get to look inside of self instead of outside of self. Everything is a learning experience.

When we go with the flow, we are **paying attention to all of the small situations**, which are found along the path, which leads to the goals we have set for ourselves. This is true, whether you have set them in this lifetime or before incarnating. **Self-Awareness**.

Shit, Damn, Hell, we are creative beings, and we are capable of visualizing where we want to be in the future, and are also capable of pursuing those same dreams. But often we get frustrated when we do not seem to be able to reach the goal, which we have set for ourselves. This happens when we have refused to pay attention to the smaller details and experiences, which are presented to us occasionally, as opportunities for growth and new understandings.

We do not pay attention to the many small details and experiences because they are not presented to us in the normal guise of opportunities. Instead, they come disguised as distractions.

We, therefore, think that they are of no value and refuse to acknowledge them, and so, often miss the very opportunities, which were offered us to reach our goals.

It is necessary to realize that each step of growth needs to be incorporated into our overall concept of where we are going, since there is no such thing as a static situation. Your dreams need to change periodically, according to the new experiences, which are had along the Way. This helps you to update and extend your goals, and to **flexibly adapt** them to the new so you can develop and grow. Remember Bruce Lee's quote? *"Be like water my friend!"*

Otherwise, once you reach the goal along the path, and you have never applied mid-course changes to, you find yourself dissatisfied and looking for something else, for you have changed and therefore where you arrive is no longer your goal. Nothing new will immediately appear, either, because you have chosen to ignore the obvious options along the way, and look only for another dream to pull you in a new direction.

You must constantly recreate your goals, based upon your everyday experiences, for your experiences provide the material for new directions and understanding. If you choose to not allow anything different or distracting into your lives, then you have only the old information to provide for the creation of your future goals and understandings.

Therefore, continue to project what you would like to have and do in the future, but recognize that the steps of growth in that direction are often disguised, and also, that once you take a few steps along the path you may want to alter your goal to include much more. Remember, *Growth means constant adaptation, not stagnation by repetition.*

CHAPTER 8

SHAME REDUCTION

> *"Shame cannot survive being spoken.*
> *It cannot tolerate having words wrapped around it.*
> *What it craves is secrecy, silence, and judgment."*
> *—Brené Brown*

> *"Shame is a soul-sucking emotion,*
> *but empathy is the antidote."*
> *—Brené Brown*

USING ALL THE TOOLS

By now, I hope you can see that codependency is a complex problem. It is the manifestation of a number of issues, with the core issue of shame. Fortunately, while the problem may be complex, the solution is fairly straightforward. I would also say it is fairly simple, which is NOT to say that it is easy.

To recap, you can use a variety of methods to do your recovery work. You might get into individual therapy, move into group therapy, develop a Recovery Family, work the Twelve steps and so on. THERE IS NO HARD AND FAST FORMULA. THERE IS NO SET TIMETABLE. I hope that by now I have made that much clear. You might try one method, get into others, get back to one, change to another, develop a twist or two of your own...But, I think you will find that recovery does come down to the principles outlined in these Six Stages: awareness of yourself and your issues; a group that you can be intimate with in doing your work; actually doing the work by writing it out and talking it out, which are means of processing; and basically creating an environment that is secure enough for you to continue your work.

As you get into that work, you will come to recognize that core issue of codependency when you see it: **Shame**. And you will learn how to reduce it. What I would like to get into in more detail here are the tools of shame reduction, starting with the Big Three: **Boundaries, Acceptance, and Love.**

Boundaries

Setting boundaries for yourself is basically a process of creating your own space. Think of it like this. A country sets boundaries. If another country crosses those boundaries, it's considered an act of aggression, an invasion.

So, it is with you. When someone crosses your boundaries, they are invading your space. They do not have a right to do that. They do not have a right to cross your boundaries without permission.

Setting boundaries, to put it in terms we already discussed, is Self-Parenting, getting your own needs met. It is also developing the adult inside of you. I'd like to give a few examples.

A person I knew who had just gotten into recovery had a dilemma. She was invited to a business event. But she had an alcohol problem that she was just getting under control, and there would be drinking at the event. Further, the *"Important Business People"* would expect her to join in the drinking. They would get on her case if she didn't match their drinking or drink at all. She didn't necessarily want them to know that she had finally decided she was an alcoholic in recovery. She thought that this information might be used against her at work (judgment, I hate judgment!) But she was in a recovery group that had sponsors, so she sat down with her sponsor and talked about it. The way these business events went, there would be speakers during the first hour or so. Then the bar would open. About an hour later, it would all be in full swing.

With her sponsor, she settled on some boundaries. She would go to the event. Listen to the speakers. Then make the rounds saying hello to the *"Important Business People"*, politely moving on from one to the next after a little small talk. Then leave without anyone noticing. No big deal. A simple plan. A way to avoid toxic shame. If you are not used to setting boundaries, you are actually going to like it. Setting boundaries is: saying NO to unwanted advances, sexual or otherwise; discussing your personal life ONLY with people you feel safe with and ONLY when you feel like it; NOT BEING PRESSURED into doing something you really don't want to do. You will get the hang of it. Think of a few examples yourself. I guarantee that the healthier you get, the easier it will be for you to set healthy boundaries. Also, the more adept you get at setting your own boundaries, the more YOU WILL RESPECT OTHERS PEOPLE'S BOUNDARIES.

I like this phrase as applied to shame reduction work:

> *The art and gift of setting boundaries is wisdom*

Acceptance
This is a concept I will cover in more detail later, but it belongs here as well as part of the Big Three. I have a theory based on my own experience:

> *95% of all recovery, of all healthy living, is acceptance!*

The Big Three work hand-in-hand. First, you set boundaries, which clears a space around you, in a sense, to do your recovery work. Then, as you actually do the work, you start to come to a point of acceptance. Acceptance of what? Acceptance of the fact that you are dysfunctional; that your OG Family is dysfunctional; that the world is dysfunctional; that neither you, nor your family, or the world have to be perfect; that you do not have to control things, including other people, to get to perfection. I'm sure you see what I am getting at. You start to accept things as they are. It's a beautiful concept, because then you let things flow, you don't try to force them. It takes a lot of pressure off you, lets you devote your energy to your own healthy recovery, instead of driving yourself crazy and beating yourself and others up trying to "cure" them. Keep a couple of things in mind when you think of acceptance, **First**, just about every major philosophical movement in the world, religious or otherwise, preaches acceptance; they often call it detachment. **Second**, when you accept the fact that you cannot control other people, you can begin working on yourself. And, when you work on yourself, everything else falls into place. With the **Big Three concept**, after you clear your space by setting **boundaries** and finally come to an **acceptance** that you are the only person you can work on, you will, probably slowly, begin to experience a sense of **love**.

Love

Let me tell you what love is not. It is not passion; passion is passion, it is not sex; sex is sex, and it is not infatuation; that's just crazy. And loving someone is not necessarily liking the way they are. Think about that last one. You can love someone and not like them.

In recovery, we refer to detaching from people, places, and things with love. It is a very difficult concept for most of us to understand. It is something that you will experience gradually as you continue working on yourself.

The problem is that we really do not understand love. For example, right now, as you read this, think of a person you think you love. What if that person stopped loving you in return? Would you then stop loving them? If so, isn't that like a business transaction: I'll love you if you love me back!

Love is something that most of us have to work on. Not that you have to work on loving a person, place, or thing, or even yourself We just have to relax and open ourselves up to what love really is. It is said that you can begin the process of loving someone by getting more knowledge of them. This applies to yourself first; get to know yourself, and you will love yourself more.

Detaching with love is tricky. It takes some practice. Let me give you an example. I knew a woman once who detached from her husband. She did it by divorcing him and moving away. If you remember, we called this a geographical detachment. But she was still obsessed with him and all the wrongs she believed he had done her, and he had done some pretty nasty things. But there she was years after the divorce. She didn't even know where he was, if he was still alive. And she was still obsessed with him. So, in effect, she hadn't detached with love, but with anger. And so she really wasn't detached from him at all. It was like he was still living with her, still married. Still very much a part of her life.

What is it, that lets one person detach from a situation with love, while another person can only detach in obsessed anger? I personally think it has to do with a conscious understanding of grieving.

The Grieving Process

Grieving is another misunderstood concept. We know we grieve when someone dies or when someone close to us discovers that they have a serious illness. In short, we understand something of grieving when it involves losing a person or something major. But do you realize that you grieve every day? Do you realize that you grieve the loss of time, or even of something as subtle as an idea? We'll look at that, but first let's look at what has become known as the grieving process. It involves five steps:

Denial>>>Bargaining>>>Anger>>>Depression>>>Acceptance

Here are a few examples of how it works:

Let's say you are driving somewhere and suddenly hear a strange noise coming from your car. Your first reaction, will be denial, something like, *"Oh, Shit, it will go away."* When it persists, you'll start bargaining: *"It isn't serious"* or *"Well, I'll make it to where I'm going then have it looked at."* When the car suddenly stops, you'll get angry; *"Shit, Damn, Hell, why me?", "Why now?"* You might just hit the steering wheel and then hang your head on the steering wheel for a while. Then you'll come to acceptance: *call a tow truck, get a mechanic, and then deal with it.*

I may as well say here that you probably won't do these steps in strict order, and that you'll probably skip back and forth among them, and that you might even do a few of them at the same time. Like say Shit, Damn, Hell, many more times. Our minds and emotions are amazing; even as we're denying something, we're already accepting it.

In the above, when you get the car fixed and some time passes, it becomes something you really accept, maybe even laugh at, which means that you actually come to love it as part of your own experience.

Now, let's look at a second example, a person faced with an unexpected divorce. First **denial**: *"My spouse can't be serious. He/she is just upset. It will pass."* When it doesn't pass, **bargaining**: approach the spouse and offer all sorts of promises in order to reconcile. When that doesn't work, **anger**: *"Bastard/Bitch, I'll make him/her pay in court, get all I can out of this."* Then **depression**: *"I'm a failure, a loser."* Then **acceptance**: *"I may not even understand this at this point, but I have to accept it and move on."* And, long after the divorce, maybe a sad night will come when the person's thinking reverts to *"Maybe we can get together again."* Or another time comes when the anger returns, or the depression. As we said, the steps play out in different rhythms and patterns for different people and circumstances.

Now let's look at a third situation, a little more subtle. Let's look at ourselves as we get into recovery. We do our personal history and we realize: *"My family is dysfunctional; I am dysfunctional."* Trust me, you will go through the grieving process at that realization. Why? Because it challenges a concept long-ingrained in you, a myth: *"My family has to be perfect. I have to be perfect. Oh, sure, we have flaws, but we're certainly not dysfunctional."*

The realization about your dysfunctionality shatters one of your expectations. It shames you. It depresses you. And, hopefully, you go through the grieving process, all the way through it, no matter how long and hard it is. Because then you heal. You move on.

You see, taking the case of the family, when you finally come to an understanding of them, you can come to love them. I have said it before: Love them, pray for them, and let them be who they are. When you go through the grieving process, you accept the fact that you cannot control your family and never could. You accept who they are, and who you were and are. That understanding is the beginning of detachment with love.

And what of those people who really did hurt you? What if you are an incest survivor? A rape victim? How could you possibly come to love the perpetrator? Is that even possible? I have friends that are children of raped mothers and they told me their mothers actually forgave the perpetrators. This is still unfathomable to me, but in talking to one of the mothers she said it took time and ultimately, she no longer wanted to be bound to him or this heinous act, she wanted to be free and live. The key is that, as you work on yourself, you understand more about all human beings, even those who have hurt you seriously. You will never like what they did to you. You may not particularly like them as people either. But understanding them is the beginning of acceptance, of accepting the fact that what they did is their issue now, not yours. What you do now, you are doing for you. And acceptance is the beginning of love. Think, for example, of the soldiers who fought in Vietnam, on both sides. It was a brutal war: napalm, booby traps, and guerrilla warfare. Yet today, in interviews, both sides reach out in reconciliation and respect. They'll never like what the other did during the war. Just as they may not like what they did during the war. But they came to understand it and accept it, which is a big step toward healing and love. What good would it do to hold each other hostage to the past?

Twelve Steps Tools of Recovery
In Twelve Steps programs, we have what we formally call "tools of recovery." We have already covered these in some detail, so I'll simply review them here. They are, basically: meetings, the phone, and journaling. I am also going to include clichés, but we'll cover them separately, looking at the concepts behind some of the key clichés.

Regarding meetings, this refers to your attending group meetings with your Recovery Family. These are people you feel safe with in discussing your issues. These are people who will also teach you to listen and learn; you listen to their stories and issues, and learn that you are not the only one with problems. These people will not shame you, make you feel as though there is something wrong with you for discussing your issues. On the flip side of this, did you ever try discussing your issues with people who are not in recovery? How did you feel afterwards? A little weird? Embarrassed? At the very least, you'll get a polite silence. At worst, you will activate your sense of shame, because your "audience" will not be interested in your problems.

At meetings, you share. Sharing is a way of processing. Processing is a way of releasing yourself from issues, of accepting your past, making peace with it, and moving on to your spiritual growth.

The phone is another tool. My therapist told me about a woman she was treating who was going through all sorts of turmoil and needed to talk it out. But she was busy. Her voice mail was on. She left several voicemails for her to please...please...please call her so she could talk to someone she trusted. By the time she got home, there was the last voicemail, telling her not to bother calling because, realizing she might not get home soon; she had called someone from a group she attended. They had talked things out. She was OK. I can't make it any simpler. The phone is a valuable tool of recovery. It is literally a line to people with whom you can share safely, people who will not activate your shame when you need to discuss personal things.

Journaling we already covered in some detail. It bears repeating, that it is a way of processing. Also, if you use the method prescribed before keeping a negative and positive journal and eventually discarding the negative you will watch your positive journal grow, even as the negative issues shrink in importance.

Clichés, WTF?
Clichés, simultaneously inspirational and annoying. By the way, you are thinking that WTF means "what the fuck?" wrong, it means, "Where's the fun?" If you have ever played sports, went to a graduation, heard someone give a wedding toast, or watched an awards show, you've heard some eye-rolling clichés. The thing about clichés, they are usually only clichés because they're true. At times, even an annoyingly basic truth. Some clichés may even be the reminder you need, when maintaining your sobriety feels a little rough. No matter if it is one of these clichés or something that you always heard your grandfather say, it's important to have reminders that you can lean back on when the skies get a little gray or black for the addict. Remember, your mind will always want to default to the old comfortable habits. Sometimes, you need a reset button. Clichés are a great tool to reboot us or to remind us or to stop us.

Next time you're struggling, remind yourself of some of these recovery-based cliché truths. Below is a quick definition of cliché, then some clichés:

Definition of cliché:
    cli·ché klēˈSHā/klee-**shey**
    noun
        1. a trite, stereotyped expression; a sentence or phrase, usually expressing a popular or common thought or idea, that has lost originality, ingenuity, and impact by long overuse.
        a. "Have an Attitude of Gratitude."

    Synonym - platitude, commonplace, banality, oldsaying, maxim, truism, stock phrase, trite phrase, a slogan;

I had some fun with these below, took some liberty because when I was knee deep in shit, just didn't feel like living, and at one time, this is how I felt. So, I thought you might want to hear what an addict sounds like in middle of recovery, or during withdrawals, or just plain High, when hearing a cliché. Just go with me on this:

1. "Actions speak louder than words."

"Actions speak louder than words, but have you ever tried having a conversation with a mime? It's like trying to decipher interpretive dance in a library."

2. "Have an Attitude of Gratitude."

"They say 'Have an attitude of gratitude,' but I once tried rhyming advice during a bad day, and someone told me to 'Get a grip, and don't be so hip.' I promptly switched to non-rhyming wisdom."

3. "Keep it Simple, Stupid."

"So, 'Keep it Simple, Stupid' becomes 'Keep it Simple, You Moron.' I'm not sure that acronym will catch on, but who knows, maybe it's the secret to recovery humor!"

4. "Easy Does It."

"'Easy Does It' is overused? Well, that's just like saying I'm overusing my couch during Netflix marathons. Let's complicate things and overanalyze 'Easy Does It' instead."

5. "If Nothing Changes, Then Nothing Changes."

"You see, 'If Nothing Changes, Then Nothing Changes' is like that elusive Zen master trying to confuse you into enlightenment. Just change something, anything, and voila – instant change!"

6. "You Are Only as Sick as Your Secrets."

"'You are only as sick as your secrets' might sound cheesy, but it's basically the 'keeping it real' rule for recovery. Plus, secrets are so last season."

7. "You are Terminally Unique."

"Remember, 'You are terminally unique,' because nothing says 'I'm special' like trying to prove you're different from every other person who's ever tried to prove they're different."

8. "One Day at a Time."

"'One Day at a Time' is a classic like a good old sitcom rerun. If it's good enough for TV, it's good enough for recovery. Just remember to change the channel once in a while."

9. "Progress, Not Perfection."

"With 'Progress, Not Perfection,' its like saying, 'I'll go to the gym, but only if I can bench press a bus on day one.' Baby steps, folks, baby steps, preferably not on a bus."

10. "This too shall pass."

"Yes, 'This Too Shall Pass.' Even that awkward moment when you tried to impress your crush with a magic trick involving spaghetti. Let's just say, pastabilities were not endless."

11. "You've got to stay strong to be strong in tough times."
"'You've got to stay strong to be strong in tough times.' It's like telling a marshmallow to toughen up in a heatwave. But hey, if marshmallows can do it, so can you!"

A FEW MORE CLICHÉs BELOW
Now on a more positive note I will now cover a few more of the Clichés below, while some are the same, it's in an effort to add more tools in your tool box of affirmations, positivity, strength activation, for support, a new way of thinking, but ultimately to help support **Shame Reduction**.

One day at a time
One Day at a Time; It is one of the most beautiful ways of doing shame reduction work, and it is very special. One other thing: it is the only way possible to do shame reduction work, or anything else, for that matter. You can only live your life one day at a time. Probably all of us want to project into the future: Where will I be in recovery seven months from now? And we will compare ourselves to other people in recovery. He/She seems to be doing so much better than me. What's wrong with me? Nothing is wrong with you. You will work things out at your own pace, one day at a time. And this goes hand-in-hand with a phrase I like: **Yesterday, Today, Tomorrow.** *Yesterday* is your teacher. *Today* is the day you try to apply the lessons you learned. *Tomorrow* isn't here yet. There is another saying I like; **Focus on the past, you will be depressed; focus on the future, you will get anxiety; all you can be is Present.** There is an Eastern philosophy and I love this one: *Live beautifully in the present, and you'll automatically have a beautiful past and future.*

Think, Think, Think
Think, Think, Think. Oh, did I have a problem with this one! As a codependent, I realized early on in recovery that one of my problems was too much thinking! Then I heard this saying telling me to think more. But that's not the message. It's not telling me to think more. It's telling me to think properly.

Don't forget that many of us are compulsive people. As such, we often make snap decisions and then regret them; in other words, the decisions shame us. So, to reduce shame, take the time to think things out. My father had a wooden plaque that he hung up in the garage where he worked. The plaque was one word; it literally was IBMs slogan for years. The word was: THINK! That was it. I had the honor and privilege to work with my father, I literally got to watch every day how he would THINK. He would think properly. He would not obsess; he wouldn't go down any funky rabbit holes. He would take the time and think. Not react, but just stop, breathe and think. It's like he knew how to check in with himself and his innate process, ask the necessary questions, and then get the necessary answers for a proper outcome. It was awesome, genius, and so much fun to watch. To see his ideas begin from a thought, a concept. Then to see the process and adjustments, all the way to completion. Genius!

So don't think you have to give answers to people right away, or that you have to respond to them at all in most cases. That's a fetish that we codependents have. The reality is, there is a more healthy approach. Someone asks a question or expects something of you, you have the right to ask for information and take the time to process it, to think about it. Then you can respond as you see fit.

But for the Grace of God
But for the Grace of God. Even if you don't believe in God, you can see the sense in this. One of the things we have done to ourselves over years and years as codependents is be very hard on ourselves, very judgmental. Guess what? We applied the same patterns to others; we were very judgmental of them. But, as we get further along in recovery, this saying reminds us how lucky we are. We are making progress. When we see someone who is not making progress, we don't criticize them.

We empathize with them. Because we have been where they are. Now, again, as when we talked about love, empathizing with someone doesn't necessarily mean that you'll like them. You see, the people who come into your life are your teachers. And some teachers are tough. You hate them. You might even want to hurt them sometimes; it gets that extreme. But they are there for you to learn. And many philosophies say that you will keep meeting the same kind of people, the same kind of situations, until you learn the lesson you are supposed to learn from them. Let me give you an example.

A businessman was having a major problem with a coworker maybe even his supervisor, who was, in fact, a very negative, critical person. Being a good codependent, the man had tried to please the other person so that person wouldn't be so critical and would actually become a friend.

Eventually, after it finally sunk in, the man realized that this other person was almost pathologically negative; he wasn't going to change. Worse, when you treated him nice, he often repaid it with bitterness, backbiting, and criticism. So, the man started getting desperate to avoid the coworker. Since that was almost impossible, he actually thought about quitting his job. When he ruled that out, he finally realized that he would have to establish some pretty definite **boundaries** in dealing with the coworker. He would have to avoid certain conversations, not get into anything personal with the coworker, and so on. The coworker was just one of those people who seemed to take politeness for weakness; he just couldn't strike a happy chord with him.

That, I think, was the lesson the man had to learn: **set boundaries**. The coworker was his teacher, even though at one point the man hated him for the misery he caused. But once the man did set boundaries, the more he got into recovery and applied the principles in that situation, the less the other person bothered him. In fact, the more the man worked on his own shame issues, the more he saw that the coworker's problem had a lot to do with shame; the coworker was, in fact, an Adult Child of an alcoholic father, though he could not admit it. The more the man understood the co-worker, the less power the coworker had to upset him; the man was detaching from the situation, realizing that whatever issues were triggering the hostility between them were the coworker's issues, not his. Eventually, he could empathize with the coworker. The coworker had become his own shame, was stuck in his issues. The man could be grateful that he wasn't in the same boat any more.

In my continued search for my recovery, I attended a week long Ayahuasca retreat. There was a small group of us, mixed woman and men, young and old. All of us looking to heal or find a way to heal. At this retreat, we were far from everything, no phone, no Internet, in a desert mountain sharing a huge log cabin which was dedicated for healing and discovery. I went in completely open minded. I seemed to get along with everyone, however there was one woman that literally from day one drove me batshit crazy. No, I am serious, so crazy. I compared her to a soul sucking horcrux. (Yep, Harry Potter Reference). She was like sick all the time, I can't do this, I can't do that. She would be in the fetal position on the couch, and had difficulty participating in the group sessions. Oh my god! It was brutal. I literally could not understand why she affected me so profoundly. I kind-a-new that if I am charged emotionally and personally with something that it is probably me and not her. But I still could not figure it out until the fifth day after so much personal work.

I figured out that in my home and in my family, in my environment, I was that soul sucking horcrux to them. This hit me like a freight train in a head- on collision. She was a mirror of me at one point. It was so powerful and so painful; I literally dropped to my knees and just cried. And at that very moment I had so much compassion for this beautiful woman who had also, endured so much shame in your life. I literally went over and gave her the biggest hug and held on to her. Just showing her understanding, love, and compassion. It was such a big moment for her and me as well. And she truly is a lovely woman, but it was not about her at all, it was totally all about me. This is one of The Seven Essene Mirror of Self, by the way. You have no idea how bad I felt. I felt so guilty and awful that I felt this way about another human being, let alone a person who is trying to better herself in a small recovery group setting.

So, this might be a little hard to understand, but everything you do to someone else is a reflection of what you are doing to yourself on the inside. You judge yourself by the same scale you judge others. So, learning the value of this saying is actually giving yourself a break, because it teaches you to be less judgmental.

Let Go, Let God
Let Go, Let God. It's amazing how many of us, when we first hear this cliché, don't know what the "Let go" part refers to. Let go of what? Basically, let go of control. The fact is that you do not control much in this life anyway. Many philosophies say this in a basic way: concentrate on the process, let the results take care of themselves. You do not control the results. But, if you make a sincere effort at something, if you work on you and your part, the rest will take care of itself. That's the general idea behind this saying, but it also has practical application for us codependents.

Another person put it to me this way:
Let Go: G.0. meaning <u>Garbage Out</u>:
Let God: G.0.D. meaning <u>Good Orderly Direction</u> in.

Let go of anything negative, anything that is sick, that eats away at me and destroys me. We talked about this in a previous cliché: We are only as sick as our secrets. Our secrets are the things we are ashamed to admit. If we follow the **HOW** of my 6 stages to freedom program, **Honesty, Openness, Willingness**, we will share our secrets with safe people, process them, and finally let them go. See how the clichés work together.

We all have skeletons in our closet. Every so often those suckers rattle around. But if we finally face them, we realize that they are just that: skeletons. They, like everything else in our lives, the positive and the negative, are our teachers. So let go of the hold they have on you and you reduce the shame in your life.

Also, let go of trying to control the process of recovery, of life. We try to force issues, face them all at once and get rid of them. It doesn't work that way. Let go of trying to force your recovery and let it happen in time. Concentrate on the process of your life, on trying to live a healthy life, and leave the results to your Higher Power, Whoever or Whatever that is.

Let's Talk About Batteries
To sum up on the tools of shame reduction, I have this Battery Theory. You see, so many of us obsess with trying to get rid of the negative in our lives. We don't want any negative in our present, but that is impossible. People and events will bring negativity into your life. You cannot control that. Often it will happen unintentionally. People will shame you without even knowing it and vice versa. We also try to deny the negative in our past, and that, too, is impossible. In fact, it leads to denial and all sorts of other psychological pathology, and that leads us into the craziness of codependency, into depression, addiction, anxiety, and all the rest. And many of us try to avoid negativity in the future, which means they live in fear of negativity. Ever live in fear? It sucks.

The only logical thing to do is accept negativity as part of life. It's like a battery. A fully charged battery is half negative, half positive. It is the balance that gives the battery its power. If you doubt this, go out and disconnect either terminal from your car battery, the negative or the positive. Guess what? Your car won't start. You need both poles. You need balance. Remember I-Ching, Yin and Yang, the balance of positive and negative forces. It's a part of our life, acceptance.

You need the same balance in your life. If we are healthy, we are 50-50, balanced, positive and negative. Does this mean we walk around acting positively half the time and negatively the other half? No. It means that we accept our negative side, learn from it, and act in a healthy way. I once heard a company executive say in time of a business crisis: *"Crunch time brings out the best or worst in a manager."* Crunch time was the crisis, a negative situation for managers to deal with. Some buckled down and worked through it. Others panicked and started doing all kinds of negative stuff, like pointing fingers at others, blaming them for not performing. It's the same with us, with all human beings. If I have a negative issue, some trauma in my past, I can face it, learn from it, and move on, or I can point fingers and wallow in it.

In my 30 days of rehab, I was in contact with maybe 100 or so individuals. I met all sorts in rehab, male, female, young, old, homeless, been in prison, that live in half-way houses, successful, etc. Some of them have done horrendous things, unspeakable things, me included. But once they began treatment, and once I began treatment and we were **honest**, **open**, and **willing**, we accepted the negative in our lives, learned from it, and grew past it. It is the person who shuts down and refuses to deal with shame issues who becomes sicker and sicker and gets caught in the spiral of drastic negative behavior.

There was this beautiful girl in rehab who didn't and couldn't honestly approach her recovery for the longest time because it was so painful. She tried to live her life but this thing, these chains; this dark passenger just wouldn't leave. Finally, in one of the group rehab sessions, she faced one of her major shame issue head-on. Her father had sexually abused her for years! She had never told anyone. She had denied it, kept it inside, and it had basically eaten her alive and ruined her life up to that point. She had been unable to sustain a close relationship with anyone. Quite simply, she didn't trust anyone. How could she, when she couldn't even trust her own father? But when she finally opened up and started talking about the issue, all sorts of other shaming episodes came out as well. It was like cracking a dam, with all the water suddenly gushing out, things she had done and other things that had been done to her that she was ashamed of. That session was the beginning of her shame reduction process.

I know first-hand, as most codependents do, what shame can do to you. Rehab was the first time I approached many of my issues. Up to that point, I had avoided the pain of facing those issues by burying myself in my work, cocaine and alcohol, and with pills. I used drugs and alcohol to mummify me, to numb my feelings. Then, when I finally faced the issues and did the inventory, all that I could write about was the negative, the negative, the negative. It was almost as though nothing positive had ever occurred in my life. That was also difficult to experience. But as time went by, as I handled my addiction and worked on shame reduction, the positive finally appeared.

I now look at life in a much, much different light. I can appreciate life as a gift. **I cannot stress enough that the core issue for codependents is shame.** Ok let me put it to you in a simple phrase; Guilt means I did something bad; Shame means that I am bad. Guilt means my actions were less than honorable, but Shame is a state of being. It's awful, so in this book, what I hope my tools in my toolbox are trying to help you do is to move feelings of shame over to guilt. Because then you can recognize triggers and behaviors and shed the lies that you are bad. You are not bad, you are beautiful, and wonderful, and amazing, and those feeling are begging you to come out.

Serenity

In closing on shame reduction, I remember something my father once told me. My father has been my greatest Idol. I had the honor and privilege to work with my father for years. He was a German immigrant that basically fulfilled the American dream. Immigrated here, started and built a successful company, he asked me to help build it more with my experience and I had the privilege of negotiating the sale of his hard earned company for millions so that he could retire. I love him and I miss him. He is a genius artist, precision machinist, and mechanic trained in Germany and could design and build anything. He was the epitome of integrity and he lived his life with integrity, he wasn't a person that told you that he loved you, he just loved you, he lived his life honestly, he wasn't the type that said look at me, and that I'm this or I'm that, he literally lived what he believed. The sad part is for me that I could not realize how beautiful, real, and truthful that was until he died and I was forced to reflect on his life (which was a good thing) and what he provided for me. He had so much wisdom. Definitely a man of few words, but when he spoke, you listened. While walking through his machine shop and talking with the machinist that worked for him, my father said, **"Karl-Heinz, if you want to know if a man is a good machinist, all you have to do is look at his tools."** A good machinist takes care of his tools, honors them. It's the same when we discuss shame reduction.

We have covered several tools you can use to do the work. They are not something that I created. They come from many sources. They work. But you have to use them, keep them sharp. Making decisions, setting boundaries, working with clichés, sharing with a Recovery Family, it all takes work.

There is one other tool I would like to introduce you to in the next chapter. It has nothing to do with religion, though it is called a prayer, the Serenity Prayer. It is, in reality, a formula for living. It is very short. Yet it contains all the principles you need to recover from codependency and all forms of addiction.

CHAPTER 9

THE SERENITY PRAYER

> *"The function of prayer is not to influence God, but rather to change the nature of the one who prays."*
> — ***Søren Kierkegaard***

> *"God speaks in the silence of the heart. Listening is the beginning of prayer."*
> — ***Mother Teresa***

My Serenity Prayer!

The Serenity Prayer is a famous prayer that is widely associated with twelve steps recovery of all Anonymous Programs. It is often recited as a mantra or used as a guiding principle for finding peace, acceptance, and strength in challenging circumstances. I promise you by virtue of saying this prayer, this mantra daily, it will activate inside of you all the necessary bits of knowledge you require for change. The prayer goes as follows:

> *"God, grant me the serenity to accept the things I cannot change,*
> *The courage to change the things I can,*
> *And the wisdom to know the difference."*

I remember the first time I recited this prayer, I actually cried. I sat down and just cried, knowing that I can change. That there is hope. Hope being so fucking powerful.

The current Serenity Prayer is often attributed to Reinhold Niebuhr, an American theologian, though its exact origin is a subject of some debate. The version we know today is a condensed version from the original. It has become widely embraced as a powerful reflection on personal growth, resilience, and finding inner peace. Here is the entire prayer as recited by Reinhold:

> "God, give me grace to accept with serenity
> the things that cannot be changed,
> Courage to change the things
> which should be changed,
> and the Wisdom to distinguish
> the one from the other.
>
> Living one day at a time,
> Enjoying one moment at a time,
> Accepting hardship as a pathway to peace,
> Taking, as Jesus did,
> This sinful world as it is,
> Not as I would have it,
> Trusting that You will make all things right,
> If I surrender to Your will,
> So that I may be reasonably happy in this life,
> And supremely happy with You forever in the next.
> Amen."

This longer version of the prayer encompasses additional elements of surrender, acceptance, and trust in God's plan. The condensed version, commonly used in recovery programs, focuses on the core message of accepting what cannot be changed, having the courage to change what can be changed, and seeking wisdom to discern the difference.

Here's my summary breakdown of the meaning behind each line of the condensed version:

1. "God, grant me the serenity to accept the things I cannot change": This line acknowledges that there are certain aspects of life beyond our control. It emphasizes the importance of finding serenity and peace in accepting these uncontrollable circumstances, events, or the behavior of others.

2. "The courage to change the things I can": This line encourages individuals to have the courage and determination to take action and make positive changes in their lives. It reminds us that we have the power to influence and shape certain aspects of our lives and encourages us to embrace that power.

3. "And the wisdom to know the difference": This line highlights the importance of discernment and wisdom in distinguishing between what can and cannot be changed. It urges individuals to develop insight and clarity to recognize which situations or circumstances are within their sphere of influence and which are not.

Overall, the Serenity Prayer promotes an attitude of acceptance, courage, and wisdom. It teaches individuals to find serenity by accepting what cannot be changed, to find the strength to make necessary changes, and to develop the discernment to recognize the difference between the two. It has resonated with people seeking guidance and comfort in navigating life's challenges, regardless of their religious or spiritual beliefs.

The most powerful Shame Reduction tool

For me, I have found the Serenity Prayer to be the most powerful of shame reductions tools. If you have a problem calling it a prayer, call it a mantra, call it a formula. If you have a problem with the concept of a God outside of yourself, think of God as yourself fully developed. Or just replace the name God in the prayer with your own name. See what happens, you are finally now giving yourself Permission. Permission to accept, permission to change, permission to love, permission to be human. The important thing is to look at the concept behind the prayer. But before we get into that, let's look at some other things that shame does to us.

First, you have probably heard it said that many of us, especially codependents, give away our power. In terms of shame, this means that we think so little of our Lives that we look to other people for approval, or praise, or confirmation. To put it in blunt terms, we need other people to like us. We can't stand it when they don't like us. We give them power over us because we give them power over our emotions. If they are nice to us, we are happy; if they are not nice, we are sad or even clinically depressed and anxious. It is as simple as that. Other people rule our emotions. If we didn't suffer from toxic shame, we wouldn't care what other people thought of us. We would have a strong enough concept of self to rule our own emotions; we would be at peace just doing the best we could.

Second, shame also changes normal events in life so that they overwhelm us. In my own experience, I swear I suffered some kind of "synaptic breakdown." Too be honest I have probably suffered from many synaptic shutdowns. But anyway, this last time was different; it was like time and space were not normal, like my chest opened up into some swirly typhoon vortex of pain and emotion. It was so intense; I literally jumped into an ice- cold lake to try and become present and did not feel the cold. Radical Intensity does not even begin to describe the experience. Every minute felt like an hour. I remember trying to watch a movie, a movie that was literally an hour and a half, but it felt like 8 hours, it was so bizarre. And it lasted like almost a week. Fucking nuts, full on metal and mental. Ironically enough, I manifested this, I literally asked for this looking back. I wanted to accelerate my change, I wanted to rush my recovery, I wanted all my repressed emotions to come out, I was sick and tired of being sick and tired, I wanted to peel back as many layers of the onion as possible, I wanted to eliminate and terminate, all of my toxic shame which contributed heavily to the breakdown. Now looking back, I don't see it as a breakdown, what really happened was a massive fucking earthquake of an emotional release, which assisted me in reducing my Shame.

But now, after a lot of shame reduction work, I see things much differently. I am actually grateful that I had the episode because it helped me continue my path to recovery. Now, instead of being paralyzed by the Shame, I see it as just another one of my teachers.

Third, shame basically intensifies our addictions, no matter what the addiction is: phones, alcohol, drugs, shopping, work, sex, social media, food. Shame makes us feel so bad that we run to our addictions to numb the pain, to mummify ourselves. I believe that almost all relapses into addictions come from being over-whelmed by our issues, particularly by shame.

We use the Serenity Prayer because it contains all the concepts we need to defuse the power of shame in our lives. I also point out that we are advised to repeat this process over and over again. **Repetition**: It's like **Kung Fu**? WTF? Why **Kung Fu**? Why do I bring up **Kung Fu**? I have always been fascinated by martial arts, my teen years were watching Bruce Lee, Steven Seagal, Jean-Claude Van Damme, and Jackie Chan. OMG are you kidding me, I wanted to do what they could do, but I found out that I loved the deeper spiritual meaning to martial arts, so I am going to offer a meaning of Kung Fu as described by Hundred Eyes (Played by Tom Wu) from the TV Series; <u>Marco Polo: One Hundred Eyes</u>. Tom Wu was absolutely brilliant as Hundred Eyes. I absolutely loved this dialogue between Hundred Eyes (Tom Wu) and Marco Polo (played by Lorenzo Richelmy);

> **Hundred Eyes:** In Kung Fu, we say, one hand lies,
> *[attempting blows]*
> **Hundred Eyes:** *the other hand tells the truth. [counter-strikes]*
> **Marco Polo:** Try that again.
> **Hundred Eyes:** If you one day you make it back to the West, what will you tell men of this strange word, "Kung Fu?" Will you tell them that it means to fight? Or will you say, like a monk from Shaolin
> *[inhales sharply]*
> **Hundred Eyes:** to summon the spirit of the crane and the tiger?
> **Hundred Eyes:** *[both grunting and panting]* Kung Fu. It means, **"supreme skill from hard work."**
> **Hundred Eyes:** *A great poet has reached Kung Fu. The painter, the calligrapher, they can be said to have Kung Fu. Even the cook, the one who sweeps steps, or a masterful servant, can have Kung Fu.* **Practice. Preparation. Endless repetition. Until your mind is weary, and your bones ache. Until you're too tired to sweat. Too wasted to breathe.**
> **Hundred Eyes:** *[continues dueling]* **That is the way, the only way, one acquires Kung Fu.** Unfortunately boy, you have not.

My prayer is and I hope you understand that you can turn this process into your own personal Kung Fu, change it for you, whatever resonates for you, make it your own, modify it, change it, update it, but make it make sense to you and then make it a *"supreme skill from hard work"*, "Practice, Preparation, and Endless Repetition. Until you are so fucking tired that your bones ache and it sticks, change will then happen permanently, progress will begin to happen and then personal evolution and enlightenment will happen. To me this makes so much sense. Launch your own Personal Revolution or your ultimate evolution.

OK, back to why I used the Kung Fu example. Because **Shame** has been programmed into us. Repetition of the prayer will begin the deprograming of Shame and then programs the healing concepts into our psyches as well. You might also experience a phenomenon with the prayer that people often report in other forms of therapy and work. They hear a concept, but they don't understand it right away. Maybe a month, six months, or a year, or even more down the road of life, they hear it again and it sinks in. It's pretty much the same with the Serenity Prayer. Its deeper meanings come to you as you repeat it sincerely, over and over and over again. Now I am going to give you long drawn version of each line of the prayer and apply it to the tools we have been talking about.

God Grant Me
Whether you believe in God or not, you are probably familiar with, have probably experienced, a very old adage: **"Seek and you shall find."** That version of it comes from the Bible, but there are other, more secular versions, like, **"The harder you work, the luckier you get."** It's a beautiful concept. Look for something and you will find it. Or, as some say, look for something, and it will find you. The mere action of seeking or looking for something, will create activation in your soul. You just have to ask, and then the seed will be planted, and it will find you.

In the first three words of the prayer, we are looking for something: God. But remember the previous definition for God I gave you. Define God as an acronym. G.O.D: GOOD ORDERLY DIRECTION. When you get a sense of order, of direction, in your life, you become calm and open, open to learn from situations, rather than be overwhelmed by them. And we said that shame tends to overwhelm us. So, we are asking not to be overwhelmed by anything, especially shame.

The Serenity to accept the things I cannot Change
This is simple to grasp but usually difficult to live by. It is a fact of life that you cannot change people, cannot "fix" anyone, cannot "rescue" anyone, and cannot save anyone. You are, in fact, powerless over most things in life, if not everything. Thank God! Once I get the concept, I can stop trying to control events and people. That's a problem with us codependents: we are control freaks. We think if we don't control everything, some catastrophe will happen. Yet the illusion of our controlling things is just that: an illusion. When you finally get that, you can also get the point that you can lower your expectations of people and things. And when you do that, you lower your own sense of shame. For example, if I do not expect everyone to like me automatically, then when I run across someone who doesn't like me, I just accept it, rather than beat myself up wondering why I'm not like-able.

Acceptance is like 95% of recovery. Accept your parents for who they are. Accept other people for who they are. Accept circumstances for what they are. Stop trying to organize them, control them, and fix them to be the way you think they should be. Does this mean that you have to accept misery? No. Remember, we said before, one of the nuances of recovery, as testified by so many people who have been through it, is that if you work on yourself everything else seems to take care of itself.

There's an old analogy comparing life to a butterfly. If you try to capture it, control its beauty, you just kill it. You have to let it be free. Maybe there are people you have been trying to control, trying to get to see things your way. Forget it. You cannot control them. So just love them, pray for them, and let them be who they are. Use your energy to work on you. To take the example further, so many of us have problems with our parents. We want them to accept us, on our terms. So, we play games with them when they don't. We try to explain to them what they're doing wrong, get them to change. But doing that implies that there is something wrong with them. It shames them. In turn, they tell us what we are doing wrong, and so we are shamed by implication as well. Remember we called it the Shame Game. But it takes two to play a game. So, if you stop, just accept them for who they are and realize that they'll never give you what you want on your terms, the game ends. The shame is diminished, or, as in the process of recovery, it is reduced.

I think of a person I met whose father wanted him to take over the family business. He didn't want to; to him it was boring. He gave up the business and went into his own profession, but only after wrangling with the father, trying to convince him that he was doing the right thing. This person finally realized that he would never convince his father; never get his approval for going into his own profession. It was understandable, from the father's viewpoint; he had built his business during hard times and it had kept his family fed. To him, keeping the business was like a matter of life and death; lose it and you don't eat in tough times. That was the father's experience. But the son finally went into his own profession and stopped trying to get his father's approval. When the father raised the subject, he'd listen for a while and then change the subject. It saved a lot of grief.

I love the following saying, because I mean it, I have lived it, and it literally helped me further my recovery; *I am sick and tired of being sick and tired!* So, in the first part of the prayer, we are asking for the direction to find acceptance of reality, of what is. We are asking to detach from things over which we have no control. Hopefully, in time, that detachment will be with Love, not anger. For example, this person mentioned above that he still loves his father, even though they can't agree on something important to both of them. If you can detach, especially with love, you will have serenity. Remember, you will probably not detach with love, but with anger, at first. The love comes later, as you grow spiritually. Serenity is not a zombie-like state. It is the foundation for happiness.

Depression, anxiety, addictions, and all the other craziness of codependency cannot exist where there is serenity.

Courage to change the things I can
Don't confuse courage with insanity. Some dude on a motorcycle charging down the interstate, way above the speed limit isn't courageous. He's insane. People who finally decide to deal with the tough issues in their lives are courageous. Being open to change and grow is courageous. In fact, if you did a psychological study on the motorcycle guy (BTW, this was a friend of mine, he crashed his motorcycle, doing 180mph, he should be dead, but now he is sober, married and working through his addictions), you'd probably find that he was acting insane because he wasn't dealing with his issues. He's showing false courage as a way to avoid his real issues. It's shame. You've probably heard the saying that the real heroes are the quiet heroes. They are the ones with inner strength.

Now, if you get the courage to face your issues, to grow and change, what is it that you change? Well, the only thing in the world you can really change is, YOU. And, to say it again, that's a relief! Once you understand that concept, you can stop worrying about trying to change anybody else. You are free to concentrate on working on yourself.

But working on what? On being open to looking at yourself, looking at what has become your normal, your patterns. Are they really healthy for you? Or are they sick? If they are sick, do you have the willingness to change and grow? If you do, you will start learning about yourself. This is the beginning of the process of developing a relationship with yourself. It takes courage, because you have to embrace everything about yourself, including your limitations and handicaps, your light-side and your dark- side. You also have to acknowledge your sick patterns and have the courage to change them, let them go, and replace them with new experiences and ways of acting. For example, many of us are constantly battling other people in our lives, like parents or spouses or children or friends or work people. We are hurting them, shaming them, and doing the same to ourselves. But guess what? Painful as it is, we don't want to let go, don't want to change, because that battling has become our normal. We do it automatically, it's are default setting. Changing will take effort, will be painful in itself, at least until we get used to new patterns in our lives.

I can draw some analogies to how this works. For example, none of us want to be in a hospital for any length of time. But guess what? People who experience long hospital stays experience anxiety when they are finally discharged. As unpleasant as the hospital stay was, it became their normal, their routine. Getting back into normal life is frightening, painful. Here is an extreme case, leaving prison. Believe it or not, long-term prisoners experience similar anxiety, and for the same reasons, when they are released. They want to change, want the freedom, but it is also anxiety-producing to give up the "normal" of prison life.

So, courage is having the willingness to change. This is such an important topic for us codependents that I will devote the last chapter to covering it in detail. As codependents, we become so wrapped up in our issues, so wrapped up in trying to change others that we have a very difficult time letting things go. It's as though we have to stay in there, battling to change people and things we can't change, so that we never change. Yet change is closure. It is healing. It is moving on. Remember the analogy of the phoenix rising from the ashes. From change, from an ending, a new beginning is born. Out of the ashes comes rebirth.

Here is an example from my own conversations. Divorce is so common now. I see just nasty divorces that affect the children and these broken families enter into new families. There was a couple that got remarried that had children from another marriage. They went through some pretty rough changes coming to grips with this new marriage, this new family. The new parent wanted them to understand, to be cooperative, and to accept the marriage, and they wanted their acceptance and understanding as soon as possible. That's codependency; that new parent wanted to control their emotions. Children in such a situation would have to be abnormal not to have a reaction. After all, their whole life, their whole world, is changing drastically, even if it was dysfunctional. They have to go through some changes with it. And it takes time and courage. If they are equipped and taught how to face the change, accept it instead of denying what is happening, they get past the mourning of the old ways, past the anger and denial, and come to peace with it. If not, it becomes a major issue for them. Just as that new parent figure wanting to control their new step children's reactions was becoming an issue for that parent.

Courage in Recovery
People in recovery are some of the most courageous people I've ever met. First, let's repeat something. I'm not just talking about recovery

from drugs or alcohol. I'm talking about recovery from any form of codependency. Recovery from depression, from anxiety, from food addictions, sexual addictions, spending addictions...Recovery from anything creating insanity in our lives. Why does it take courage? Let's look at a few scenarios.

For example, people who decide to put down the drink...That probably means that the whole direction of their lives, everything they know as normal, will change. To get to that point, they already went through a grieving process. They stopped denying that alcohol was a problem. They stopped bargaining that they could still drink occasionally, have the proverbial—and mythical—one or two drinks. They went through the anger and depression coming to grips with their addiction, and finally came to accept it. What then? They could no longer rely on alcohol to numb themselves in times of stress; they had to feel their feelings. They had to give up their bar room friends. They probably had to face the fact that they were lacking true intimacy in their other relationships, because they were avoiding that with alcohol, and work on developing that. All strange, all new and I am sure very painful. And it takes courage.

A friend of mine complained to me that he had stopped drinking, stopped drugs, and his life was in turmoil. I said, **"Congratulations, you're on the right path."** He had to find the courage to stay on the path, stay in recovery, even when he slipped once in a while.

If you stick with recovery, you will discover something: THE GREATEST HEALING SPOT IN THE WHOLE WORLD IS INSIDE OF YOU, NOT ON THE OUTSIDE. That means that you are going to start to feel differently, feel a power you never had, or only had so long ago that you virtually forgot it. You will probably realize that much of this strength comes from reducing your feelings of shame; the negative is going out, the positive coming in. You will experience and be conscious of your own personality changing. And you will see how courage builds on itself; ever hear the successful sports teams talking about how winning is contagious? It's the same principle. I call people in true recovery, walking miracles, because I see them developing the courage to change and grow, to be open, to listen, to take Good Orderly Direction. I see the contagious positive effects this has on them, and their family, and all people around them.

So "Courage to change the things I can..." means the courage to change
YOURSELF

And Wisdom to know the difference

Wisdom is a gift. It only comes from experience, from openness, from learning, from hard hits, from scars, and from all the growth we go through in the course of our lives.

Wisdom is the art and gift of being able to set boundaries

The wisdom of recovery gives you balance. Balance is not criticizing other people for what they do. Sometimes we tend to get so self-righteous: *"I don't drink. So, the rest of the world shouldn't drink either!"* That's not balance. Balance is working on yourself and letting other people be where they need to be. And the beauty of the program can be summed up in that very brief phrase:

Work on YOU and everything else will take care of itself

Practicing the Prayer

Do we always do what the prayer says? Of course not, *we slip sometimes, we relapse sometimes, we forget sometimes.* That's part of life and recovery, too. You slip. You get hurt. You relapse. You learn from the pain. You go back and do what you need to do. Set your boundaries and work within them. When you don't, you wind up reactivating your shame and the shame in other people.

Another way of putting it is, work within your limitations. Limitations are natural boundaries. Not only are they a normal part of life; they also free you from trying to do too much.

For example, look at the prayer in relation to your own OG Family, whatever that is. Maybe you are in recovery and part of you, that child within, desperately wants them to be in recovery too. That's a very normal feeling for us to have. The child in us wants to make everything better. But wisdom, the adult in us, reminds us that we cannot control anyone else. We cannot make them be where we want them to be. So, we set our boundaries with our family accordingly.

We do what is healthy for us. We do not shame them in the process. So certain things, for example, you'll be able to talk about with them, share with them. But some things you will not be able to share with them. It might make things a little superficial between you sometimes, but that is OK.

So, one thing the Serenity Prayer has taught me, and that I try to practice, is that you solve problems through healing and gentleness and kindness. Living the Prayer also means knowing that I need direction. Not just sometimes. Not just until I'm *"cured"* of my codependency; wisdom tells me that recovery is not only process, but also a life-long process. I need direction in my life. And I need courage to follow that direction. I need the wisdom to know that I can only work on me and that I need to work on me for ten days, one hundred days or even ten thousand days, and I need courage to do the work. Prayer has also taught me that if I run into something I need to do, but can't Do myself, then I get help. You keep it that simple. That's what living the Serenity Prayer is all about.

There is another aspect of the Prayer, of wisdom, that we experience as we work on ourselves. I call it *"Letting go of Taboos."* It's not easy for codependents to do that. It causes a lot of pain and anxiety. The taboos come from the most powerful rules ever laid on us: childhood rules. They are deep, deep in our psyche. As I cover them in the next chapter, I think you will see the wisdom in the Serenity Prayer when it asks for the courage to change the things we can. Letting go of taboos is painful. Facing that pain, getting through it, takes courage.

CHAPTER 10

GOD, AS I UNDERSTAND GOD

"There is no God higher than truth."
— *Mahatma Gandhi*

"Our higher power only puts in front of us what we are capable of overcoming."
— *Unknown*

The Taboos

The Taboos in our lives are part of the Shame process. They are part of the Original Shame messages given to us in the very early stages of our lives, so they become part of our deepest fiber. They are presented to us as something sacred. They are never to be challenged. And when you come to the point in your life that you do challenge them, as you inevitably must, they cause you a great deal of pain, usually in the form of depression and anxiety fueled by Guilt and Shame and Fear. The taboos are given to us by the Family Systems that we talked about in: **(Chapter 2: OG Family, Society, Religion, Peer Groups, and All Media.)** The taboos are basically presented to you as absolute truth, with the warning that if you ever challenge them something bad will happen to you.

As an example, when I was a kid, I was taught that you never question God. If you do, He will punish you. So, I spent most of my life being afraid of God. After all, I was human. I was making my share of mistakes and questioning things about God and life, so I kept looking over my shoulder, wondering when He was going to get me. Even the term "He" in referring to God was a stumbling block. Today I realize that God, as I understand Him, works out of reality, and, as such, can be a He, She, or even something beyond those labels, anything that helps us better understand the Higher Power.

Taboos are absolutes if you live your life around absolutes; you are putting yourself in a position of judging. Shame naturally flows from judging, because when you find someone who doesn't agree with your absolutes, you try to invalidate their point of view, try to make them feel that there is something fundamentally wrong with them. By the way, that's called Control. Also, if you have to try to convince everybody that you are right, it means that you yourself are not convinced, otherwise, you would simply stand back and let people find the truth for themselves; you wouldn't feel a need to force it on them. It's amazing to watch posts on Facebook or whatever about politics or any opinion you might have. Friends will read the post and reply with opposing opinions and if you don't share their opinion, you can no longer be friends. This blows me away, why can't I believe what I believe, you believe what you believe and we can still be friends? Crazy, right? Because of our Sacred Ideals, our Taboos.

Taboos Keep you from your higher Power
I call my personal Higher Power "God." As we said before, you can identify your Higher Power as you understand your Higher Power. But generally, you come to understand your Higher Power through the workings of yourself and your environment, including the people and things you experience. Since the entire world including you, is constantly changing, you can see where absolutes rule, the Taboos, can keep you from understanding your Higher Power. Basically, absolutes and change don't go well together. If your whole experience is telling you one thing, and your taboos insist on something else, and you insist on clinging to your taboos, you will experience shame. It's a simple concept: Either the taboos are wrong, or you are wrong; if you insist on honoring the taboos, you invalidate yourself, make you think there is something wrong with you, which is shame.

What makes the taboos so strong is that they are usually given to us as Original Shame Messages. They are deeply rooted into the earliest parts of our life, the roots of our psyche. Let's look at some of the common ones.

Most of us are taught that God is a God of fear, of guilt, of trepidation and punishment. If you believe in that concept, you begin to look at the world as something to be feared, as something bad. And you begin to experience yourself that way; after all, you are part of this world. What greater shame experience can you have than to think of yourself as something bad?

Why was God described to us that way? Control. Religion wanted to control us. Society wanted to control us. So, God was used as a God of guilt to control us. *"If you do something wrong, go against the rules, you will be punished."* For those of us who accepted that, we constantly looked over our shoulders to see if we were doing the right thing or if someone was coming to punish us. That, by the way, is a form of anxiety. In my own case, I was constantly in fear, and did not know it, and very hard on myself.

What I realize today is that this concept of the Higher Power is a taboo, something used to control people through fear. It is unhealthy. Today, I realize that I am allowed to have a God of my own understanding. A God of my belief process. A God that works for me. I am allowed to develop in my life whatever is healthy for me. That is part of what the Higher Power is to me, as I understand Him or Her. He is a God of health. She is a God of Love. He is a God of forgiveness. She is a God of compassion. He or She, it doesn't matter, this is now a God of my understanding.

I still have twitches of guilt that reveal themselves as I continue to peel back new layers. Every once in a while, the fact that I challenge the old taboos, the old concept of God, brings back those nervous twitches. It is something I continually work on as I grow. It's something you all need to work on as you grow.

I'll give you another example, what I call an outrageous example. When I was growing up, in my teens and young adult years, one of the taboos that was forced on me was I could not stay out past like midnight on a Saturday, because Sunday, being the Sabbath was the next day. I was taught the Holy Spirit or Holy Ghost for me goes to bed at midnight and bad things will happen to me if I continue living past midnight. That I would leave myself unprotected, and that it's my fault if I make that decision to defy or break this taboo. OMG, I hated this so much growing up, I literally could not reconcile it. So, what you're saying is God is going to abandon me after midnight. I know, right? Crazy!!! So, once I was out of the house, Jesus Christ help me, I was out all night, all day, and the next night. Yep, I rebelled and tested if God would abandon me.

Think of your own taboos. Think of your personal outrageous taboos, as well as those passed on to us by society and religion and peer groups.

Think of Church, organized religion. I'm not saying that what they have to say doesn't have validity, they do. There are so many beautiful teachings of Christ, if Christian, whatever religion is important to you or a part of your life and past. But sometimes we are taught that our religion cannot be wrong. Whatever it teaches us is infallible. I had put my religion on a pedestal. I never challenged it. Yet, when I was a missionary in Italy, I had Italians challenge me and say, *"Me and My family have been Roman Catholics for 2000 years since Christ, who the Hell (insert Italian profanity) are you? Some 19-year-old telling me that you speak only the truth and that your religion is the only true religion on earth. I am not going to be the first in my family to break tradition."* And then in true Italian Spirit, they would feed me the most amazing Italian Dishes, I miss Italian food.

I remember one beautiful Italian woman, a mother. It was such a profound moment for me. She said *"I love God, and I see him my way, I can see that you love God the way you do, let's just sit and eat and drink and talk about our Gods that we love so much!"* OMG, I loved this woman. Do you know what it is like to sell GOD as a 19-year-old. Fucking crazy, like it was crazy. I really did have the most amazing experiences on my Mormon mission. I do not regret one day. It literally pushed me and forced me to challenge my taboos, my normals, my belief system. I learned so much. I grew. I evolved. Again, this is my personal history, my story, my own life movie.

One Ultimate Authority
Today, I have come to understand that there is only one legitimate ultimate authority: your Higher Power as you understand your Higher Power. You come to understand your Higher Power by being open to learning, to growth, which means that sometimes you have to be open to discarding the taboos in your life. Let's look at a few more examples to illustrate.

Just like my missionary story, we codependents set people and things on an improper level. Basically, we set them above us, on pedestals. What we are doing is giving our power to them. What we want in exchange is to avoid the pain of growth. We put people on pedestals, make gods of them, and basically want them to tell us what to do, how to live. When you do that, you are doing a grave disservice to them and to yourself, because ultimately no one can live up to that god-like expectation. The people you put on pedestals will ultimately fall off the pedestal, will let you down. Then what? You are worse off than when you started. You see this often in relationships. We want someone who can tell us how to live, give us the answers. What you learn in recovery is that no one can do this for you. You must find your own answers. And sometimes you will not learn the answers to everything. That's OK. You'll find the answers you need to know at the moment you need to know. The remaining bits you don't know, the bits you might struggle with, you will eventually will let go. That's ok, they will show up when its time. It's a simple philosophy. You don't have to analyze everything to death.

What makes that simple philosophy difficult to live with is that we are conditioned to feel that we can't possibly run our own lives, find our own answers. **First**, we are used to being given the *"rules."* **Second**, we feel so personally insignificant that we cannot possibly accept that we have the power to run our own lives. But we do. We are each unique, special. We each count. We each have the power to manage our own lives and make our own decisions.

Of course, we don't just give our power away to people. We also look to institutions to run our lives for us. One of these institutions is recovery itself; some people get into it and create the taboo that it has to be one way and one way only or it won't work. They never see that their own rigidity in approaching recovery is creating insanity for them. It's almost as though, instead of having the goal of joy and freedom from unhealthy things, their goal is following the rules, no matter what feelings that brings them.

The point is that things change. Even your **Sacred Ideals** change, whether or not you want them to. Even recovery changes for each of us. We must be open to grow and discover new things and put aside the old taboos.

Three Principles
I would like to share three basic principles that I learned in my own recovery:

First Principle: this one we already touched on: Nothing is absolute. Life is change. Life is a process. Being open to change is healthy.

Second Principle, there are no **Sacred Ideals**. If you put a person, place, or thing on a pedestal, if you expect that person, place, or thing to run your own life, you are doing yourself and that person, place, or thing a disservice. An example for me is that when I was growing up. I was taught that you only went to one Church, one denomination. If you violated that, something would happen to you. I still to this day don't know what was supposed to happen to me, but it was something vague and bad. Today, I realize that I can learn from any Church, from any source, if I am open to learn from it. For example, Buddhism, Kabbalah, Chinese I-Ching, Astrology, Chakras, all of these are so different and foreign to my own culture and upbringing, but they can teach me something if I am open to the teaching. And when I was open to their teachings, I started seeing so many similarities. In fact, that is when the Gene Code and Human Design came to me. Human Design came to me a critical time when I was asking again, *"why am I, the way I am."*

Also, in regard to being open in recovery, even people who are not in recovery can teach me. They can be your teachers. They might not be pleasant to be around. You might not like them or what they do. It might be painful. But you can learn from them if you are open. People around you are literally mirrors of what you are trying to figure out for yourself. *Again see (Seven Essene Mirrors of Self)*. Look at everyone as a mirror to what you are feeling, wanting, needing, it will open your eyes big time. This is how you start learning and becoming so self-aware of yourself.

So many times, people will discuss how certain people or situations resurrect their codependency issues, for example, how they try to please people or institutions, even when this is unhealthy for them personally, or how they try to control other people or situations to get the approval they so desperately need, or think they need. These are just some of the common codependency issues, of course. What you hear by interacting with people around you and in your life, even at the grocery store, or gas station, or work. You need to be self-aware and become open to learn about your issues by listening to others issues, they can become your teachers, your mirrors, and not even know it.

We are taught, and I think it is true, that all of us are created in the likeness of a Higher Power. All of us. No matter who the person is.

Third Principle: God As I Understand Him. It's sort of an open-ended principle, because what it means is that I learn about my Higher Power by watching the unfolding of the people around me. Or, to put it another way, if we work on ourselves, discover who we are, build a relationship with ourselves, discover the gift of ourselves as unique people and participate in the process of life, and then we will discover a God as we understand a God through us, through our own experience.

It might not be an easy concept to grasp. That's OK. It's not as simple, as telling you that, Yeah, you see God as this really old grandfather type, tall with a white beard and long white hair, who lives in the universe, amongst the stars, watching us and then and punishes us for some things and rewards us for others and only wants to be worshiped by one name and in one way and all the rest are wrong, and so on. Because the fact is that God as I understand Him is how He unfolds in my own life, how I came to be open and then saw my life change from depression and anxiety and addiction and care-taking and fantasizing and isolation and all sorts of other unhealthy behaviors to a healthy, fulfilling experience.

And God as I understand Him also comes from having watched the same thing happen to other people, through their own individual paths, as well. That's why I call people in recovery walking miracles. It's like a miracle to see the change in people from the misery of codependency to the serenity of recovery.

GUT Theology - I can feel it in my gut!
By my examples, which I take mostly from my own experience, you can also see that I didn't get the principles on the first, second, third, or even tenth pass. I had to experience a lot of change, a lot of pain, a lot of growth before they started to sink in. I don't mean *"sink in"* to the brain; most of us can understand things on an intellectual level. I mean sink into my gut, into my feelings, into my soul. If you look at depression and anxiety and the other manifestations of codependency as these terrible, hopeless feelings they are, you can understand that if the principles sink into the gut, if they cause my feelings to change for the better, they bring their own peace and serenity, which sure beats depression and anxiety. I call this the *"GUT Theology"* Like any theology, it takes practice.

Theology means the study of the nature of God and religious beliefs; religious beliefs and theory when systematically developed. So GUT Theology would be to me, the study and belief of what God means to me in my Gut, in my core. So, I am going to pose a question, To you all, *"I want you to describe God."* Who and what is God. Write down your answer and say it out loud so you can confirm what you believe that answer to be. Below is my kind of textbook answer as per the masses.

The concept of God varies across different religions and philosophical traditions, and perceptions of God can be deeply personal and subjective. However, here is a general description of the concept of God:

God is often understood as a supreme being, a transcendent and immanent presence that is believed to have created and governs the universe. In many religious traditions, God is considered to be all-powerful (omnipotent), all-knowing (omniscient), and all-present (omnipresent). God is seen as the ultimate source of truth, wisdom, love, and goodness.

Different religions have different names and understandings of God. For example, in Christianity, God is often referred to as the Holy Trinity—The Father, The Son (Jesus Christ), and The Holy Spirit. In Islam, God is known as Allah, while in Hinduism, there are multiple deities that represent different aspects of the divine.

Beyond religious conceptions, some philosophical and metaphysical perspectives define God as an ultimate reality, a universal consciousness, or a higher power that underlies and sustains the universe. These concepts often transcend specific religious beliefs and may be rooted in philosophical reasoning or personal spiritual experiences.

Many religious traditions and philosophical perspectives also emphasize that God is beyond human comprehension and cannot be fully understood or described by human language or concepts. The nature and attributes of God are often considered to be mysterious and beyond the limitations of human understanding.

It's important to note that this description of God is a general overview, and different individuals and religious traditions may have unique and nuanced interpretations of the divine. I feel that the understanding of God is a **deeply personal** and **subjective** matter, **shaped by personal beliefs**, religious teachings, cultural influences, and **individual spiritual experiences**.

Now, let me ask the question a little differently. *"What is it that you love to do the most in your life?"* *"Maybe even right at this moment?"*

There are so many things I love to do; in fact, one of my favorite things is to go boating at Lake Powell, a large lake that spans Utah and Arizona. I love to literally cruise through all the beautiful petrified sand dune canyons, weave in and out of every little finger and offshoot from the main channel. It's truly spiritual. It will take your breath away. So, to look at God a little differently maybe God for me is those moments in my life. Boating on a beautiful lake, on a hot day, winding through 200-foot canyons.

It's not exactly a textbook definition. But oddly this makes sense to me. And I can understand it much better today. What I am trying to say, as I am getting in touch with my own life, I realize that God is connected deeply inside of me, and that as I begin to experience a sense of myself as a person, I will begin to experience a God as I understand God and begin to develop a belief process that works for me. And what works for me this week might change next week.

Slowly, I am developing a much richer and deeper relationship with myself, and so I am also developing a relationship with my God, as I see him/her, this Higher Power, because I believe God created me. To state it yet another way, so many times I went outside of me looking for the answers when I should be looking inside of me for the answers that already exist.

In relationships, in family, when we remove the **Sacred Ideals**, we experience growth, and so come to know our Higher Power, and ourselves better as we understand that power, better. For example, whether or not we realized it, or do realize it, we held it sacred to give our families all of our power, total loyalty. That translated into certain rules that we never broke. One was that the family could never show its dysfunction, not even to one another, not even when that dysfunction was driving everyone crazy. Everything had to be OK. There wasn't supposed to be any conflict, any struggle, and any disagreement, at least any meaningful disagreement.

Now we know better. We know that we are all dysfunctional, the world is dysfunctional, and so relationships are dysfunctional. And since family relationships are among the most powerful, their dysfunctionality is powerful. We can go around denying it or trying to make everything perfect, but I think we know where that leads. Or I can adjust. I can learn and unlearn things from my family and from any relationship.

I know a man whose father is eighty-one and he has been an alcoholic for probably a better part of sixty years. And the man keeps trying to *"fix"* his father. He's been trying for the fourteen years that I've known him.

He is obsessed with changing his father before his father dies. He feels that it's his duty. As a result, he beats himself and his father half to death. He has no life of his own. He's blaming himself for his father's dysfunction, and his father doesn't have the slightest idea what he's talking about. The father just shakes his head when he sees him and says, here comes my crazy son again, here he comes preaching. He even told the son that he should find a church and become a preacher. Basically, the father also told him that yes, he's numbed himself with alcohol but that's the way he wants to be, he's too old to change, and anyway this way they won't have to embalm him after he's gone. At least the father has a sense of humor.

But the son can't accept that, can't let go. As a result, he's put his father, or, more accurately, his father's alcoholism on a pedestal. He's made a god out of it. He's given his life to it. After all, his life revolves around it. He has basically said it's his job to fix his father and if he doesn't, there's something wrong with him as a son. Recognize the issue? Shame. If the father doesn't change, there's something wrong with the son. We said that shame is hard to get over. It is no easy thing for the man to find the serenity in letting go of what he cannot change, in grieving his situation and letting it go, accepting it, and then moving on with his own life. If he did, he might even come to laugh at the situation. As a good codependent I never understood that; you can get to the point where you laugh at things, even when they're not funny. You can process shame and learn from it and grow from it. I laugh all the time now.

In learning the GUT Theology, you start to see things, FEEL things. You look at expectations, yours and others. You look at the status quo, traditions, things that have become our *"normal."* All addicts in recovery have experienced it. They used to go down to the bar to see their friends, they hung out, they got drunk. It was normal. It was called fun. Now they see it as insane. Part of the reason they did it was in honor of the **Sacred Ideals**; if they didn't do it, their friends wouldn't like them, they'd be isolated. As good codependents, they had that desperate need for approval, for acceptance, to fit in. In recovery, they finally get the feeling in their GUT: they don't need to look outside for approval. They can do what's healthy for them and experience serenity.

They also know that they don't have to go around preaching to the guys who still go down to the bar and get drunk. They have no control over them. Everybody works on their own life, in their own way. And somehow serenity flows from that, from doing what you can, making your best effort. In GUT Theology you learn from your old pain and you experience new pain, but you don't stop there. For example, take someone, like me, who was an addict for 10 to 12 years. The old pain was the misery of the addiction, of numbing myself with drugs and alcohol then feeling shamed and guilty and depressed and anxious about it, and then doing it again. The new pain is the pain of grieving, of realizing what I had been doing, of what it had cost me in life, how my life could have been without the addiction. But you work through that, you realize that, first, there's nothing I can do about it now, and, second, that it was a teacher when I became open to learn from it, and that there was life after the addiction.

The experience of Simplicity

Ok, I am going to try and simplify all this shit we just talked about to a few basic points, all of which are centered around simplicity. Because, when you think about it, as complicated and strange and different as some of the things we covered sound, they really boil down to a simple process. We feel pain in our lives, the pain of shame and guilt and fear and anger and whatever else. If we open ourselves to learning from the pain, we realize that we have to let go of things, have to take certain people, places, and things down off their pedestals, have to replace some old Sacred Ideals with a new, open way of living. We basically realize that what we learned and lived by maybe is not healthy for us. We realize that we can't change what we were taught, or experienced, or did, or didn't do. We pray for the courage to change our behavior to something healthy; we deal in the present. When we do that, as we do it, we experience something new, something very positive, something that brings a real joy to living.

I personally have lived this experience. Now, as good codependents, especially those of you going through addiction, depression, and anxiety as you read this, you're thinking, *"Yeah, Karl, that was you. You're different. You don't know me. I just don't have it in me, don't feel it in me."* Bullshit, Whatever, I felt the same way. I was just like everyone in pain. Helpless, Hopeless, etc. etc. etc.

Let me share two FACTs with you. There are many programs, and all I am asking you, is to pick one to start, update it, modify it, simplify it, like I did. Make it your own. Alcoholics Anonymous (AA) occurred in the 1930's. It started with two drunks, both of whom had been diagnosed incurable-hopeless-alcoholics by the medical profession and themselves.

Now here are the two facts.

First, as of 1993, there were 96,000 AA groups worldwide. Now add to that all the other groups that use the Twelve Steps method: codependents, incest survivors, gamblers anonymous, overeaters anonymous, debtors anonymous, sex, there is even and emotions anonymous, and so on. How many millions of people are experiencing their recovery through these programs? The Reason I keep referencing twelve steps and all the different programs is because this is now global, it is world-wide, so wherever you are in the world, you can start here, and begin your **Discovery to Recovery** Journey, no matter your personal affliction.

Second, Twelve Steps, Buddhism, Daoism, and Kabbalism, all state, *"Having had a spiritual awakening..."* Having had...Not if. That is what is formally called **"the Promise"** of doing your work; you will have a spiritual awakening. If you put into practice these principles, and if you apply them consistently and persistently with compassion and patience and acceptance of any or all of these teachings, you will see that they specifically address, by name, depression and anxiety and anger and addiction and all the things you are experiencing that is making life seem helpless, hopeless, and unmanageable. Having a spiritual awakening means getting beyond the suffering, getting into life, finally getting your own **GUT Theology**.

Those are just two facts. I am not saying that there is the only way to recovery. I have used Twelve Steps, Daoism, Buddhism, Kabbalah, Chinese I-Ching, Gene Code Therapy and Human Design Methodology (which is Buddhism, Kabbalah, I-Ching, and Astrology combined) all integrated into one beautiful specific teaching for me. But let's not set up another Sacred. I am only saying that I have experienced and witnessed these methods work and apparently so have millions of other people just like me, like us. And let's face it...No matter how unique we think our problems are, no matter how much our codependency convinces us that we are hopeless and helpless, somewhere in those millions is someone who was just like us. Same problems. Same Pain. Same Recovery.

It's a simple program. I am trying to even make it more simple. Watching it work shows me God as I understand Him. And it begins with a simple principle:

Simple doesn't mean without effort

CHAPTER 11

WILLINGNES TO CHANGE AND GROW

"To improve is to change; to be perfect is to change often."
— **Winston Churchill**

"The art of life is a constant readjustment to our surroundings."
— **Kakuzo Okakura**

"If you're not willing to learn, no one can help you. If you're determined to learn, no one can stop you."
— **Zig Ziglar**

The simplest Principle

All of these ideas, and principles are not new; they have been around for thousands of years, across many different cultures. All I wanted to do is to organize them in a way that simplifies it and I wanted it to make sense to me. I hope this makes sense to you, and to some of you it will. To some of you, it might not make any sense. That's ok. If you're like me; I'm constantly looking for an end to codependency; an end to depression and anxiety; and the beginning of a fulfilling life. At this point you might seem overwhelmed. You might be asking yourself, or just freaking the fuck out, "What will I do when I finish these last few pages? How can I actually begin to change my life?" My response is this: start by trying and to be willing to change and grow. That's all. JUST BE WILLING!.

Fun fact and at some point, you have to act. To have to DO! This is the same for Siddhartha Gautama (who is the OG Spiritual teacher - Buddha) He was next level. He was rich, well-educated, born absolutely privileged, servants, the palaces (yep, plural), I'm talking totally set. But, in all his welloffness (wealth). He was still disturbed by Old Age, Homelessness, Suffering, Simplicity, etc. He could not reconcile a life in uncertain socioeconomic conditions. So, at the age of 29, He literally left is 3 palaces, his family, without a word to them. Just took off to become a monk, a beggar, in search for peace and enlightenment, answers and knowledge, a new state of being. But seriously, I'm sure his family was fine with all that wealth, but I'm sure his wife wanted her husband, and kids wanted their father. They had no idea for years where he was, alive or dead!

Rough! But this helped me enjoy his teachings even more. I'm not saying what he did was right, but He showed me that Buddha (Siddhartha Guatama) is and was human, he wasn't perfect, and he was just like me. And even though his path is absolutely his own, no judgment, I can reach my own enlightenment: freedom from codependency, freedom from addiction, by choosing my own path, and putting these principles to work. Buddha even says, don't listen to me, figure this shit out on your own. You have to put the work in. But he gives you guidelines and wisdom from HIS experiences, so you are not on your own. He shared what he learned. And, now, I want to do the same.

That's it. To begin your recovery or take it to the next level, just try to be willing to change and grow. And trust the process from there. The process works. I said at the close of the last chapter that it's a simple principle. I also said that simple doesn't mean easy. Again, if you're like the rest of us, you will resist change, and you might not even be aware that you are resisting. So, by trying, you develop a willingness to change and grow. **DESIRE** to change. That's how you start.

Don't forget, when you start to change, you are going to challenge things that you have accepted as your **Normals**. There might be things that cause you a lot of pain, but they are your normals; they are *"comfortable", in a perverse way.* When you move away from them, you move into unfamiliar ground, and, though that might be healthier and happier for you, it's 'going to be scary at first. That's why we resist change.

The point is that, when something new comes along, it shakes you up. Seriously, like every time for me it was like this. Even when that something new is good, something positive, it can shake you up. As noted earlier, even people freed from prison after so many years, experience anxiety. Extreme example I know, but Freedom is new to them. It scares them. People being released from the hospital after a long stay experience anxiety. They have become used to the hospital. The outside world is a change, is scary. Being in Rehab and then living in half way homes for 30 days to a year, and now I have to go do it myself. Shit, Damn, Hell, You got to be fucking kidding me? But you can do it, you have been learning and living a program of your choosing, now just extend that outside of that structure, and create your own healthy support system, your foundations, your program.

Here is a great story, I call it a parable: It is about a man who won the lottery. He had serious heart problems. He didn't know he won because he was in the hospital. The family had the ticket and they went to his cardiologist and said, *"Hey, we have a problem. We're afraid that when he finds out he won, the shock could kill him, his heart's so weak."* The cardiologist said, *"Yes, you're right. The shock might kill him. Let me handle this. I'll break it to him gently."* So, the cardiologist, in making his normal rounds, just struck up a conversation with the man and casually asked, *"Hey, what would you do if you ever hit the Lottery?"* The man laughed. *"Doc, I have never won anything. I've been playing the lottery for years and never even got a hit. I don't think I'll ever hit the lottery."* But the cardiologist kept pressing him, asking what he would do if he did hit the lottery. The man thought for a moment, then said, *"Well, Doc, one thing I would definitely do. You've taken such good care of me. I feel I owe you, my life. If I did hit it, I'd give you half."* And the cardiologist keeled over with a heart attack.

Change is hard. None of us codependents just become open to change. And none of us just decide that we're going to grow. Most of us kick, scream, battle, drive ourselves totally crazy, beat ourselves into the ground until we finally agree to try change.

It requires change, giving up the familiar. But in the familiar, no matter how unhealthy it is; we have the illusion that we can control things. Oh my god, we convince ourselves that things aren't as bad as they feel, that all we need is time, a few minor adjustments, and then we'll be OK. When we're finally **sick and tired of being sick and tired**, we get in touch with just how insane things have become. We call that our dysfunctionality; we get in touch with that. We realize that we are dysfunctional, our families are dysfunctional, the whole fucking world is dysfunctional. We mourn that. We grieve that. Then we accept that. And then we become ready to try change and growth.

I'll share a last example of this: a person in a shitty relationship. We are not stupid as humans. Usually, we know when a relationship is dead, when its absolute shit, when it's unhealthy for us, causing us all kinds of pain. Yet we say things like, *"I will leave when the kids are legal adults. I don't want to upset them."* We're suffering, but we're afraid of upsetting the kids, upsetting our families, upsetting the way we were brought up, our family systems. And we beat ourselves to death. We martyr ourselves. We make ourselves into victims. And we shame ourselves because we don't want to upset anyone else. So, who do you hurt the most? Yep! You, You, and you!

Continuing with the example, change is hard. It's not easy to walk away from a relationship that you've invested in and that reflects everything you've ever been taught by your OG Family, your culture, your religion, your peer groups, and the media, literally your Identity. Which is why we said that, before you begin to try to change, **build your base, a beautiful foundation**. Don't go on your journey alone. Develop a recovery family. Use your recovery tools. Connect with other people making the same journey. In recovery circles, there's a simple illustration I loved, to help guide us into change and growth.

The Recovery Triangle
This is the Recovery Triangle. Each side of the figure represents a core element in recovery: *your **Higher Power**; your **Recovery Family**; and your **Relationship***. Or, to put it clearly: **Faith, Family, Relationship**. Now, by relationship, we mean your relationship with life, with the fundamental concepts of life. We need to keep that in mind. We do not define relationship by the old tunnel vision definition; relationship means more than having interaction with just a person or persons. Relationship means how you interact with life itself. These three components of the triangle make up a total person. If you eliminate any one of the three, you experience codependency.

For example, if you eliminate **Faith**, you may be in a recovery family, but recovery will be difficult, if not impossible, because you do not have faith that any process will work for you. On the other hand, if you have the element of faith in a Higher Power, no matter how you define that power, your recovery family gives you support and you relate to life, drawing lessons from all the relationships you experience, whether it's with people or its with events. In short, you learn from all areas of life, and you have faith that it will work.

For some, as we already noted, the concepts of Higher Power and faith might be tough to swallow. I suggest reading an explanation of the Twelve Steps. There are all sorts of versions on the Internet, Amazon, bookstores, especially sites that specialize in recovery literature. But all versions are essentially the same. They all explain that many of us struggle with these concepts because our experiences were so bad, maybe are still so bad, that we just cannot accept the idea of a Higher Power or faith. However, the beauty of the Twelve Steps is that you really do not have to accept anything. All you need do is try. Start the work. Then, if you benefit, take the next step. In other words, you get paid as you go, so to speak. Don't try to analyze what you're doing, don't analyze what the Steps prescribe or how they even work. Just try them. See what happens. The concepts of a Higher Power and faith will become more clear.

But we can make this approach even simpler. Let's give it and acronym, why not? Let's call it **H.O.W**. Who doesn't love acronyms!

H.O.W. (Honesty, Openness, Willingness)

Now, please, note the order of the words and initials. It's not WHO, or WOH. It's HOW. The first step in all growth is shame reduction work. That comes from honesty (See chapter 12 - **Tools**, Radical Honesty). And a lot of what we know about honesty in regard to this program comes from the Big Book. By the way, if you're still hung up about that, still saying *"Hey, I'm not an alcoholic, what does that book have to do with me?"* let me remind you again that the Big Book lays out the precepts, the model, that has been adapted to treating all sorts of psychological and emotional problems. **And let me say again that if you have a problem thinking of yourself as an addict, think of an addict as someone who lives in fear, as opposed to love, someone who is not happy with life.**

The Big Book was basically put together by a bunch of drunks. They were desperate. Traditional medicine couldn't help them. So, Dr. Bob and Bill W. and the others in the earliest groups got together and hung on to each other, and out of their struggles and pain came some concepts. They all put those concepts down in a Book, which is why there is no author listed. From the pain of a group came a Book. A recovering addict gave me a Narcotics Anonymous book and she considered it a sacred book. It saved her life. It offers the gift of life in its principles. Its first principle is shame reduction, which is accomplished by honesty. And also remember the other saying:

You are only as sick as your secrets

So, to start your recovery, you strive for **honesty**. The more honest you become, the clearer you become, the cleaner you become, the more peaceful you become. Oh, and don't get hung up on *"total"* honesty. It's a rare person who achieves that, if anyone ever does. The program asks for Progress, Not Perfection. And, again, you start by trying.

You have to start with an **honest inventory** of yourself. You basically write out a personal history. We already covered some of this in journaling. There are no hard and fast rules to it. Basically, you just try to get things out on paper. This is another area where a Twelve Steps book can give excellent guidance. The purpose of the exercise is to learn about yourself: your history, patterns, emotions, traumas, secrets, guilts...You are striving for self-knowledge.

There are many ways in which this process works. For example, a person, I know, and I know him really well, he never identified himself as a controlling person. He thought of *"controlling"* people as those who demanded things. In doing his inventory, he finally saw that he tried so much to please other people. Often, he said yes to things, swallowed his feelings, did what other people wanted, just so he could please them. And he realized: he did this in order to control them, to get them to like him. So, he identified control as an issue to work on. Holy Shit, this is Me!

Another thing, you might want to do a personal inventory more than once. Most people do. In my own case, I did my first one in rehab. I was as honest as I could be. I did another inventory later and noticed that I was a hell of a lot more honest. Why? Because of the second part of **HOW: Openness**. Gaining knowledge about ourselves is one thing. But it is only one level. Openness is like the second level. We become open to learn from all areas of our lives. Some say that when that happens, when we add openness to a searching honesty, the process begins to take on a life of its own. And don't forget: it is a healing process. It will not hurt you. It evolves.

As you become more open, you will learn more about yourself. And, you will not see anything about yourself until you are ready to handle it. Take, for example, people who have serious abuse issues, maybe sexual abuse, even incest. They have buried the experiences, forgotten them, at least consciously. As they begin this process, become more open, the experiences come back to them, so they can finally face them and learn from them. Please note, though, that you are not working this process in a vacuum. Do not just sit down and take this little part of this book and say, *"Hey, I'll start here and see what happens."* You might not be able to handle what you bring up, which is why you develop your recovery family and arrest your addictions and have professional help available at arm's length in case you need it.

The **Honesty** and **Openness**, when coupled with a **Willingness** to learn and grow, complete the HOW of the program. You are **honest**, and you **learn**. You **open** up more, your **knowledge** expands from other sources. Then you become **willing** to **grow**, you make the effort consciously to **accept** GOD: Good, Orderly, Direction. And please do not confuse willingness with will power. From my own experience with my drug addiction, I can tell you that will power is kill power. You decide that you're just going to put your foot down, stop your codependent behaviors by sheer force on will alone.

OMG, I did this so many times, and failed every time, I could not reconcile why I could not intellectualize my healing. It just doesn't work that way. You have to build your recovery system, including connecting to other people in recovery, and then you do the **HOW** and let things happen at their own pace. This same principle is reflected in many philosophies: When you are ready, a teacher will appear. **HOW** makes you ready. And, please, don't complicate this process, and *"For God's sake, keep it simple."*

If you have a mind to try this program, just do it. Don't analyze it. Don't try to figure out where it will lead you. Don't compare yourself with other people doing it. Don't put a time limit on it. Don't try to fit it into a preset format. Be honest. Be open. Be willing. Let go.

Ownership

When I discovered that control is one of my issues, I also discovered something else as I tried to work into my program. I learned something about the concept of ownership. In this case, it didn't come from a written inventory, but from attending an Anonymous meeting. It happened while one of the group attendees was sharing one of her experiences. She had just moved to the area from a different part of the country. She talked of how she at first saw things in her new environment as depressing and strange. Then she opened up one day and saw things differently. For example, where she had come from, cities and developments were fairly new, there were virtually no old buildings. Her new location had many old structures, which she saw as depressing. However, when she opened up, became willing to look at things differently, she appreciated the history of the old structures, part of the culture of her new environment.

Just hearing that triggered something in me. I realized that when I looked back in my life, I mostly focused on the negative. For example, in high school, I had bad experiences with some teachers and some class mates. When I thought of high school, I thought of them. Automatically. Like an addiction. In fact, I learned later that I was caught in this negative-view addiction; negativity is a sign of codependency. But in the meeting, hearing the woman, I suddenly realized that I could focus on the good things in my past, the positive. I could choose to do that. Or, to put it in different terms, I could finally take *"ownership"* for my own actions and feelings.

Now, I didn't just get to this point, too this realization, automatically. It took working my personal program. The program helped me process the negative feelings in my past, *"defuse"* them, in a sense, and permit me to see the good in my past. Listening to the woman in the meeting triggered the realization that I could now choose, now take ownership for the present.

Ownership comes from **openness**, because **openness** simply means that everything in life is your teacher. If you do not take ownership for your present circumstances, all you are doing is renting space in your head to someone or something or some institution that hurt you ten, twenty, thirty years ago, or more. You are a prisoner of your past, instead of learning from it and moving on. If you do not take ownership, you get stuck in the Blame Game. You walk around with all kinds of resentment and anger inside of you. You become your issues. And that is the essence of codependency, with its depression, anxiety, and addictions.

I am not saying that it is easy to let go of the past. It is not easy to let an ex-wife, ex-husband, the child who is driving you insane, or someone who perpetrated abuse on you, to become your teacher. It is not easy to let someone you don't like become your teacher. It is not easy to let death or trauma or serious abuse or something else horrible become your teacher, But, you do not have to like your teachers in life. I said this before, some of them might drive you crazy. But, from the point of view of ownership, you have a choice.

You can choose to continue playing victim, playing the Blame Game, and being miserable, which is ironic, since it doesn't make any difference whatsoever to those who hurt you in the past. Or you can say, *"OK, I couldn't do anything about what was happening then and how I felt about it, but I can take responsibility for what I do with it now."* My Grandfather, who survived two world wars, being tortured, being blown up, etc. would always say; *"you get one"*, *"you can complain, you can blame anyone, you can use any excuse you want, Once, Just Once! Then you have to own it and change it."* He never believed in being the Victim, he had more right than most. That's called ownership. And, if you want to change, you get H.O.W: **Honest, Open, Willing.**

Many of us in recovery discover something about this process. It seems to take on a life of its own. As it should, it needs to be personal, we need to be willing to create and own our own process. Where change was so scary for us before, it actually becomes fun and rewarding.

The Greatest Movie you'll ever See
I always wanted to be an actor. I always wanted to be in the movies. So, **The greatest movie star, you will ever meet is: YOU!** we are all actors in our own life movie. Each and every one of us is like a movie in the making, in process. We are actors in our own movie, we have our own script, we have to research are character so that we can give our best performance, we have to dig deep so we can go so method that we truly can show the audience the real us. Be open to your growth, to your story as it unfolds. People come into your life. Some stay. Some leave. Things happen. Things change. It is all there for one purpose: **So, you can learn, act, evolve, and move on.**

Learn from your personal story as it has been written so far. Try and pull yourself away and watch your past and present like you are watching a movie, without the attachment. Embrace every aspect of your history, no matter how painful that is for you at first. Don't try to do it alone. In my own case, now that I finally understand that recovery is a process, an ongoing process, I really see the value of my recovery system. I still attend occasionally an NA or AA Anonymous group. Even when I'm traveling, in whatever city, I can look up the local groups and attend the meetings. So, I'm never alone in "writing" and embracing my personal story. And once you start learning from that part of your story that is already written, the past, you also start learning from the present. You can help this along by taking a daily inventory, by reflecting on each day. As I said very early in this book, is that it gives you something to do. It is not just an intellectual exercise. It changes you at the gut level.

You do not need to force your story. I heard a funny story in rehab. About this old dude named Frank. He had been an active alcoholic for most of his life. He finally got sober and into recovery, and some of the other people in the center would try to push him along. But Frank would tell them, *"Hey, it took me 50 years to work Step One and that's enough. I'm not drinking. My life's a little saner. That's enough. Let me die in peace."* I laughed at that. It reminded me to accept being where we were at, not to force things. He kept it simple to stay sober. As codependents, we need that reminder. We are addicted to forcing things. We try to organize and control everything, including confusion.

You know when I was in my 20's. I thought I had all the answers. That was an amazing place to be. Nobody could tell me anything. Even in my 30's I was so good, I had a beautiful wife, 3 beautiful children, a job that paid silly money. But, in my 40's I realized I was conflicted and that I had questions and no answers. Fun fact, I did not start really drugging and drinking until my mid-40s. Yep, right up to that point, I went to church and all kinds of good Mormon boy stuff. Like, Shit, Damn, Hell, you got to be fucking kidding me? No really, seriously! Now, in my 50's, with over 10 years of hard-core addiction and all its glorious consequences. So, now starting with rehab and having a willingness to learn and change by any means or program necessary, I finally learned, *"So what? Don't force things. Don't try to figure it all out and organize it."* I hear that in your 60's it really gets exciting because then you don't give a damn one way or another. You just work on you and trust that everything else will fall into place. I can't wait. That last statement about not trying to figure it out and organize it, this is a lie for me, the truth is that this has been part of my process, this is my willingness, my openness, my honesty. This book is my tool and set of tools, to liberate myself from drugs, alcohol, codependency. Again, the journey is personal, I decided to **"be like water"** and adapt and let it flow so that I can change.

You see, that's the thing about your personal story, about the movie you are starring in, that is unfolding in you: It doesn't end. If you are HOW: **Honest, Open, and Willing**, you will learn till the day you die. Along the way, if you put together your personal recovery program, you will grow past codependency. You will experience serenity and the joy of living. That is the Promise of recovery. Trust your process, it will work for you.

CHAPTER 12

Tools: What's in your toolbox?

> *"a master craftsman always, keeps his tools sharp!"*
> — ***Heinz G. Augat***

You want to borrow one of my tools?

Everything that I included in this chapter has become one of my tools in my toolbox. I discovered each and every one of these teachings when I needed it most. This is why I included them. Everything I have included in this book was critical to my recovery and now I share them with you. Why? Because **Sharing is Caring**! (Yep, another cliché)

12- Steps (as per The Big Book)

The 12 steps of Alcoholics/Narcotics Anonymous (AA/NA) are a set of guiding principles and actions that form the foundation of the AA recovery program. They are as follows:

1. We admitted we were powerless over alcohol—that our lives had become unmanageable.
2. Came to believe that a Power greater than ourselves could restore us to sanity.
3. Made a decision to turn our will and our lives over to the care of God as we understood Him.
4. Made a searching and fearless moral inventory of ourselves.
5. Admitted to God, to ourselves, and to another human being the exact nature of our wrongs.
6. We're entirely ready to have God remove all these defects of character.
7. Humbly asked Him to remove our shortcomings.
8. Made a list of all persons we had harmed and became willing to make amends to them all.
9. Made direct amends to such people wherever possible, except when to do so would injure them or others.
10. Continued to take personal inventory, and when we were wrong, promptly admitted it.
11. Sought through prayer and meditation to improve our conscious contact with God as we understood Him, praying only for knowledge of His will for us and the power to carry that out.
12. Having had a spiritual awakening as the result of these Steps, we tried to carry this message to alcoholics and to practice these principles in all our affairs.

These 12 steps serve as a guide for individuals seeking recovery from alcohol addiction and encourage self-reflection, acceptance, spiritual growth, and making amends to those harmed by one's actions. They are often worked through with the support of a sponsor—a more experienced member of AA who provides guidance and support along the journey of recovery. It's important to note that while the original 12 steps were specifically designed for alcohol addiction, variations of the steps have been adapted for other addiction recovery programs as well.

12- Steps (as per Russel Brand)

I prefer this demystified version of the 12-step program. More direct, Clearer. Russell Brand, in his book "Recovery: Freedom from Our Addictions," presents his own version of the 12-steps based on his personal experiences and interpretation. So fucking genius. Here are the 12-steps as described by Russell Brand:

1. **Are you a bit fucked?** Be honest and willing to accept that your life has become unmanageable due to addiction or destructive behaviors.

2. **Could you not be fucked?** Believe that there is a power greater than yourself that can help restore you to sanity and provide guidance in your recovery.

3. **Are you, on your own, going to unfuck yourself?** Make a decision to turn your will and life over to the care of a higher power or a greater sense of purpose.

4. **Write down all the things that are fucking you up or have fucked you up or have ever fucked you up and don't lie, or leave anything out**. Make a searching and fearless moral inventory of yourself.

5. **Honestly tell someone trustworthy about how fucked your are.** Share your inventory with someone trustworthy. Admit to yourself, to a higher power, and to another human being the exact nature of your wrongs.

6. **Well that's revealed a lot of fucked up patterns.** Do you want to stop it? Seriously? Are you ready to let go of all the fucked up shit you've done? Be entirely ready to let go of your character defects and negative patterns of behavior.

7. **Are you willing to live in a new way that's not all about you and your previous, fucked-up-ness?** You have to ask your higher power to remove your shortcomings. Humbly ask for assistance in overcoming your destructive habits and attitudes.

8. **Prepare to apologize to everyone for everything affected by your being so fucked up.** Make a list of all the people you have harmed and become willing to make amends to them all.

9. **Now apologize. Unless that would make things fucking worse.** Make direct amends to those you have harmed, except when doing so would cause harm to them or others.

10. **Watch out for fucked up thinking and behavior and be honest when it happens.** Continue to take personal inventory, promptly admitting when you're wrong and making amends when necessary. Self-Awareness is critical here.

11. **Stay connected to your new perspective.** Seek to improve your conscious contact with your higher power through prayer, meditation, or other practices. Ask for guidance and the strength to carry out your higher power's will.

12. **Look at life less selfishly, be nice to everyone, help people if you can.** Having had a spiritual awakening as a result of these steps, carry this message to others struggling with addiction and live by these principles in all areas of your life.

It's important to note that Russell Brand's interpretation of the 12 steps is aligned with his personal journey and perspective on recovery. While inspired by the traditional 12 steps of Alcoholics Anonymous, his adaptation reflects his own experiences and spiritual beliefs. Now you can do the same for you with your own experiences and your new spiritual beliefs. Buddha actual said, I am paraphrasing now:

"Do not take my word for it, you have to discover this for yourself!"

Be Like Water! Bruce Lee

The quote *"Be like water"* is a famous statement attributed to the martial artist and philosopher Bruce Lee. It encapsulates a core principle of his martial arts philosophy and serves as a metaphor for adaptability and fluidity in life.

When Bruce Lee said, *"Be like water,"* he was emphasizing the idea of flexibility and adaptability. Water is a substance that can take various forms, conforming to the shape of its container and flowing around obstacles. Similarly, Lee encouraged individuals to cultivate a mindset that allows them to adapt to different situations, circumstances, and challenges.

Here are a few key interpretations of the quote:

1. Adaptability: Water can effortlessly adjust to its surroundings, whether it's flowing around rocks in a stream or filling the space of a container. Similarly, Lee advocated for individuals to be adaptable and flexible in their approach to life, relationships, and problems. By being open to change and willing to adjust their strategies, people can navigate obstacles more effectively.

2. Flowing with Life: Water flows naturally and follows the path of least resistance. Bruce Lee suggested that individuals should avoid resisting or fighting against the natural flow of life. Instead, they should learn to go with the flow, embracing change and finding harmony in the ever- changing circumstances.

3. Formlessness: Water has no fixed shape or form; it can transform from a gentle stream to a powerful wave. In a similar way, Lee encouraged people to transcend rigid patterns and preconceived notions, allowing themselves to be formless and adaptable in their thinking and actions.

4. Simplicity and Simultaneity: Water is simple in its essence, yet it can manifest its power in many ways simultaneously. Lee highlighted the importance of simplicity in one's approach, as well as the ability to harness multiple skills or qualities at once, just like water can be calm, gentle, and powerful all at the same time.

Overall, Bruce Lee's quote *"Be like water"* serves as a reminder to embrace flexibility, adaptability, and an open mindset in our lives. It encourages us to flow with the changes and challenges we encounter, finding strength in our ability to adjust and transform as needed.

Radical Honesty, How free do you want to be?

Radical honesty is a concept that emphasizes open, direct, and unfiltered communication. It encourages individuals to express their thoughts, feelings, and opinions truthfully and without reservation, even if it means potentially causing discomfort or conflict. Radical honesty aims to create authentic and transparent relationships by eliminating deception, social niceties, and the withholding of information. If is funny because I love radical honesty, and when you ask people if they want radical honesty, they say absolutely, but when you give them that, no one is ready.

Here are some key characteristics and principles associated with radical honesty:

1. **Truthfulness**: Radical honesty prioritizes telling the truth in all circumstances, even when it may be uncomfortable or socially unconventional. It encourages individuals to express their genuine thoughts, emotions, and experiences without filtering or distorting them.
2. **Authenticity**: Radical honesty promotes authenticity by encouraging individuals to be true to themselves and their feelings. It rejects societal expectations and norms that might suppress or manipulate one's expression of personal truth.
3. **Transparency**: Radical honesty emphasizes open communication by removing barriers and veils of secrecy. It encourages individuals to share information openly, allowing others to have a complete understanding of their thoughts, motivations, and intentions.
4. **Emotional Honesty**: In addition to sharing factual information, radical honesty encourages the open expression of emotions. This involves honestly communicating one's feelings, desires, and reactions, without suppressing or hiding them for the sake of social harmony.
5. **Vulnerability**: Radical honesty often requires individuals to be vulnerable and willing to expose their true selves, even if it means risking judgment, rejection, or discomfort. It values authenticity and personal growth over the fear of potential negative consequences.
6. **Self-Reflection**: Practitioners of radical honesty often engage in self-reflection to understand and communicate their own emotions and experiences more effectively. This process encourages individuals to be introspective and aware of their own thoughts and motivations.
7. **Responsibility**: Radical honesty places importance on taking responsibility for one's own actions and words. It encourages individuals to acknowledge and address any harm caused by their honesty, seeking resolution and growth through open dialogue and understanding.

It's important to note that radical honesty is not about being intentionally hurtful or using honesty as an excuse for rudeness or insensitivity. It requires a delicate balance of expressing oneself honestly while considering the impact of one's words on others. Successful implementation of radical honesty requires a mutual understanding and agreement within relationships or social settings, as it can challenge established social norms and expectations.

Shame vs. Guilt

Guilt and shame are two distinct emotions, although they are often related and can be experienced together. Understanding the difference between guilt and shame is essential as they have different impacts on individuals' emotional well-being and behavior. Here are the main differences between guilt and shame:

1. Focus of the Emotion:
- **Guilt**: Guilt is primarily focused on a specific action or behavior. It arises when a person feels remorseful and responsible for having done something they believe is wrong, hurtful, or against their moral or ethical values. Guilt is about feeling bad about what one has done.
- **Shame**: Shame, on the other hand, is more about the self rather than a particular action. It is a deeply internalized feeling of being flawed, unworthy, or fundamentally inadequate. Shame makes individuals believe they are inherently bad or defective, regardless of their actions.

2. Internal vs. External:
- **Guilt**: Guilt is often more of an internal emotion, where the focus is on the person's behavior and actions. It can be seen as a signal that prompts individuals to reflect on their behavior and consider making amends or changing their actions in the future.
- **Shame**: Shame, on the other hand, is an internalized belief about the self, which can be triggered by both internal and external factors. Shame makes individuals feel that they are flawed or unworthy as a person, regardless of their actions or behaviors.

3. Adaptive vs. Maladaptive:
- **Guilt**: Guilt can be considered a more adaptive emotion as it can motivate individuals to correct their mistakes, learn from their experiences, and make positive changes in their behavior. Healthy guilt helps guide moral development and interpersonal relationships.
- **Shame**: Shame is often considered a more maladaptive emotion because it tends to be more self-destructive. It can lead to feelings of worthlessness, withdrawal from social interactions, and even exacerbate mental health issues like depression and anxiety.

4. Expressions:
- **Guilt**: People experiencing guilt might apologize for their actions, try to make amends, or take steps to correct their behavior. Guilt can be seen as remorseful behavior focused on the specific action.
- **Shame**: Individuals experiencing shame might avoid social interactions, withdraw, or engage in self-punishment. Shame can lead to attempts to hide or deny perceived flaws and an overwhelming sense of unworthiness.

5. Relational Aspect:
- **Guilt**: Guilt often involves a focus on repairing relationships with others. It emphasizes acknowledging one's actions and how they affect others, and seeking forgiveness or reconciliation.
- **Shame**: Shame tends to be more isolating and self-focused. It can interfere with relationships, making it difficult for individuals to connect with others due to feelings of inadequacy.

To summarize, guilt and shame are distinct emotional responses to wrongdoing. Guilt is tied to a specific action or behavior, whereas shame is a state of being. It is crucial to address and process both guilt and shame in a healthy manner, fostering emotional resilience and positive self-esteem. The ultimate aim should be to shift feelings of shame towards guilt, enabling productive action to take place.

Guilt

Humans will always choose what they understand over what they do not. What is a person but a collection of choices? Where do those choices come from? Do I have a choice? If you keep pretending, you are not going to remember who you are? Guilt is a complex and powerful emotion that arises when an individual believes they have done something wrong or violated their moral or ethical standards. It is a natural response to actions or inactions that conflict with one's values, leading to feelings of remorse, regret, and self-condemnation. Guilt can manifest in various ways and have a profound impact on a person's emotional well-being and behavior. Here is a detailed description of guilt:

1. Emotional Response: Guilt is primarily an emotional response, often characterized by feelings of sadness, shame, and discomfort. It can be accompanied by a sense of heaviness or a knot in the stomach, and individuals may experience a desire to withdraw or isolate themselves.

2. Cognitive Dimension: Guilt involves a cognitive aspect as well. It stems from the recognition that one's actions have caused harm or transgressed their internal moral code. This cognitive dimension may lead to rumination and persistent thoughts about the wrongdoing.

3. Types of Guilt: Guilt can be classified into different types based on the circumstances that trigger it. Two common types are:

• **True Guilt:** This type of guilt is experienced when an individual genuinely recognizes their responsibility for a harmful action or behavior. It can be a healthy response that encourages reflection and a commitment to making amends or changing behavior.

• **False Guilt:** False guilt is when a person feels guilty for something that is not their fault or responsibility. It may stem from irrational beliefs or excessive self-criticism, leading to feelings of guilt even when no wrongdoing has occurred.

4. Sources of Guilt: Guilt can arise from various sources, including:

• Actions that caused harm to others: Guilt is often triggered by behavior that has hurt or negatively impacted someone else physically or emotionally.

• Violation of personal values: Guilt can emerge when individuals act in ways that conflict with their deeply held beliefs, morals, or ethics.

• Inaction or failure to help: Sometimes, guilt can arise from not taking action or failing to help others when we believe we should have.

• Survivor's guilt: This form of guilt is commonly experienced by individuals who have survived a traumatic event while others did not. They may feel guilty for being alive when others suffered or died.

5. Impact on Behavior: Guilt can influence behavior in different ways. Some individuals may seek to make amends for their actions, apologize, or attempt to rectify the harm caused. Others might avoid situations or people associated with the guilt-triggering event.

6. Psychological Effects: Prolonged or intense feelings of guilt can lead to negative psychological effects such as anxiety, depression, low self-esteem, and a diminished sense of self-worth.

7. Coping Mechanisms: People may cope with guilt in various ways, including seeking forgiveness, engaging in self-punishment, or attempting to suppress the guilt altogether.

8. Resolving Guilt: Resolving guilt often involves acknowledging the wrongdoing, accepting responsibility, and taking steps towards making amends or learning from the experience. Seeking forgiveness from others and oneself can be an important part of the healing process.

It is essential to differentiate between healthy guilt that leads to growth and learning, and destructive guilt that can be detrimental to mental well- being. Addressing and processing guilt in a constructive manner can be a crucial step towards personal growth and emotional well-being. Seeking support from friends, family, or a mental health professional can be beneficial in dealing with overwhelming feelings of guilt.

Blame

Blame is an emotional and cognitive process that involves holding someone or something responsible for a perceived fault, mistake, or negative outcome. It is a common human response to events or situations that have caused harm, disappointment, or frustration. Blame can have both interpersonal and intrapersonal dimensions, affecting individuals' behaviors, emotions, and relationships. Here is a detailed description of blame:

1. Identifying Responsibility: Blame arises when individuals or groups attempt to identify the party they believe is responsible for a particular event or outcome. It involves attributing fault or causation to a specific person, organization, circumstance, or even oneself.

2. Emotional Response: Blame is often accompanied by a range of emotions, including anger, frustration, disappointment, and resentment. People might experience these emotions towards the perceived responsible party or themselves if they believe they are at fault.

3. Attribution Errors: Blame can sometimes be influenced by cognitive biases, such as the fundamental attribution error. This error occurs when individuals attribute the cause of someone else's actions to internal factors (their personality or character) rather than external factors (the situation or context). In other words, people may be quick to blame others' personality flaws rather than considering external factors that contributed to the situation.

4. Interpersonal Aspects:
• **Accusation**: Blame often involves accusing someone of wrongdoing or holding them accountable for their actions or decisions.
• **Conflict**: The process of blame can lead to conflict between the parties involved, as the accused may defend themselves or counter-blame, leading to a defensive and confrontational atmosphere.
• **Breakdown of Trust:** Frequent blaming can erode trust within relationships, as individuals may become wary of admitting mistakes or taking responsibility for fear of being blamed or judged.
• **Communication Barriers:** Blame can hinder effective communication, as individuals may be more focused on defending themselves or attacking others rather than seeking solutions or understanding.

5. Intrapersonal Aspects:

- **Self-Blame:** Blame can be directed inward, leading to feelings of guilt and self-condemnation. Individuals may hold themselves accountable for negative outcomes, even when external factors beyond their control contributed to the situation.
- **Impact on Self-Esteem**: Excessive self-blame can significantly affect a person's self- esteem and self-worth, leading to feelings of inadequacy or worthlessness.

6. **Coping Mechanisms:**
- **Projection**: Sometimes, people engage in projection, a defense mechanism where they attribute their own faults or mistakes to others. This can be a way of avoiding personal responsibility and projecting their negative feelings onto someone else.
- **Avoidance**: When confronted with blame, some individuals may choose to avoid the situation or the person they believe is blaming them to protect themselves emotionally.

7. **Role in Problem-Solving:** While blame can provide some initial emotional relief by attributing responsibility, it may not contribute constructively to problem-solving. Constructive problem-solving involves identifying causes, finding solutions, and taking corrective action without resorting to excessive blame.

8. **Cultural and Social Factors:** Blame can also be influenced by cultural norms, social dynamics, and institutional practices. In some cultures or societies, the tendency to assign blame may be more prevalent, while in others, there might be a stronger emphasis on forgiveness and collective responsibility.

In summary, blame is a multifaceted response that involves attributing fault or responsibility for negative events or outcomes. While it can serve as a mechanism to identify causes and hold individuals accountable, excessive or misplaced blame can lead to negative consequences such as conflict, damaged relationships, and emotional distress. Recognizing the role of blame in our interactions and being mindful of its effects can contribute to healthier and more empathetic communication and problem- solving.

Self-awareness is a fundamental cognitive ability that allows an individual to recognize and comprehend their own existence, emotions, thoughts, and actions. It goes beyond basic consciousness, as it involves the ability to introspect and understand one's own mental and emotional states. Here is a detailed description of self-awareness:

1. Consciousness of the Self: Self-awareness starts with the recognition of one's own existence as a separate and distinct entity from the external world. This understanding enables individuals to identify themselves as "I" or "me" and to perceive their thoughts, emotions, and experiences as their own.

2. Introspection: A key aspect of self-awareness is the ability to introspect and look inward. Individuals with self-awareness can examine their thoughts, beliefs, attitudes, and emotions, and assess how these factors influence their behavior and decision-making processes.

3. Emotional Awareness: Self-awareness includes being conscious of one's emotions and understanding their causes and effects. This means recognizing when we feel happy, sad, angry, anxious, or any other emotional state, and comprehending the reasons behind these feelings.

4. Recognizing Patterns and Traits: Self-aware individuals can identify recurring patterns in their thoughts and behaviors. They are able to discern their strengths, weaknesses, preferences, and tendencies, which helps them make informed choices and adapt their behavior accordingly.

5. Understanding Impact on Others: People with self-awareness are mindful of how their actions, words, and emotions can impact others. This empathetic understanding allows them to be more considerate, compassionate, and respectful in their interactions with others.

6. Acknowledging Limitations and Mistakes: Self-awareness involves recognizing one's limitations and areas for improvement. When errors are made, self-aware individuals take responsibility for their actions and are open to learning from their mistakes.

7. Perspective-Taking: A high level of self-awareness enables individuals to step into the shoes of others, understanding their perspectives and emotions. This ability fosters empathy and facilitates more effective communication and cooperation with others.

8. Self-Reflection and Growth: Self-aware individuals regularly engage in self-reflection, contemplating their values, goals, and aspirations. This process allows them to set personal development targets and work towards becoming the best version of themselves.

9. Tolerance of Ambiguity: Being self-aware means being comfortable with uncertainty and ambiguity. Individuals who embrace self-awareness are more likely to tolerate the complexities of life and are open to exploring new ideas and perspectives.

10. Enhanced Decision Making: Understanding one's own thoughts and emotions enables better decision-making. Self-awareness allows individuals to align their choices with their values and long-term goals, leading to more meaningful and purposeful outcomes.

Suffering

Suffering, as described in the I-Ching, Kabbalah, and Buddhism, shares some common themes while also offering unique perspectives on its nature and purpose.

1. Suffering in the I Ching (Book of Changes):

The I Ching acknowledges suffering as an inevitable part of the ever-changing and cyclical nature of life. It recognizes that both joy and suffering are interconnected aspects of existence, represented by the principles of Yin and Yang. Suffering is seen as the Yin aspect, contrasting with the Yang aspect of joy. The I Ching teaches that experiencing suffering can lead to growth and transformation. By maintaining a balanced and composed mindset, individuals can navigate through difficult times, just as water flows around obstacles with adaptability and resilience.

2. Suffering in Kabbalah:

In Kabbalah, suffering is understood in the context of Tikkun, the concept of rectification. The material world and the human soul are considered fragmented and imperfect due to a primordial event. Suffering is seen as a consequence of this brokenness, and the human soul's purpose is to participate in the process of Tikkun by elevating and reuniting divine sparks through acts of kindness and ethical living. Suffering is also viewed as an opportunity for purification and spiritual growth. Challenges and difficulties in life are seen as opportunities to refine the soul, learn valuable lessons, and develop virtues.

3. Suffering in Buddhism:

Buddhism identifies suffering as the core problem of existence, referred to as Dukkha. It encompasses physical suffering, emotional dissatisfaction, and existential unease. Buddha's Four Noble Truths explain suffering as arising from craving and attachment, leading to the cycle of birth and rebirth (Samsara). The path to liberation (Nirvana) involves recognizing the nature of suffering, understanding its cause, and cultivating the Noble Eightfold Path, which includes ethical conduct, mental development, and wisdom. In Buddhism, suffering is a central concept that guides practitioners to seek enlightenment and transcend the cycle of suffering and rebirth.

In summary, all three traditions recognize suffering as an intrinsic part of human life. While the I-Ching emphasizes the balance between suffering and joy in the context of change, Kabbalah links suffering to the process of Tikkun and the elevation of divine sparks. In contrast, Buddhism identifies suffering as the core problem and focuses on its understanding and cessation through the Four Noble Truths and the Noble Eightfold Path. Despite the different approaches, these traditions share a common thread of seeking wisdom, transformation, and spiritual growth as individuals navigate the challenges of suffering.

Kabbalah on Suffering

Yes, suffering is indeed addressed and explained within the context of Kabbalah, the mystical and esoteric tradition of Judaism. In Kabbalah, suffering is viewed as an essential aspect of the human experience and is intricately connected to the understanding of the spiritual journey and the nature of the Divine.

The concept of suffering in Kabbalah can be understood through several key principles:

1. Tikkun (Rectification): According to Kabbalistic teachings, the material world and the human soul are believed to have become fragmented and imperfect due to a primordial event known as the "Shattering of the Vessels" or "Tikkun." This event resulted in the dispersal of divine sparks throughout creation, leading to a world filled with both light and darkness. Suffering is seen as a consequence of this brokenness, and the human soul's purpose is to participate in the process of rectification (Tikkun) by elevating and reuniting these divine sparks through acts of kindness, compassion, and ethical living.

2. The Descending Sefirot: Kabbalah describes the structure of the Divine emanations as ten Sefirot (attributes or spheres) through which God interacts with creation. These Sefirot are arranged in a descending order, representing the progressive "hiding" of the Divine light. The lower Sefirot, which are closer to the material world, are associated with more limited and constrained aspects of God's presence. This limitation creates the space for human free will and the possibility of experiencing suffering as a consequence of moral and spiritual choices.

3. The Veil of God's Presence: In Kabbalistic thought, the physical world is considered to be veiled by God's presence, making it difficult for humans to perceive the Divine directly. This veiling contributes to a sense of separation from the Divine source, and the yearning to reconnect and experience the Divine is seen as a driving force in the spiritual journey.

4. Purification and Growth: Suffering is also seen as a means of purification and spiritual growth in Kabbalah. The challenges and difficulties encountered in life are viewed as opportunities for the soul to refine itself, learn valuable lessons, and develop virtues such as patience, resilience, and compassion.

5. Kabbalistic Meditation and Transformation: Kabbalistic practices, including various forms of meditation and contemplation, are designed to help individuals transcend the limitations of the material world and connect more deeply with the Divine source.

These practices can offer insights into the nature of suffering, its purpose, and how to transform its negative aspects into spiritual growth and awareness.

Overall, in Kabbalah, suffering is seen as an integral part of the human journey and the process of spiritual development. It is viewed through the lens of divine purpose and the potential for elevating one's consciousness and reuniting with the Divine. By understanding the deeper meanings and lessons behind suffering, individuals are encouraged to embrace the challenges of life and use them as opportunities for personal and spiritual evolution.

I-Ching on Suffering

Yes, suffering is addressed and described in the I-Ching, also known as the Book of Changes. The I-Ching is an ancient Chinese divination text and one of the oldest books in Chinese literature. It consists of a set of hexagrams, each made up of six lines, that represent different states or situations in life. The book provides guidance and wisdom on various aspects of life, including the understanding of suffering and how to deal with it.

In the I-Ching, suffering is recognized as a natural part of the human experience and is often associated with the concept of change and transformation. The book teaches that life is characterized by a constant cycle of change, and both joy and suffering are inevitable parts of this cycle. The I-Ching acknowledges that everyone experiences difficulties, setbacks, and challenges in life.

One of the central teachings of the I-Ching is the principle of Yin and Yang, representing the duality of existence. Yin and Yang are opposite but complementary forces, and they are in a perpetual state of dynamic balance. Suffering is often seen as the Yin aspect of life, which contrasts with the Yang aspect of joy and contentment. The book emphasizes that one cannot fully appreciate joy without experiencing suffering, as they are interdependent and part of the natural order.

The I-Ching also offers guidance on how to navigate through difficult times and suffering. It suggests that during challenging moments, it is essential to maintain a balanced and composed mindset. The book encourages individuals to act with resilience, patience, and adaptability, much like the water that flows and adjusts its course around obstacles. By cultivating these qualities and embracing change, one can find inner strength and wisdom to endure suffering and overcome life's difficulties.

The hexagrams in the I-Ching often contain specific wisdom and insights related to various life situations, including those that involve suffering. People consult the I-Ching for divination or seek its guidance to gain clarity and understanding in times of uncertainty or distress.

Overall, the I-Ching acknowledges the reality of suffering and provides a philosophical and spiritual framework for understanding it as an integral part of the human experience. Through its teachings, it offers valuable insights on how to navigate suffering with wisdom, patience, and acceptance while seeking harmony and balance in the face of life's challenges.

Buddhism on Suffering

When Buddha said, *"To be free, you have to go back to the beginning,"* he was referring to the concept of returning to the root or source of suffering and delusion in order to attain liberation or enlightenment. This statement is closely related to the fundamental teachings of Buddhism, which emphasize understanding the nature of suffering and the path to its cessation.

In Buddhism, the core problem is considered to be the cycle of suffering known as Samsara, which is characterized by birth, aging, illness, death, and rebirth. This cycle is perpetuated by ignorance (ignorance of the true nature of reality), craving, and attachment to desires and worldly pleasures.

To break free from Samsara and achieve liberation (Nirvana), Buddha taught the Four Noble Truths:

1. The Truth of Suffering (Dukkha): Acknowledge the reality of suffering and dissatisfaction in life. This suffering can be physical, emotional, or existential.

2. The Truth of the Origin of Suffering (Samudaya): Recognize that the root cause of suffering is craving (**Tanha**) and attachment to desires, which lead to a never-ending cycle of discontent.

3. The Truth of the Cessation of Suffering (Nirodha): Understand that liberation from suffering is possible by eradicating craving and attachment, breaking the cycle of birth and rebirth.

4. The Truth of the Path to the Cessation of Suffering (Magga): Embrace the Noble Eightfold Path, which is a set of ethical and mental guidelines to lead a life of wisdom, ethical conduct, and mental development. By following this path, one can attain liberation from suffering and achieve enlightenment.

So, when Buddha said, *"To be free, you have to go back to the beginning,"* he meant that true liberation from suffering can be achieved by understanding and addressing the root cause of suffering, which is craving and attachment. By going back to the origin of our desires and uncontrolled thoughts, one can break free from the cycle of suffering and attain the state of ultimate freedom, known as Nirvana. This journey often involves self-awareness, introspection, and the cultivation of wisdom through meditation and the practice of the Noble Eightfold Path.

Kabbalah

Kabbalah, a mystical and esoteric tradition within Judaism, offers various teachings and practices that can support the journey of self-love and freedom. While there isn't a specific step-by-step process outlined in Kabbalah for this specific purpose, there are principles and practices that can be applied in this context. Here are some elements from Kabbalah that can contribute to the journey of self-love and freedom:

1. Self-Awareness and Understanding: The Kabbalistic tradition emphasizes the importance of self-reflection and self-awareness. Engage in introspective practices such as meditation, contemplation, or journaling to gain insight into your thoughts, emotions, and behaviors. Seek to understand yourself on a deeper level, exploring both your strengths and areas for growth.

2. Unification of Opposites: Kabbalah teaches that reality is composed of complementary and interconnected forces. Embrace the understanding that within you, there may be conflicting aspects or polarities. Recognize that self-love and self-acceptance involve embracing and integrating all aspects of yourself, including your light and shadow qualities.

3. Divine Spark Within: According to Kabbalah, every individual possesses a divine spark or essence within them. Nurture a connection to your inner divine nature and recognize the inherent worth and potential within yourself. Cultivate practices that help you connect with your inner essence, such as meditation, prayer, or acts of kindness and compassion.

4. Tikkun Olam - Repairing the World: Kabbalah teaches the concept of Tikkun Olam, which means "repairing the world." Recognize that your journey of self-love and freedom is not solely for personal benefit but also has an impact on the collective. Consider how your growth and self-acceptance can contribute positively to the world around you.

5. Love and Compassion for Others: Kabbalistic teachings emphasize the importance of love and compassion towards others. Extend love, understanding, and forgiveness not only to yourself but also to those around you. Recognize the interconnectedness of all beings and strive to cultivate a compassionate and loving attitude towards others.

6. Study and Contemplation: Engage in the study of Kabbalistic texts and teachings to deepen your understanding of the mystical aspects of self-love and freedom. Reflect on the teachings and contemplate how they apply to your own journey. Seek guidance from qualified teachers or mentors who can offer insights and support along the way.

It's important to note that Kabbalah is a complex and deep spiritual tradition. If you are interested in exploring Kabbalah further and integrating its teachings into your journey of self-love and freedom, it is recommended to seek guidance from knowledgeable practitioners, teachers, or study groups who can provide proper guidance and interpretation of the teachings.

The I-Ching, Book of Changes

The I-Ching, also known, as the Book of Changes, is an ancient Chinese divination text and philosophical system. While it is not explicitly focused on the journey of self-love and freedom, its wisdom and principles can offer guidance and insights that may support such a journey. Here are some ways you can incorporate the I-Ching into your process:

1. Consult the I-Ching: Use the I-Ching as a divination tool to gain guidance and insights into your journey of self-love and freedom. Formulate a clear and specific question related to your process and consult the I-Ching by casting coins or yarrow stalks, following the traditional methods outlined in the text. Reflect on the hexagram and its associated teachings as they relate to your situation and seek to apply the wisdom in your life.

2. Reflect on Hexagrams: Study the hexagrams and their associated meanings within the I-Ching. Each hexagram represents a unique combination of Yin and Yang lines, symbolizing different situations, archetypes, and energies. Explore the hexagrams that resonate with the themes of self-love and freedom. Reflect on their teachings and contemplate how they can offer insights and guidance for your journey.

3. Inner Reflection and Contemplation: The I-Ching encourages introspection and self-reflection. Take time for quiet contemplation, meditation, or journaling. Ask yourself thought-provoking questions related to self-love and freedom and contemplate the insights that arise. Allow the wisdom of the I-Ching to inform your reflections and guide your inner exploration.

4. Embrace the Yin and Yang: The concept of Yin and Yang is central to the I-Ching. Embrace the understanding that self-love and freedom involve finding balance between opposing forces within yourself. Embody both Yin (receptive, nurturing) and Yang (active, assertive) qualities, recognizing the importance of integrating and harmonizing these energies within your journey.

5. Embody the Teachings: Apply the wisdom of the I-Ching to your daily life. Take the insights and guidance you receive from the I-Ching and translate them into action. Implement practices, behaviors, or mindset shifts that support your journey of self-love and freedom. Reflect on the hexagrams' advice and consider how you can embody those qualities in your relationships, choices, and self-care practices.

6. Seek Guidance and Study: Engage in the study of the I-Ching to deepen your understanding of its philosophy and teachings. Seek guidance from experienced practitioners or scholars who can provide insights and interpretations. Explore books, commentaries, or online resources to expand your knowledge and gain a broader perspective on the I-Ching's wisdom.

Remember that the I-Ching is a **tool** for contemplation and guidance, and its interpretation is subjective. I loved that it is referred to as the Book of Changes. Essentially that is what the I-Ching is supporting you to do.
I-Ching asks you to consult the Universe and listen. It is essential to cultivate your own understanding and integrate the teachings in a way that resonates with your personal journey of self-love and freedom.

A Fathers Journey

I was in so much pain and in my darkest hours, I started writing and trying to manifest my success story. I love music, poetry, and movies; and I wanted to write a song or poem about a father in his 50s (obviously me) and his ability to overcome his demons and show his family and himself, that he had WON. Here it is;

In the twilight of his years, a father stands,
A battle fought, a victory in his hands.
In his fifties, a chapter turned anew,
Overcoming darkness, embracing skies of blue.

Once lost in the haze of substance's hold,
His spirit weary, his heart felt cold.
But within his core, a flame ignited bright,
A flicker of hope, a longing for the light.

He faced the demons that plagued his soul,
Confronting the past, taking back control.
With every step, he shed the chains that bound,
A strength within him, gradually found.

His children's eyes, filled with doubt and fear,
Witnessed a transformation, a father so near.
They saw him rise from the depths of despair,
A beacon of hope, showing them he cared.

With each passing day, he built a new foundation,
Drawing on love, seeking liberation.
He forged ahead, hand in hand with grace,
A journey of healing, finding his rightful place.
Through trials and temptations, he stood tall,
Breaking the shackles of addiction's call.
He embraced sobriety, his spirit reborn,
A testament to the strength he had sworn.

Now he walks with purpose, his soul set free,
A shining example of what one can be.
A father in his fifties, a beacon of light,
Guiding others toward the path of right.

In his eyes, a twinkle, a spark of pride,
For he knows the depths from which he did stride.
With love as his compass, he charts a new course,
A legacy of resilience, a father's unwavering force.

So let his story inspire, let it be known,
That in the face of addiction, seeds of hope are sown.
For a father in his fifties can find redemption's embrace,
And in his triumph, find solace and grace.

www.ingramcontent.com/pod-product-compliance
Lightning Source LLC
Chambersburg PA
CBHW070326010526
44107CB00004B/437